Gender Camouflage

Gender Camouflage

Women and the U.S. Military

EDITED BY

Francine D'Amico and Laurie Weinstein

New York University Press

NEW YORK AND LONDON

NEW YORK UNIVERSITY PRESS
New York and London

© 1999 by New York University
All rights reserved

Library of Congress Cataloging-in-Publication Data
Gender camouflage : women and the U.S. military / edited by Francine
D'Amico and Laurie Weinstein.
p.   cm.
Includes bibliographical references and index.
ISBN 0-8147-1906-6 (alk. paper). — ISBN 0-8147-1907-4 (pbk. :
alk. paper)
1. United States—Armed Forces—Women.   2. Women and the military—
United States.   I. D'Amico, Francine.   II. Weinstein, Laurie Lee.
UB418.W65G46   1999
355'.0082'0973—dc21   98-40841
                        CIP

New York University Press books are printed on acid-free paper,
and their binding materials are chosen for strength and durability.

Manufactured in the United States of America

10 9 8 7 6 5 4 3 2 1

Contents

Preface

Francine D'Amico and Laurie Weinstein

Many people whose names do not appear in the table of contents contributed to this book in many ways. Linda Grant DePauw of the MINERVA Center provided logistical and moral support throughout the project, sharing information and contacts through the H-MINERVA e-mail discussion list and publishing valuable research in the center's journal, *MINERVA: Quarterly Report on Women and the Military*, and several books, including Donna Dean's *Warriors without Weapons: The Victimization of Military Women* (1997), which we have excerpted with permission. Our conversations with people in the MINERVA network of academic researchers and military personnel have shaped this anthology in profound ways. We also thank C. Dixon Osburn and Michelle Benecke of the Servicemembers Legal Defense Network for permission to reprint portions of SLDN's 1997 and 1998 reports on the "Don't Ask, Don't Tell" policy, and author Winni Webber and her publisher, Diane Benison of Madwoman Press, for permission to reprint her story from *Lesbians in the Military Speak Out* (1993). We are also grateful to Temple University Press for permission to reprint selections from *The Women's Encampment for a Future of Peace and Justice: Images and Writings* (1988), edited by Mima Cataldo, Ruth Putter, Bryna Fireside, and Elaine Lytel. Thanks also to contributors to the volume who provided photographs; other photographs are courtesy of the Geneva Historical Society, P. B. Oakley Collection.

Many researchers and servicemembers came together face-to-face through a series of workshops and conferences on issues relating to gender and the military, and we are grateful to the organizers of these events. First, thanks to Professors Mary Fainsod Katzenstein and Judith V. Reppy and the Ford Foundation for three engaging workshops: "Institutional Change and the U.S. Military: The Changing Role of Women" (November 1993) and "Race, Gender, Sexuality, and Military Culture" (January 1996), both held at Cornell University in Ithaca, New York, and "Military Culture, Military Policy: Issues of Race, Gender, and Sexuality" (April 1997), held at the University of Maryland in College Park and cosponsored by Women in International Security (WIIS). Second, thanks to Captain Georgia Clark Sadler (U.S. Navy, retired) and the other members of the "Women and the Military" Project of the Women's Research and Education Institute (WREI) and, again, the Ford Foundation, for the conferences on "Women in the Military" (December 1994) and "Women in Uniform: Military, Police, and Fire-Fighting Services" (December 1996), held in Washington, D.C. Third, thanks to Lieutenant Commander Anne Flammang (U.S. Coast Guard) and Professor Gwendolyn Stevens for organizing the conference "Leadership in a Gender-Diverse Military" (March 1997) at the U.S. Coast Guard Academy in New London, Connecticut.

Our conceptualization of the military's gender camouflage has been shaped by the participants at these workshops and conferences, including Frank Barrett, Carolyn Becraft, Johnnie Boynton, Kathleen Bruyere, Carol Cohn, Cynthia Enloe, Patricia Gormley, Gwendolyn Hall, Beth Hillman, Dana Isacoff, Barbara Lee, Rosemary Mariner, Brenda Moore, Madeline Morris, Paul Mottola, Dee Norton, Doris Price, Paul Roush, Vicki Sadler, Elaine Scott, David Segal, Mady Weschler Segal, Judith Hicks Stiehm, and Patricia Thomas. We are grateful for their engaging analyses. We and the contributors to this volume, of course, are responsible for its contents. The views expressed in these pages are those of the named author(s) and not of any government department, institution, or service branch with which they may be affiliated. Some contributors have used pseudonyms to protect their privacy.

Many other people contributed their expertise to make this book a reality. Francine wishes to thank the following people at Hobart and William Smith Colleges: Dawn Feligno, for her administrative support; the library reference staff, especially Janie Wilkins, Michael Hunter, and Dan Mulvey, for their research assistance; Beverly Ilacqua, Barry Jones, and Ron Rhodes for their computer wizardry. She also thanks her life partner, Douglas Roll, for his support; their sons, James and Patrick, for their inspiration; and Caly, for her companionship. Laurie wishes to thank Michelle Benecke of the Service Members Legal Defense Network and Captain Lynn Meola for their research assistance. She also wishes to thank Kroeber, Darwin, Franz, Rufus, Goodie, Peter, Margaret, Marvin, Janis Slomka, Beverly Dumonski, Katy Wiss, Susan Maskel, Ingrid Pruss, Jerry Bannister, Paul Simon, Ross and Allen Kopfstein, and especially Cathie and Russ Reynaga for their continued friendship and support. Laurie also wishes to thank Marilyn Kuruz whose expertise in editing and indexing made this book a reality.

Finally, thanks to our publishing editor at New York University Press, Jennifer Hammer, for her belief in the value of our proposal, her enthusiasm for the project, and her patience with the process.

Introduction

Laurie Weinstein and Francine D'Amico

Imagine you are a civilian coming onto a military base for the first time. It's like entering a foreign country and not knowing the culture: the language, the dress code, the rules of behavior. The base is surrounded by tall fencing and bright yellow lights that eerily light up the evening sky. A guard stops your car as you pull up to the gate. If you have an officer sticker on the car, the guard salutes and allows you to pass. If you have an enlisted sticker, you are merely waved through. All others—*outsiders*—require a pass or special permission to enter.

The base is a maze of one-way streets. Even the PX (post exchange or general store) has one-way signs painted on the floor. The widest aisle at the PX is the one for diapers and baby products, and pregnant women or women with babies in tow make negotiating that aisle a mission impossible. Should you wander too far afield on the base, a security patrol will ask for your military identification (ID). If you are a military wife, that ID bears your husband's name, rank, duty station, and/or unit assignment. It also lists you, the wife, as a military dependent: you are *dependent* on your husband for your identity in the military institution.

All the officers on the base look like carbon copies of one another and are distinguished from enlisted personnel, that is, those with lower rank and pay, by their dress: uniforms, insignia, and even style of hat differ. Dress also reveals a person's specific rank, military job specialty, previous assignments and awards, and even season of the year.

For example, if you are on a Navy base, you might notice a fellow wearing a white uniform and a white cap with a gold design on the brim that looks like scrambled eggs. If you understand the culture, you would recognize that officer's rank and position by his style of uniform, the number and size of stripes on his sleeve, the insignia on his collar, and the amount of scrambled eggs on his cap. You would also know it was spring or summer because *dress whites* are worn only then. For those who know the code, the series of ribbons and pins above the right chest pocket of his jacket reveal the accolades he has earned: sharpshooter awards, an "E" for excellence, hazardous duty assignments, and so on.

If you are observant, another thing you would notice on base is that most of the uniformed people you see are men. That's because in 1997 women were only about 14 percent of the total U.S. armed forces personnel. Of the women who serve, very few ever get a chance to wear the scrambled eggs on their hats because practices grounded in ideas about gender-appropriate behavior, such as combat restrictions in each service, prevent women from competing successfully with men. The nonuniformed women you will see on base are either wives of military service members or civilian employees of the Department of Defense (DOD).

Laurie began to study gender and the military because she is a former military wife:

> I truly felt as if I were living in a foreign country whenever I stepped on base. I was not allowed an identity of my own, even though I had a professional degree and an academic career. When my husband's ship went out to sea, I was expected to send care packages, to make holiday placemats for his meals, and to send cheery, upbeat greetings from the home front. I was expected to socialize with the other wives and to attend all kinds of boat functions to stimulate our own morale as well as the morale of the men at sea. I was known as *Mrs.* or as a *dependent*, but never Dr. or Professor. My research on women and the military has enabled me to come to grips with my own situation and to deal with the anger I felt as a woman whose gender made her less valuable than a man.

Francine became curious about women's role in the military when the U.S. Congress ordered the nation's federal military academies to admit women for the first time:

> As a high school senior in 1975–1976, I was worried about how to pay for college and what kind of job I would get when I graduated. Some military recruiters who visited the school urged me to apply to be among the first class of women cadets. This appealed to my sense of patriotism, my working-class financial fears, and my nascent feminism: I would serve my country, get the best college education in the country tuition-free, and have a job guaranteed when I graduated—and I'd be a pioneer and make my family proud. My only question was "Where do I sign?"
>
> I had no qualms about the idea of entering military service. Although I wasn't a "military brat,"[1] I had been around uniforms all my life. My father had served in the Army and then became a civilian police officer. Uncles and cousins had been in the Navy, and my older sister married an Air Force serviceman. And my hometown in upstate New York had an active Army National Guard unit and an active military base nearby. I saw the military as a normal part of my family and my community, so I was surprised by my family's reaction to my announcement that I wanted to go to a military academy. My mother cried, and my father tore up the recruiting brochure. "No daughter of mine," he said, "is going to be one of *those* women in the military." I didn't dare ask what he meant. So I did not join the service. Since then, I have found that many people shared my father's negative perception of "those military women," and I have worked to understand why these perceptions exist and how they can be dispelled.

This book is a step on the path to that understanding. In the pages that follow, you will read the story of one woman who did defy convention and entered the first class at West Point to include women. You will also read about women's contributions to the maintenance and operation of the military institution as nurses, servicewomen, veterans, wives, civilian employees in the Department of Defense, civilian workers in industries that provide the military with goods and services, and volunteers in civilian organizations that support and/or advocate for the military in particular ways. We also examine the ways women confront the military as advocates of demilitarization and how decisions about the military affect women with no apparent connection to the institution.

Understanding the relationship between women and the military is important not only because we are individuals with particular histories who have experienced the military in particular ways. We—*and you*—need to understand how the military works in our society because we are *citizens*. As citizens, we are responsible for the policies and actions of our government. Whatever the government does, it does in our name and with our authorization. To be responsible citizens, we must make sure that our government acts in ways that are compatible with our needs, interests, and values.

Citizens of the United States must ensure that the American government respects the rights and reflects the values and diversity of all people, both within our national community and in the larger global community. U.S. military policies *directly* and *indirectly* affect the lives of millions of people both within and beyond our country's borders. We have a responsibility to investigate how this public institution carries out its functions and to hold the military accountable for its policies and actions. We must require the military to change if neglect, mistreatment, or abuse occurs, as in the rape of an Okinawan schoolgirl by U.S. military personnel in 1995 and in sexual harassment of women trainees by their supervisors at Aberdeen Proving Grounds in 1997.

Citizens of other countries need to understand the U.S. military, too, because of its role in world affairs and its presence in specific countries. If you are a citizen of a country allied with the United States, you should be aware that U.S. military advisers may be shaping the policies of your own country's military, using American practices as models and taking lessons from American experiences. If there are U.S. military bases in your country, they impact the daily lives of people in your communities. If your country has been the site of U.S. military operations, you, too, need to understand the full scope of how the military's culture has affected your people and culture.[2]

Americans also need to understand the relationship between the military and society because the military both reflects the larger society and serves as one avenue to change society. Historically, *outsider* groups have seen military service as a way to assimilate into mainstream America. Military policies of *exclusion* have been challenged by African Americans, Asian Americans, and, recently, gays and lesbians, and these challenges have reverberated throughout society. The quest for *inclusion*—for acceptance—is echoed in the stories of many of the women in the pages that follow, such as Margaret "Maggie" Gee, a Chinese American defense industry worker and later WASP (Women's Airforce Service Pilot) during World War II.

In recent years, the U.S. military has come under increasing public scrutiny for its policies of exclusion regarding women. Although Congress rescinded the laws barring women from combat aircraft and ships after the Gulf War, women are still excluded from infantry and artillery posts and service on submarines and in special forces, despite actress Demi Moore's role as a Navy SEAL in the recent movie *G.I. Jane*.[3] And women's exclusion has been accompanied by harassment and victimization at the federal service academies, on military bases, and at military conventions. Perhaps if the exclusion ended, the harassment might as well.

Women have been excluded in another way: their work for the military—whether as warriors, wives, civilian employees, volunteers, defense workers, or prostitutes/sex workers—has often been unacknowledged. Few women appear in the historical chronicles of the official "war story" except as victims of or witnesses to military violence.[4] Women's military roles and contributions are made *invisible*—until women make themselves visible by challenging gender boundaries. Consider the case of Captain Linda Bray, who was celebrated by the media but discredited by military officials for her role in the U.S. invasion of Panama in 1989 because women weren't supposed to be in combat. A military woman may also make herself visible by appearing to make a mistake or to fail; she is then judged as representative of all women, as in the case of Navy pilot Kara Hultgreen, whose tragic death in an aborted carrier landing became a battle in what some observers call the military's "gender war."[5]

Contributors to this volume are working to make women's multiple relations to the military *visible*. In doing so, we reveal how our understanding of the military as a sociopolitical institution is shaped by our conceptualization of *gender*. Beyond the simple physiological fact of sex differences between male and female, *gender* defines the hierarchical relations between *men* (that is, people gendered *masculine*) and *women* (that is, people gendered *feminine*). Each of us is born male or female and taught what behavior is appropriate, what roles are acceptable to become a man or a woman in our society: Big boys don't cry. Nice girls don't hit. These behavioral expectations establish a range of boundaries for what we can do without incurring social censure. An example of these boundaries may be seen in the apparently inconsistent treatment of personnel who engage in extramarital affairs, as discussed in chapter 2.[6] Other factors, such as class/rank, race/ethnicity, and sexuality, as well as the particulars of each case and the general political climate, have to be considered, but the overall gender pattern of permitting—and even encouraging—heterosexual promiscuity for servicemen and prohibiting it for servicewomen is well established by decades of military policy and practice.[7]

Gender boundaries also establish and maintain a division of political power in society, because the behavior and roles associated with one gender are more valued than those associated with the other. Traits considered *masculine*, such as aggression, are seen as the qualities needed in politics and business—and the military. Traits considered *feminine*, such as compassion, are seen as beneficial for personal relationships but not professional success. Sometimes efforts to meet gender expectations endanger our health and well-being, as well as disqualify us from positions of power in society. For example, people diagnosed with eating disorders—which afflict mainly females trying to fit the model of desirable femininity in U.S. society—"may be medically disqualified from being commissioned" at a military academy.[8]

As coeditors of this project, we approach our analysis of gender and the military as feminist scholars trained in the disciplines of anthropology and political science. From these perspectives, we see that the military plays a critical role in the creation and maintenance of a particular pattern of gender relations in the wider society. The military has a unique position in society because of the "close identification of the military to the state" and the "financial, labour, and material resources" at its command.[9] The military's privileged position makes it not just a mirror of gender relations in society but a fundamental site for the construction of gender, that is, the defining of the boundaries of behavior—indeed, of life possibilities—for people we call *men* and *women*.

For example, when American women enter the United States military institution, they enter hostile territory: it is, quite literally, No-*Woman's*-Land. To survive in this hostile environment, servicewomen adopt one of a variety of coping strategies for self-protection. These strategies differ in the gendering of the subject. Each day, the servicewoman must (re)construct her gender identity: Should I try to be "one of the guys," that is, adopt a passing strategy, hoping for male bonding to extend to include me? Or should I be "one of the girls," that is, become ultrafeminized, hoping for brotherly affection or chivalric protection? Should I try to be a "soldier," that is, aim for a seemingly gender-neutral professionalism, hoping for mutual respect? Or should I be a crusader, mounting a conscious—and personally and professionally risky—challenge to the structure of gender relations in the institution?[10]

In this sense, gender is a costume we put on, or a type of *camouflage*, to militarize the metaphor. We hope that the meanings of the various gender camouflage outfits we select are understood as we intend them in the context in which we will portray them. Yet our gendering strategy may be interpreted differently by those around us. These different interpretations occur because gender as a pattern of social relations is ubiquitous but not uniform. The range of gender-appropriate behaviors is shaped by other social hierarchies, most prominent among which are race/ethnicity, class/rank, and sexuality. Because of these other hierarchies, gender camouflage comes in different colors, shapes, and sizes, and some gender camouflage may not be available to some people, that is, certain gender strategies may be foreclosed to them. For example, a white lesbian officer may need to be "one of the girls" to mask her sexuality and avoid the risk of exposure and discharge. An African American straight enlisted woman might try to be "one of the guys" because of white society's assumptions about her sexual availability.[11] Gender is thus not only an identity we adopt but also a place we get put or a way we are identified by others.

Although individual women don gender camouflage to survive in a hostile institution, the military itself must camouflage the multiple ways in which it depends upon the skills, talents, energies, and support of people gendered feminine. The military must camouflage its reliance on *woman*power in order to maintain its self-image as a quintessentially *masculine* institution in society, the place where boys become men and no girls are allowed. To do this, the institution denies women an official place and marginalizes them through the use of sexual harassment and assault, professional disparagement and dequalification, and distinctions between combatant and noncombatant, servicemember and dependent, insider and outsider.

About the Book

For this project, we brought together a diverse array of authors to examine the experiences of women who are differently situated vis-à-vis the U.S. military institution and to explore the ways the concept of gender is used in policing the boundaries of who belongs and who does not, of who counts and who does not, of who defines the institution's identity and social significance.

This analysis is organized locationally, that is, in reference to women's constructed relation to the military institution: on the *inside*, at the *margin*, or on the *outside*. The format for this book was inspired by the work of Nancy McGlen and Meredith Reid Sarkees on women in foreign policy, which juxtaposed analytic chapters and interviews.[12] Here, analytic chapters by academics, retired servicewomen, former military wives, and policymakers are accompanied by autobiographical essays by or oral histories of the women who occupy these locationally defined spaces of inside/margin/outside. They speak their stories in their own words, so that we may hear their voices and understand their experiences.

In part 1, we focus first on women most visible in their location *inside* the institution: military nurses and women in the uniformed services. To explore contemporary issues relating to women's service, we include individual chapters on women veterans, military education, and lesbian exclusion. These chapters make it clear that although many women are located *inside* the institution, some do not accept them as *insiders*.

In chapter 1, Lieutenant Colonel Connie L. Reeves (U.S. Army, retired) argues that military nurses remain largely invisible in the contemporary public debate over women's military participation. In the original autobiographical essay accompanying the chapter, Lieutenant Colonel Karen Johnson (retired), an African American Air Force Nurse Corps veteran, describes how her experiences as a military nurse during and after the Vietnam War transformed her into an advocate for women's rights.

In chapter 2, Captain Georgia Clark Sadler (U.S. Navy, retired) explores the establishment of the women's auxiliary services, the regularization of those services, their integration into the institutional hierarchy, and the experiences of contemporary servicewomen. Captain Barbara A. Wilson (U.S. Air Force, retired) discusses her twenty-two years of military service, detailing her rise from enlisted to officer rank, in an original autobiographical essay.

In chapter 3, Dr. D'Ann Campbell considers what lessons on gender integration the federal military academies may have for public state-supported institutions for military education, including the Citadel and Virginia Military Institute (VMI). In the companion essay, Major Lillian A. Pfluke (U.S. Army, retired) recounts her experiences as a member of the Class of 1980 at West Point—the first class to admit women—and the highlights of her fifteen-year military career.

Chapter 4 focuses on the 1.2 million women veterans in the United States who remain a nearly invisible part of the population. Only recently has some formal recognition of women's military contributions been paid with the erection of the Vietnam Women's memorial in 1993, and, more recently, the dedication of the Women in Military Service for America (WIMSA) Memorial at Arlington National Cemetery on October 18, 1997. Chapter 4 excerpts the executive summary of a recent conference on women veterans, reprinted with the permission of Joan A. Furey, director of the Center for Women Veterans. The chapter is followed by two veterans' voices. In an excerpt reprinted from *Warriors without Weapons* with permission from the MINERVA Center, Navy veteran and clinical psychologist Dr. Donna M. Dean discusses the sexual violence and dehumanization she argues are common to the experiences of military women.[13] In an original essay, an enlisted Army veteran using the pseudonym Anne Black to protect her identity describes her reasons for joining—and leaving—military service.

In chapter 5, Laurie Weinstein and an active-duty military officer writing under the pseudonym Captain Lynn Meola consider the experiences of lesbians currently in military service under the "Don't Ask, Don't Tell" policy and of women discharged for their sexuality. Women discharged under gay/lesbian exclusion rules are perhaps the most invisible of women veterans, for their service and dedication have been negated because they loved the wrong person, not because they didn't do their jobs. The Servicemembers Legal Defense Network (SLDN) has provided information on recent discharge cases for the chapter, which is accompanied by a previously published autobiographical essay by an active duty Army officer using the pseudonym Winni S. Webber, reprinted with permission from Madwoman Press.[14]

In part 2, our focus shifts to women *with* the military, that is, women whose relationship to the military is less visible or less formal but—as the authors demonstrate—no less essential to the institution. Each of the chapters and essays in this part explores how the work of women seemingly *at the margin* is in fact *central* to both the support of the military institution and the maintenance of social gender boundaries.

Dr. Doreen Drewry Lehr analyzes the invisibility of the wives of service personnel in chapter 6 and reveals the extent and value of their work for and support of the military institution. Dr. Joan I. Biddle (U.S. Army, retired) describes her life as an Army officer's wife *and* as an Army officer herself in the accompanying autobiographical essay.

In chapter 7, Dr. Diane Disney examines the roles of women civilian workers in the Department of Defense. Professors Gale Mattox and Helen Purkitt analyze their experiences as the first two female civilian instructors at the U.S. Naval Academy at Annapolis, Maryland.

Chapter 8 describes a few of the numerous support and advocacy groups and programs related to military service, such as the United Service Organizations (USO) and the Defense Advisory Committee on Women in the Service (DACOW-ITS), a watchdog organization of civilian appointees established by the federal government that advocates on behalf of servicewomen. Servicewomen themselves have established professional organizations and have organized to ensure that women's military contributions are recorded in an organization called Women in Military Service to America (WIMSA), whose work is described in an original essay by WIMSA curator Judith Lawrence Bellafaire.

In part 3 we examine the experiences of women who are ostensibly *outside* the military yet who, upon closer examination, are affected by the military, are integral to its functioning, or, alternatively, challenge its position.

In chapter 9, Joan E. Denman and Dr. Leslie Baham Inniss argue that women workers were essential for the operation of defense industries in wartime but were mobilized in such as way as to maintain rather than to challenge traditional gender roles. Their analysis is illustrated by the oral history of defense worker and WASP pilot Maggie Gee, compiled by Dr. Xiaojian Zhao. In chapter 10, Dr. Katharine H. S. Moon analyzes the role of the so-called military comfort women, from the traditional camp followers to prostitutes/sex workers employed around contemporary U.S. bases.

Other women located *outside* the military but important to consider in analysis of gender and the military are women who engage in peace work. In chapter 11, Dr. Gwyn Kirk catalogues the many ways women have organized to oppose militarism. Her chapter is accompanied by a narrative compiled by Francine D'Amico, which includes the stories of two women who participated in antinuclear demonstrations by the Women's Encampment for a Future of Peace and Justice in upstate New York, reprinted with permission from Temple University Press.[15]

In chapter 12, researcher Marion Anderson examines how military spending in the federal budget impacts women's employment. Anderson argues that women workers, who tend to be concentrated in the service sector of the economy, are displaced when federal spending on the military increases.

In the conclusion, we consider the consequences of the military's gender camouflage and suggest areas for further research, analysis, and action.

NOTES

1. Mary Edwards Wertsch, *Military Brats: Legacies of Childhood Inside the Fortress* (Bayside, N.Y.: Aletheia, 1991).

2. See Cynthia Enloe, *Does Khaki Become You? The Militarization of Women's Lives* (London: HarperCollins, 1983), 123–31; Cynthia Enloe, *Bananas, Beaches, & Bases: Making Feminist Sense of International Politics* (Berkeley: University of California Press, 1989), 65–92.

3. "Pentagon Denied 'G.I. Jane' Request," *Finger Lakes Times* (Geneva, N.Y.), 17 August 1997, 6D.

4. See, for example, Miriam Cooke, *Women and the War Story* (Berkeley: University of

California Press, 1996); Miriam Cooke and Angela Woollacott, eds., *Gendering War Talk* (Princeton: Princeton University Press, 1993).

5. Linda Bird Francke, *Ground Zero: The Gender Wars in the Military* (New York: Simon & Schuster, 1997), 46–72, 256–57.

6. "Double Standards, Double Talk," (editorial), *New York Times*, 6 June 1997, A30; "Sex and the Military" (editorial), *Washington Post*; reprinted, *Finger Lakes Times* (Geneva, N.Y.), 6 June 1997, 8.

7. Leisa D. Meyer, "Creating G.I. Jane: The Regulation of Sexuality and Sexual Behavior in the Women's Army Corps During World War II," *Feminist Studies* 18, no. 3 (fall 1992): 581–602; Melissa S. Herbert, "Guarding the Nation, Guarding Ourselves: The Management of Hetero/Homo/Sexuality among Women in the Military," *MINERVA: Quarterly Report on Women in the Military* 15, no. 2 (summer 1997): 60–76.

8. Mary O'Brien, U.S. Air Force Academy graduate, H-MINERVA electronic discussion network H-MINERVA@H-NET.MSU.EDU (2 May 1996).

9. Enloe, *Does Khaki Become You?*, 10–12.

10. Melissa S. Herbert, *Camouflage Isn't Only for Combat: The Management of Gender and Sexuality among Women in the Military* (New York: New York University Press, 1998); Francke, *Ground Zero*; Billie Mitchell, "The Creation of Army Officers and the Gender Lie: Betty Grable or Frankenstein?" in *It's Our Military, Too! Women and the U.S. Military*, ed. Judith Hicks Stiehm (Philadelphia: Temple University Press, 1996), 35–59.

11. Nell Irvin Painter, "Hill, Thomas, and Racial Stereotype," and Paula Giddings, "The Last Taboo," in *Race-ing Justice, En-Gendering Power: Essays on Anita Hill, Clarence Thomas, and the Construction of Social Reality*, ed. Toni Morrison (New York: Pantheon, 1992), 200–214, 441–70.

12. Nancy E. McGlen and Meredith Reid Sarkees, *Women in Foreign Policy: The Insiders* (New York: Routledge, 1993).

13. Donna M. Dean, *Warriors without Weapons: The Victimization of Military Women* (Pasadena, Md.: MINERVA Center, 1997).

14. Winni S. Webber, *Lesbians in the Military Speak Out* (Northboro, Mass.: Madwoman Press, 1993).

15. Excerpted from Mima Cataldo, Ruth Putter, Bryna Fireside, and Elaine Lytel, *The Women's Encampment for a Future of Peace and Justice: Images and Writings* (Philadelphia: Temple University Press, 1988).

Part I

Insiders
Women *in* the Military

One

Invisible Soldiers
Military Nurses

Connie L. Reeves

Our nation continues to debate whether women should be in war, whether their presence inhibits men from carrying out their mission, whether the American public can stomach women's return in body bags, and whether women can endure lack of privacy, serious privation, being surrounded by violent deaths, or being prisoners of war. Either people aren't paying attention to history or historians aren't telling the story, because these questions have been answered by the experiences of thousands of women who have served the military as nurses.[1]

Foundations of Military Nursing

When the Revolutionary War began, General George Washington asked that one female nurse be employed for every ten patients—to relieve men for battle—and one nurse matron for every hundred patients. Surgeon's mates performed skilled nursing tasks, and female nurses emptied chamber pots and cleaned wards and patients, though nurses might occasionally give medication or assist with diets. Nurses were paid two dollars a month, nurse matrons fifteen, surgeon's mates fifty, and senior surgeons one hundred twenty. When the war ended, seven female matrons and thirty nurses were treating four thousand men in seven hospitals. Maryland records show that one woman, Mary Pricely, served aboard a navy ship. After the war, the Medical Department was eliminated, and a few surgeons and surgeon's mates, along with military wives and female laundresses, provided medical care to soldiers.[2]

Nursing in the United States was greatly influenced by the work of Florence Nightingale in the Crimean War (1853–1856). At the British government's request, Nightingale and a select group of female nurses traveled to the Crimea to care for sick and wounded British soldiers. Her philosophy of improved nutrition and basic sanitation procedures improved the survival rate for casualties.[3] Mary Grant Seacole, an African American nurse, traveled to the Crimea, established a hospital ward in a public house, and volunteered alongside Nightingale. After the war, the British government honored her with a medal for saving the lives of countless soldiers.[4]

When the U.S. Civil War broke out, the Army had no ambulance corps, no field hospitals, no nursing corps, and few surgeons. Protestant nursing groups and Catholic nuns volunteered their services, tending sick and wounded soldiers in hospitals and on the battlefields. In 1861, the U.S. Sanitary Commission coordinated relief efforts by assigning nurses, inspecting hospitals, raising money, providing supplies, and building hospitals.[5]

In June 1861, the Secretary of War appointed Dorothea Lynde Dix as Superintendent of the female nurses of the Union Army. Dix recruited nurses, established an Army nurse corps, assigned nurses to military hospitals, and disbursed supplies. In August 1861, Congress authorized the employment of women nurses in military hospitals, paying them twelve dollars a month and a daily ration to serve for six months or the war's duration. The nurses were given an administrative rank equivalent to surgeon but no military rank. Many surgeons and other officers resented women's presence in the hospitals and initially used them for only menial housekeeping tasks. Over time they became more accepted and provided skilled nursing. By the end of the war, Dix had placed six thousand nurses in military hospitals and on the battlefields.[6]

Louisa May Alcott served briefly as a Union Army nurse in a military hospital in Washington, D.C., until she fell ill from typhoid fever. In 1863, Alcott published the letters she had written home while serving as a nurse, furnishing one of the earliest first-person accounts of caring for the wounded; the letters were reprinted in newspapers across the North.[7] Mary Edwards Walker served in the Union Army as first a nurse and then a doctor; she was captured by the Confederates, spent four months as a prisoner of war, and was the first woman awarded the Medal of Honor.[8] Under the auspices of the Sanitary Commission, Mary Ann Bickerdyke—widow and mother of two—cared exclusively for enlisted men, and they called her "Mother Bickerdyke." After the war, she distributed clothing from the Sanitary Commission and then devoted herself to helping freedmen in Chicago. In honor of her service, the United States launched the hospital ship *Mary A. Bickerdyke* in 1943.[9]

African Americans also served as nurses, particularly for the Union Army. The abolitionist Harriet Tubman served off the coast of South Carolina in the Sea Islands as a nurse for the Union Army; she later received a pension for her war work as spy and scout. Sojourner Truth—a former slave, abolitionist, and women's rights advocate—served as a nurse and counselor for the Freedmen's Bureau and in Freedmen's Hospital in Washington, D.C. Susie King Taylor, married to an Army noncommissioned officer, was a paid laundress in her husband's unit and volunteered her nursing services alongside Clara Barton in South Carolina in 1863.[10]

Clara Barton, the most famous nurse of the Civil War, was not a Union Army nurse. An office clerk in Washington, D.C., when the war began, Barton immediately began nursing wounding soldiers when they appeared in April 1861 in the nation's capital. Barton established an independent organization to provide food, clothing, and medical supplies to the military, raising money and spending her own. She nursed Union and Confederate soldiers, black and white, in hospitals and on the battlefield. Her service continued after the war as she ensured the identification and marking of twelve thousand graves, in addition to founding the American Red Cross.[11]

In the South, religious groups and individual women also volunteered to nurse the wounded, turning their homes into hospitals and convalescent centers. Sally Louisa Tompkins was a nurse superintendent in a private hospital and required military rank to acquire needed supplies for military patients. President Davis appointed her a captain in the Confederate Army and kept her hospital open when all other private hospitals were closed. Ada Bacot wrote a six-volume diary during the war detailing her experiences as a nurse.[12]

The first Navy hospital ship is considered to be the *Red Rover* on which four Catholic nuns and five African American women served as nurses. Wounded men could be removed from battlefield areas more quickly and transferred to general hospitals or convalescent centers. By 1862, the Union Army had thirty-two hospital steamboats.[13]

An estimated ten thousand women served as nurses during the war, as Army nurses, as members of religious orders, with the Sanitary Commission, or independently. Ten percent of all nurses who served became ill from disease or overwork, and twenty Union nurses died. Although some persons recommended that nurses be granted pensions, Congress did not do so until thirty years later. Despite Army nurses' contributions in the war, all were discharged.[14]

During the Spanish-American War, insufficient numbers of male nurses were available to care for the patients. The Surgeon General appointed Dr. Anita Newcomb McGee an acting assistant surgeon general in the Army and designated her the head of the new Nursing Corps Division. Congress authorized the recruitment of contract nurses for thirty dollars a month and a daily ration. Some twelve hundred female nurses served in Army hospitals in Cuba, Puerto Rico, the Philippines, China, Japan, and Hawaii, as well as in stateside hospitals and on the USS *Relief*, a hospital ship anchored off Cuba. No nurses died from military action, but twelve died of typhoid fever, and Clara Louise Maass died participating in a experiment.[15]

Subsequently, in 1901, Congress created the permanent Nurse Corps (female) as an auxiliary of the Army. Nurses would neither possess military rank nor receive retirement or veteran's benefits, and their pay would be far less than that of male officers. In 1908, the Navy Nurse Corps was established, and twenty Navy nurses reported for duty. In 1909, the Red Cross Nursing Service was founded to provide a reserve of trained nurses for the two new military nursing corps and the Red Cross.[16]

World War I Era

On the eve of World War I, there were 400 nurses in the Army Nurse Corps and 170 in the Reserve Corps. Red Cross nurses departed for Europe in 1914, bound for all belligerent nations. Four hundred nurses arrived in France in 1917 to serve with the British Expeditionary Force. Nurses often worked during air attacks or traveled the high seas under threat of torpedo or mine attacks. In the field, nurses encountered horrible, unfamiliar wounds that resulted from mustard gas and machine-gun fire. Before the war ended, Congress raised nursing pay to sixty dollars a month.[17]

Approximately 21,500 Army nurses served during the war, with almost 9,000 of these serving overseas. No nurse died from enemy action, but 200 died during the influenza epidemic and 60 of other causes. Thirty-eight were buried overseas. Three nurses were awarded the Distinguished Service Cross (a combat medal, second to the Medal of Honor) and 23 the Distinguished Service Medal (the highest noncombat award). Two nurses received the British Military Medal, 69 the British Royal Red Cross, and 28 the French Croix de Guerre. Many nurses remained in Germany as part of an occupation force until 1923.[18]

The Navy Nurse Corps expanded from 460 nurses prior to the war to a high of 1,551 on Armistice Day; 327 of those served overseas in Britain or France. Some Navy nurses performed transport duty, providing care to troops as they sailed the Atlantic. Four were awarded the Navy's highest decoration, the Navy Cross. The first Navy nurses served on a hospital ship, USS *Relief*, after the war, in 1920.[19]

Altogether, more than 23,000 Army and Navy nurses served on active duty during World War I. After the Armistice, 18 African American nurses were assigned to the Army Nurse Corps because the influenza epidemic created a nurse shortage. These new nurses worked in integrated hospitals but lived in separate quarters. As the corps was demobilized after the war, they were discharged.[20]

Between the world wars, military nursing was a better-paying profession for women than most civilian ones. In addition, the military provided education, travel, and medical care, as well as room and board. Military nurses received "relative rank" in 1920, in honor of their wartime contributions. This gave them officer status and authority to wear officer-rank insignia; however, they still did not receive the same pay or privileges as their male peers. Finally, in 1926, nurses were eligible for retirement benefits and, in 1930, disability benefits, but army nurses who married and/or became pregnant were discharged. Nursing pay increased to seventy dollars a month. However, civilian nursing dropped in prestige, and a national shortage of nurses grew as demands for hospital care increased.[21]

World War II Era

More than one hundred Army and Navy nurses were serving in the Philippines when Japanese forces captured Manila in January 1942. Navy nurses still in Manila were imprisoned immediately; Army nurses were evacuated to Bataan and then Corregidor. In May, twenty-one Army and Navy nurses escaped safely to Australia by submarine and seaplane, but fifty-five Army nurses were taken prisoner after Corregidor's surrender. The nurses were liberated in 1945 after three years of imprisonment. Each received the Bronze Star and a promotion before returning to the United States. Another five Navy nurses captured on Guam in 1941 spent five months in a Japanese prison camp, for a total of eighty-three military nurse POWs in the Pacific.[22]

As Allied forces regained control of the Pacific, military nurses were moved forward and they braced themselves for new onslaughts of wounded men. Navy nurses on board hospital ships were often just a few miles offshore from island fighting, ready to take on battle wounded, provide triage, and transport them to hospitals further to the rear. During the Okinawa landing, two of the seven hospital ships offshore, the *Relief* and the *Solace*, were attacked. Once the fighting was over on an island, Army nurses were moved in to staff hospitals. Army nurses were aboard the USS *Comfort* at Okinawa in 1945 when it was hit by a kamikaze plane; six were killed.[23]

Air evacuation was a new and dramatic development during the war that saved thousands of lives. Both the Army and the Navy developed training programs for flight nurses to serve on transport planes ferrying the wounded from battlefield to hospital. Altogether, more than five hundred flight nurses evacuated almost 1.2 million patients to Pacific hospitals, Hawaii, and the United States; their dedication ensured that only forty-six died. Seventeen flight nurses, however, did not survive. Second Lieutenant Ruth M. Gardiner, the first Army-nurse fatality, died in an air-evacuation plane crash in July 1943.[24]

Other nurses were in the midst of action in Africa and Europe. When U.S. troops assaulted the North African beach in November 1942, sixty Army nurses landed with them and immediately set up medical support operations with no electricity, no running water, no beds, and few medical supplies. They shared their rations with their patients and donated their own blood. The hospitals and nurses moved forward with the units, on occasion finding themselves behind enemy lines. Lieutenant Mary Ann Sullivan received the Legion of Merit for staying with her patients in the Kasserine Pass until they could be evacuated.[25]

Two hundred Army nurses landed at Anzio in January 1944 with the invasion force. Four received the Silver Star—one posthumously—for evacuating patients during a German bombing in February 1944; six nurses died. Nurses landed four days after the Normandy invasion in June 1944, providing medical care throughout the European theater. Reba Z. Whittle, wounded when her air-evacuation plane crashed in September 1944, was held captive by the Germans for five months—the only nurse POW in Europe.[26]

In December 1943, the War Department stopped recruiting nurses. A few months later, however, an additional ten thousand nurses were needed. The situation appeared desperate, and President Roosevelt called for a draft of nurses in January 1945. While Congress debated the nurse draft bill, thousands of women joined the nurse corps, alleviating the shortage. The war ended before the bill could be passed.[27]

A record number of 57,000 Army and 12,000 Navy nurses were on active duty in 1945. Five hundred African American nurses served in the war, both in the

United States and overseas. Two hundred male nurses were drafted but 40 percent ended up serving in nonmedical positions or performed only corpsmen's duties. Nurses served everywhere that soldiers and sailors could be found and received every medal except the Medal of Honor; 1 out of 40 nurses was decorated. Of Army nurses, 201 died during the war, and 17 are buried overseas. Five hospital ships and one general hospital used during the war were named for Army nurses who died. After the war, the Army Nurse Corps was reduced to 8,500 nurses and the Navy Nurse Corps to 7,500, and both would continue to shrink until the Korean conflict. The Naval School of Air Evacuation for Navy flight nurses was closed.[28]

The military status of the nursing services was changing. Navy nurses received relative rank in 1942, and the Army could promote a nurse to lieutenant colonel. Married women were permitted to join the Army Nurse Corps in 1942 and the Navy Nurse Corps in 1944. During the war, military nurses received temporary commissions and full pay and privileges. Afterward, they received veterans' benefits. In 1947, the Army and Navy Nurse Corps became permanent staff corps. Their superintendents had the temporary rank of colonel or captain and full pay. In 1949, the Air Force Nurse Corps was formed with 1,199 nurses from the Army Nurse Corps.[29]

The Korean Conflict

Only one U.S. Army nurse, Captain Viola B. McConnell, was stationed in Korea in June 1950. She evacuated 700 Americans to Japan and received the Bronze Star. Combat troops arrived on 1 July, and 57 Army nurses on 5 July. Within days, 12 nurses moved forward with a Mobile Army Surgical Hospital (MASH), to treat the critically wounded prior to air transport to Army evacuation hospitals or Navy hospital ships. By August, 100 Army nurses were in Korea; by 1951, 540. Most were World War II veterans who had joined the reserves upon demobilization. Major Genevieve Smith, killed in a plane crash en route to be the Army's chief nurse in Korea, was the only Army nurse to die in the war.[30]

In 1950, only 1,950 regular and 440 reserve Navy nurses were serving on active duty. They were assigned in the United States, overseas, and aboard two hospital ships and eight Military Sea Transport Service (MSTS) ships, which carried soldiers and dependents to foreign duty posts. In August, the USS *Consolation* arrived in Korea, and the USS *Repose* and *Benevolence* were taken out of the Reserve Fleet. Fifteen Navy nurses were aboard the *Benevolence* during a trial run in San Francisco Harbor when it sank; one Navy nurse died. In September 1950, 11 Navy nurses were killed when their plane crashed in the Pacific en route to their new duty station. By 1951, the USS *Haven*, with 30 Navy nurses on board, was also on station, and the three ships rotated between Korea and Japan.[31]

After a major military battle, the hospital ships would be overwhelmed with casualties from the United Nations multinational force as well as U.S. personnel. Many nurses serving aboard these ships despaired over the number and kinds of casualties and the youth of the soldiers, many not yet twenty years old. As one nurse recalled: "Some had a leg or arm blown off, or both. Some were hit in the face, some were blinded, and one had half his brains blown out."[32]

Convalescent patients were sent to Yokosuka, Japan, where a dispensary that had 6 Navy nurses before the war had been transformed into a complete hospital with 200 nurses. Other Navy nurses continued to serve on transport ships carrying troops into Korea or as flight nurses on air-evacuation planes between Korea and Japan. The number of regular and reserve Navy nurses on active duty peaked in July 1951 at 3,200. Male nurses were still not eligible to join the Navy Nurse Corps.[33]

The Air Force Nurse Corps, the newest military nursing service, received its baptism by fire in the Korean War. Flight nurses had to load 30 to 40 patients onto a plane, arranging them to care for their wounds or illnesses efficiently. Sometimes extra litters dotted the floor, hampering movement. Nurses had to be prepared for unusual circumstances at high altitudes: wounds and bodily functions reacted differently, and engine noise drowned out patients' calls for help. Due to air evacuation and the Army's MASH, fewer than 2,000 of the 78,000 men who were wounded in Korea died. Air Force nurses had evacuated 350,000 patients by war's end and continued to serve in Korea through July 1953. A total of 2,991 were on active duty in June 1953.[34]

Changes in military nursing policy and practices were ongoing. A new policy stated that registered nurses could not be used to perform nonnursing tasks such as housekeeping and food service. Men were finally permitted to be in the Army Nurse Corps; Edward L. T. Lyon arrived in 1955. Legislation in 1957 permitted more colonels, lieutenant colonels, and majors in the corps. Nurses were authorized retirement pay equal to that of other Army officers, and the permanent size of the corps was increased to 2,500.[35]

After the Korean War, nurses served around the world providing support to victims of natural disasters and epidemics in Yugoslavia, Alaska, Iran, and Honduras, as well as to casualties of political violence and military action, including the Hungarian uprising, the Lebanon crisis, the Berlin crisis, the Cuban missile crisis, the U.S. occupation of the Dominican Republic, and an insurrection in Jordan (male nurses only).[36]

The Vietnam Era

Military nurses in Vietnam encountered men with vicious wounds from punji sticks, booby traps, claymore mines, and high-velocity bullets. Helicopters would whisk soldiers out of a combat area to a hospital in minutes, often overburdening the medical capability of the staff. In triage, nurses had to choose who should receive treatment based on who was expected to survive—by all accounts, an emotionally wrenching task. Patients sometimes arrived with live grenades in their stomachs or their clothing burned onto their skin—nurses had to handle these problems, often while under rocket and mortar attack and sometimes without having rested for days. Nevertheless, nurses refused to be evacuated from combat areas and often volunteered to go to firebases or Vietnamese villages.[37]

The first Army nurses arrived in Saigon in 1956 to train South Vietnamese nurses and to provide care to the U.S. Military Assistance Advisory Group. As U.S. troop strength increased, more nurses were deployed. By the end of 1963, 17,000 troops had been deployed and 215 Army nurses were in-country, working in MASH, field, and evacuation hospitals in Vietnam and Thailand. The highest number of Army nurses in Vietnam occurred in 1969, when more than 900 were in-country.[38]

At the Army's Cu Chi base, a fifteen-minute helicopter ride from Saigon, 50 nurses supported 15,000 men. It was a remote and harsh assignment; heavy fighting was always near at hand. Nurses were not allowed to ride in convoys because they were often ambushed and hidden mines and booby traps were everywhere around Cu Chi. Captain Clara Schoen said, "Young guys arrive full of holes or with an eye missing. Some come in with just two big stumps, their legs blown off by a mine. They're so young—that's what gets you."[39]

In 1963, 7 Navy nurses reported to the new U.S. Naval Station Hospital, Saigon. In 1964, 4 Navy nurses were off-duty in their quarters in Saigon when a car bomb exploded. Although all were injured, they provided first aid to others and then worked on emergencies at the hospital. They were the first military women to receive the Purple Heart in Vietnam, and the first Navy nurses ever to have received it. When offered an opportunity for less hazardous duty, each refused. In 1965, 29 Navy nurses arrived aboard the USS *Repose*, and in 1966, another 29 arrived on the USS *Sanctuary*.[40]

The Navy built a hospital at Da Nang in 1966, and 4 female nurses arrived the next year. The facility was a frequent target of mortar attacks and was shelled during the Tet offensive in 1968. The following year, the operating rooms were being used twenty-four hours a day.[41]

In 1964, Air Force flight nurses were stationed in Saigon, and clinical nurses were assigned to other locations in Vietnam and Thailand. The Air Force had one ground hospital in Cam Ranh Bay with 55 nurses. The hospital was far from the fighting, and most patients suffered from tropical and routine illnesses, not combat casualties. Nurses worked regular shifts, and many volunteered to assist Vietnamese villages or teach classes in health care.[42]

Two teams flew air evacuation during Vietnam: the Military Airlift Command (MAC), with 67 flight nurses who escorted patients aboard C-141 planes to the United States; and the Pacific Air Force (PACAF), with 54 flight nurses aboard camouflaged C-130 aircraft that delivered patients to the Philippines, Japan, or Okinawa. In unsecured areas, the nurses always wore weapons and were trained to use the M-16 machine gun. First Lieutenant Jane A. Lombardi loaded patients onto a plane under enemy fire in Da Nang and was awarded the Bronze Star for her heroism. A total of 550 Air Force nurses served in Southeast Asia from 1964 to 1973, reaching a peak of 129 in 1967–1968.[43]

Between 1965 and 1970, only 2.6 percent of the 133,000 patients treated died, in large measure due to the nurses, the mobile hospitals, the hospital ships, and the air-evacuation system.[44] An estimated 6,000 military nurses served in Vietnam from 1962 to 1973. All received combat pay, and many received combat medals. Nine Army nurses—7 of them women—died in Vietnam. First Lieutenant Sharon Ann Lane, killed by shrapnel from an enemy rocket attack on her hospital, was awarded the Purple Heart and Bronze Star posthumously. Two died in a helicopter crash in 1966, 4 in a plane crash in 1967, and 2 from illness.[45]

Military nursing policy and practice continued to evolve. In 1964, Margaret E. Bailey became the first African American Army nurse promoted to lieutenant colonel; in 1970, she was the first to make colonel. In 1964, married women could receive appointments directly into the regular Army; male nurses were authorized commissions in the regular Army in 1966. In 1970, a married pregnant officer could stay on active duty. In that same year, the Army Nurse Corps had 1,000 male nurses and promoted the first female nurse to general.[46]

Legislation in 1957 increased the number of Navy commanders. In 1965, Ensign George M. Silver became the first man to be commissioned in the Navy Nurse Corps. In 1972, Alene Duerk was the first Navy nurse promoted to admiral. Pregnant women could remain in the military, although it was still considered a disability until 1975.[47]

All-Volunteer Force

When the draft ended in 1973, women made up less than 2 percent of the military, but they were breaking many gender barriers. Navy nurses with children were allowed to stay on active duty, and the Navy gave appointments to women who already had children. In 1978, Joan Bynum became the first African American Navy nurse promoted to captain. In 1980, Captain Frances T. Shea became the first female Navy nurse to command a naval hospital; in 1985, Clarence W. Cote became the first male Navy nurse to command a naval hospital, and the following year, Captain Julia O. Barnes became the first black Navy nurse to command a naval hospital. The Navy deployed its nurses all over the globe, including Greece, Ethiopia, Sardinia, and England; on aircraft carriers; and with troops on training missions to Korea and elsewhere.[48]

Army Nurse Corps officers also made great strides in the years after Vietnam. In 1979, Hazel W. Johnson became the first African American general officer in the entire military. The first major Army hospital to be named for a woman or a nurse was dedicated in 1982. In 1983, the Pentagon honored military women with a permanent exhibit of their contributions over the years, in which military nurses figured prominently.[49]

Like Navy nurses, Army and Air Force nurses were also deployed throughout the world, including Germany, Italy, Belgium, Korea, Japan, Okinawa, and Panama. Army nurses provided support to Cuban refugees in 1980 and were assigned to the United Nations Sinai peacekeeping force for the first time in 1982, including one female among the three Army nurses. In October 1983, sixteen

Army nurses of the 5th MASH and 307th Medical Battalion at Fort Bragg deployed to Grenada; six of the nurses were decorated for their efforts. In 1984, a change in policy permitted a total of two hundred Army nurses to be assigned to medical treatment facilities in the field supporting tactical units, and in December 1989, Army nurses of the 44th Medical Brigade from Fort Bragg deployed to Panama. Air Force Reserve and Air National Guard nurses flew air-evacuation missions, commanded aeromedical evacuation units, and staffed clinics and hospitals in the wake of Hurricane Gilbert.[50]

In the 1980s, defense planners considered the numbers of military nurse reserves to be inadequate, estimating a wartime need of an additional thirty thousand nurses with operating-room, surgical, emergency, critical-care, trauma-care, or anesthesia experience. To recruit nurses, the Defense Department offered financial assistance for nursing study, gave credit for education and experience, and raised upper age limits.[51]

Medical support for Desert Shield began in the second week of August 1990 when Army, Navy, and Air Force mobile medical units were airlifted to the Persian Gulf. The Navy hospital ships USS *Mercy* and USS *Comfort* left their home ports in California and Maryland for the gulf. Safety was not assured because missiles and floating mines were threats, and hospital ships usually traveled without fleet protection. Medical personnel set up facilities to decontaminate and treat victims. Two female prisoners of war, Major Rhonda Cornum and Specialist Melissa Rathbun-Healy, were treated aboard the *Mercy*.[52] One observer noted: "The staffing of these theater facilities, ashore and afloat, was very different from that in previous wars, in that the age-old sex stereotypes—wherein women were nurses and all other medical personnel were men—had all but vanished."[53]

The Army Medical Department (AMEDD) was tasked with both continuing its military care in the United States and worldwide and deploying to Southwest Asia. The Army needed more nurses and, in September 1990, authorized the AMEDD Enlisted Commissioning Program, which sent 100 servicemembers a year to pursue a bachelor's degree in nursing and authorized incentive pay for nurse anesthetists. By mid-January 1991, the Army had established forty-four hospitals to support the war: sixteen Active Component, seventeen Army Reserve, and eleven Army National Guard. One hospital deployed to the Iraqi border in advance of casualties was further forward than allied infantry units before the ground war began. By February 1991, 2,265 Army nurses had deployed to Saudi Arabia.[54]

Fortuitously, Rear Admiral Mary A. Fields Hall, who became Director of the Navy Nurse Corps in 1987, had increased the Reserve Nurse Corps from 1,100 to 2,750 by the end of 1990. Half of the reservists were called to active duty in support of Desert Shield/Storm, enabling the Navy Medical Department to support deployed and nondeployed forces adequately. For her efforts, Hall was the first Navy Nurse Corps officer to be awarded the Distinguished Service Medal. The first Reserve Nurse Corps flag officer, Rear Admiral Maryanne T. Gallagher Ibach, was promoted in 1990.[55]

Of the 5,304 Air Force nurses on active duty during the Gulf War, 336 served in the Southwest Asia theater, almost evenly split between the active component (162) and reserve nurses (174).[56] Approximately 100,500 medical support personnel were on active duty in December 1990 and, although their numbers decreased to 99,700 by the following year, women's representation in the total force had actually increased slightly.[57]

Despite earlier concerns, Desert Storm did not result in high casualty rates for the U.S. military. Almost 300 persons died from their participation in Desert Storm, with battle deaths (148) almost equivalent to nonbattle deaths (145). Fifteen women died as a result of the war: 5 killed in action and 10 from other causes. A total of 467 U.S. military members were wounded.[58]

Since the Gulf War, military nurses have continued to participate in areas of international and intense conflict. Army nurses were dispatched to Zagreb, Croatia, in November 1992 as part of a UN peacekeeping force; another hospital unit deployed there the following year. In December 1992, additional Army nurses deployed to Honduras on rotating six-month tours. Army nurses deployed to Somalia from January 1993 to March 1994 as part of Operation Restore Hope lived and worked in a hostile environment, treating the largest influx of combat casualties experienced on a single day since the Vietnam War. In 1994, Major Nelly Aleman-Guzman became the first female Army nurse since Vietnam to be awarded the Purple Heart, for injuries incurred during her 1989 service in El Salvador.[59]

In other developments, the Air Force's 50th Flight Nurse Course included Army nurses for the first time since World War II, and Army nurse Major Mary Burman was an honor graduate. Rear Admiral Mariann Stratton, Director of the Navy Nurse Corps from 1991 to 1994, provided advice about military nursing and training in Egypt at the request of the Egyptian minister of defense. In 1994, the Navy had six female rear admirals, two of whom were nurses—one on active duty and one in the reserves.[60]

Following Desert Storm and the end of the Cold War, the number of active duty personnel, including all medical personnel, decreased dramatically. Today, almost one-third (30 percent) of all female military officers are nurses, 7 percent are doctors, and 10 percent are health care professionals. In other words, 46 percent of all female military officers serve in the health care field. Only 13 percent of all male officers are in health care positions and, of those, 42 percent are doctors.[61]

In the event of a major conflict, current active-duty and reserve nursing personnel may prove insufficient to tend to both continuing-care and combat needs. Currently, the military is finding it difficult to recruit nurses, and the low supply of nurses in the civilian world compounds the problem. Major General Jeanne Holm (USAF, retired) predicts that major mobilization will require a draft of female nurses because 98 percent of all nurses in the United States are women.[62]

Each of the military services has recognized that its nursing history needed to be written. The Navy Nurse Corps was first on the scene with a comprehensive history, *In and Out of Harm's Way: A History of the Navy Nurse Corps*, written by

Captain Doris M. Sterner. In 1992, the army selected Colonel Mary T. Sarnecky to write the Army Nurse Corps history, a project as yet uncompleted. The Air Force Nurse Corps has no firm plans yet to write its history but has acknowledged that it must be done.[63]

In October 1997, the Women in Military Service to America Memorial was dedicated in Washington, D.C. Representatives of the military nursing corps were present in full force to be recognized for their efforts and to honor all those who passed before. The *Spirit of Nursing* statue in Arlington National Cemetery was the site of a special ceremony. Deceased female Vietnam nurses have been honored on the Wall; all nurses in Vietnam have been honored with the Vietnam Women's Memorial; and nurses are a proud and large contingent of the women being honored by the new Women's Memorial. At long last, their contributions are being made visible.

NOTES

1. See Connie L. Reeves, "The Military Woman's Vanguard: Nurses," in *It's Our Military, Too! Women and the U.S. Military*, ed. Judith Hicks Stiehm (Philadelphia: Temple University Press, 1996), 73–114, for more on the earlier days of military nursing.

2. Richard A. Gabriel and Karen S. Metz, *A History of Military Medicine*, vol. 2, *From the Renaissance Through Modern Times* (Westport, Conn.: Greenwood Press, 1992), 106–7, 131, 134–36, 143; Elizabeth A. Shields, ed., *Highlights in the History of the Army Nurse Corps* (Washington, D.C.: U.S. Army Center of Military History, 1981), 7; M. Patricia Donahue, *Nursing, the Finest Art: An Illustrated History*, illus. ed./comp. Patricia A. Russac (St. Louis: C. V. Mosby, 1985), 284–85; Linda K. Kerber, *Women of the Republic: Intellect and Ideology in Revolutionary America* (Chapel Hill: University of North Carolina Press, 1980), 58–60, 74; Josephine A. Dolan, *Nursing in Society: A Historical Perspective*, 14th ed. (Philadelphia: W. B. Saunders, 1978), 108, 110, 115–16; Linda Grant De Pauw, *Seafaring Women* (Boston: Houghton Mifflin, 1982), 91; Louis A. Meier, *The Healing of an Army, 1777–1778* (Norristown, Pa.: Historical Society of Montgomery County, 1991), 17–19, 24, 28, 32–34, 36; Jeanne M. Holm, *Women in the Military: An Unfinished Revolution*, rev. ed. (Novato, Calif.: Presidio Press, 1992), 3.

3. Matthew Naythons, *The Face of Mercy: A Photographic History of Medicine at War* (New York: Random House, 1993), 42; Dolan, *Nursing in Society*, 159–61, 163–65, 167; Donahue, *Nursing, the Finest Art*, 242–45, 247–48, 251, 253; Gabriel and Metz, *From the Renaissance*, 170, 173.

4. Mary Elizabeth Carnegie, *The Path We Tread: Blacks in Nursing, 1854–1984* (Philadelphia: Lippincott, 1986), 1–4; Mary Grant Seacole, *Wonderful Adventures of Mrs. Seacole in Many Lands*, intro William L. Andrews (1857; reprint, New York: Oxford University Press, 1988).

5. Gabriel and Metz, *From Renaissance*, 187, 193; Naythons, *Face of Mercy*, 48, 74; Dolan, *Nursing in Society*, 175–76, 179, 186; Donahue, *Nursing, the Finest Art*, 280, 282–83, 285, 290–92; Lavinia Dock and Isabel Stewart, *A Short History of Nursing: From Earliest Times to Present Day*, 2d ed. (New York: G. P. Putnman's Sons, 1925), 129, 146.

6. Dolan, *Nursing in Society*, 177–78, 180; Donahue, *Nursing, the Finest Art*, 230–31, 292–94; Naythons, *Face of Mercy*, 42, 74; Holm, *Women in the Military*, 8; Nina B. Smith, "Men

and Authority: The Union Army Nurse and the Problem of Power," *MINERVA: Quarterly Report on Women and the Military* 6 (winter 1988): 25–30; Victor Robinson, *White Caps: The Story of Nursing* (Philadelphia: Lippincott, 1946), 250.

7. Louisa May Alcott, *Hospital Sketches*, ed. Bessie Z. Jones (1863; reprint, Cambridge: Harvard University Press, 1960).

8. Charles McCool Snyder, *Dr. Mary Walker: The Little Lady in Pants* (New York: Arno Press, 1974); Allen D. Spiegel and Andrea M. Spiegel, "Civil War Doctress Mary: Only Woman to Win Congressional Medal of Honor," *MINERVA: Quarterly Report on Women and the Military* 12 (summer 1994): 27–29; Holm, *Women in the Military*, 6–7; Gabriel and Metz, *From the Renaissance*, 192; Dolan, *Nursing in Society*, 184; Naythons, *Face of Mercy*, 74.

9. Nina Brown Baker, *Cyclone in Calico, The Story of Mary Ann Bickerdyke* (Boston: Little, Brown, 1952); Adele Deleeuw, *Civil War Nurse: Mary Ann Bickerdyke* (New York: Simon & Schuster, 1973); Nancy B. Samuelson, "Mother Bickerdyke: She Outranked Everybody but God," *MINERVA: Quarterly Report on Women and the Military* 5 (summer 1987): 114–19. See also L. P. Brockett and Mary C. Vaughan, *Women at War: A Record of Their Patriotic Contributions, Heroism, Toils and Sacrifice During the Civil War* (1867; reprint, Stamford, Conn.: Longmeadow Press, 1993), 172–86.

10. Susie King Taylor, *Reminiscences of My Life in Camp with the 33rd United States Colored Troops Late 1st South Carolina Volunteers* (1902; reprint, New York: Arno, 1968); John P. Dever and Maria C. Dever, *Women and the Military: A Hundred Notable Contributors, History to Contemporary* (Jefferson, N.C.: McFarland, 1995), 146. See also Donahue, *Nursing, the Finest Art*, 301, 206–7; Naythons, *Face of Mercy*, 75; Dolan, *Nursing in Society*, 183–84; Carnegie, *Path We Tread*, 1–11.

11. Percy H. Epler, *The Life of Clara Barton* (1919; reprint, New York: Macmillan, 1953); Stephen B. Oates, *A Woman of Valor: Clara Barton and the Civil War* (New York: Free Press, 1994); Dolan, *Nursing in Society*, 175; Naythons, *Face of Mercy*, 42; Donahue, *Nursing, the Finest Art*, 294; Holm, *Women in the Military*, 7.

12. Jean Berlin, *A Confederate Nurse: The Diary of Ada W. Bacot, 1860–1863* (Columbia: University of South Carolina Press, 1994); Glenna R. Schroeder-Lein, *Confederate Hospitals on the Move: Samuel H. Stout and the Army of Tennessee* (Columbia: University of South Carolina Press, 1994); Gabriel and Metz, *From the Renaissance*, 193; Donahue, *Nursing, the Finest Art*, 304–6; Dolan, *Nursing in Society*, 185.

13. "The U.S. Hospital Ship *Red Rover* (1862–1865)," *Military Surgeon* 77, no. 92 (August 1935), quoted in Donahue, *Nursing, the Finest Art*, 288. See also Naythons, *Face of Mercy*, 42; Gabriel and Metz, *From the Renaissance*, 181–82, 185–87, 189–90, 194–95; De Pauw, *Seafaring Women*, 101.

14. Naythons, *Face of Mercy*, 74–75; Donahue, *Nursing, the Finest Art*, 287; Carnegie, *Path We Tread*, 9.

15. Holm, *Women in the Military*, 8–9; Shields, *History of the Army Nurse Corps*, 8–11; Dolan, *Nursing in Society*, 220–21; Donahue, *Nursing, the Finest Art*, 327–33; Dock and Stewart, *A Short History of Nursing*, 181. See also Barbara Brooks Tomblin, *G.I. Nightingales: The Army Nurse Corps in World War II* (Lexington: University of Kentucky Press, 1996), 2.

16. Shields, *History of the Army Nurse Corps*, 10–16; Donahue, *Nursing, the Finest Art*, 297, 327, 329, 331, 333; Dolan, *Nursing in Society*, 221, 285–286; Tomblin, *G.I. Nightingales*, 2–3; Holm, *Women in the Military*, 9; Mary E. Gladwin, *The Red Cross and Jane Arminda Delano* (Philadelphia: W. B. Saunders, 1931), 42.

17. Shields, *History of the Army Nurse Corps*, 14; Donahue, *Nursing, the Finest Art*, 397–98; Holm, *Women in the Military*, 10; Jo-Anne Mecca, " 'Neither Fish, Flesh, Nor Fowl': The World War I Army Nurse," *MINERVA: Quarterly Report on Women and the Military* 13

(summer 1995): 5, 6; Carolyn M. Feller and Constance J. Moore, *Highlights in the History of the Army Nurse Corps* (Washington, D.C.: U.S. Army Center of Military History, 1995), 3–5; Tomblin, *G.I. Nightingales*, 3–5; Dolan, *Nursing in Society*, 287–90; Donahue, *Nursing, the Finest Art*, 399–402, 404; Gabriel and Metz, *From the Renaissance*, 240, 243, 250; Gladwin, *Red Cross*, 45–46, 61–63; Robinson, *White Caps*, 225, 288–89.

18. Donahue, *Nursing, the Finest Art*, 404–5, 407; Shields, *History of the Army Nurse Corps*, 14, 16; Holm, *Women in the Military*, 10; Dolan, *Nursing in Society*, 287.

19. Holm, *Women in the Military*, 11; Donahue, *Nursing, the Finest Art*, 407.

20. Feller and Moore, *Highlights*, 5.

21. Holm, *Women in the Military*, 16–17; Donahue, *Nursing, the Finest Art*, 331, 407–8, 432; Shields, *History of the Army Nurse Corps*, 18–19; Doris Weatherford, *American Women and World War II* (New York: Facts on File, 1990), 3, 16.

22. Judith A. Bellafaire, *The Army Nurse Corps: A Commemoration of World War II Service* (Washington, D.C.: U.S. Army Center of Military History, 1994), 4–7; Barbara B. Tomblin, "Beyond Paradise: The U.S. Navy Nurse Corps in the Pacific in World War II (Part One)," *MINERVA: Quarterly Report on Women and the Military* 11 (spring 1993): 33–40; Tomblin, *G.I. Nightingales*, 28–37; Weatherford, *American Women and World War II*, 2–7; "RN Notes and Quotes," *RN* 34, no. 5 (May 1971): 19; Holm, *Women in the Military*, 45, 91, 97; Shields, *History of the Army Nurse Corps*, 20–24; Feller and Moore, *Highlights*, 8.

23. Tomblin, "Beyond Paradise (Part One)," 41–48; Weatherford, *American Women and World War II*, 11–12; Barbara B. Tomblin, "Beyond Paradise: The US Navy Nurse Corps in the Pacific in World War II (Part Two)," *MINERVA: Quarterly Report on Women and the Military* 11 (fall/winter 1993): 37–8; Tomblin, *G.I. Nightingales*, 42–45; Bellafaire, *Army Nurse Corps*, 24–27.

24. Feller and Moore, *Highlights*, 8; Bellafaire, *Army Nurse Corps*, 14–15, 28; Shields, *History of the Army Nurse Corps*, 22; Donahue, *Nursing, the Finest Art*, 416; Weatherford, *American Women and World War II*, 12; Tomblin, *G.I. Nightingales*, 42–45.

25. Bellafaire, *Army Nurse Corps*, 9; Weatherford, *American Women and World War II*, 9; Holm, *Women in the Military*, 80, 91; Shields, *History of the Army Nurse Corps*, 22.

26. Weatherford, *American Women and World War II*, 8–9; Bellafaire, *Army Nurse Corps*, 11–14, 16–24.

27. Bellafaire, *Army Nurse Corps*, 7–8; Dolan, *Nursing in Society*, 306–7; Donahue, *Nursing, the Finest Art*, 306, 408, 414, 419–20; Shields, *History of the Army Nurse Corps*, 22–4; Holm, *Women in the Military*, 108–9; Weatherford, *American Women and World War II*, 19–21.

28. Tomblin, "Beyond Paradise (Part Two)," 50; Shields, *History of the Army Nurse Corps*, 25; Holm, *Women in the Military*, 91–92; Donahue, *Nursing, the Finest Art*, 395, 415–16; Bellafaire, *Army Nurse Corps*, 16, 19, 31; Feller and Moore, *Highlights*, 7, 10; Dolan, *Nursing in Society*, 307.

29. Donahue, *Nursing, the Finest Art*, 306, 331, 408, 414, 418–20; Dolan, *Nursing in Society*, 306–7; Shields, *History of the Army Nurse Corps*, 22–4, 28, 31; Holm, *Women in the Military*, 108–9; Bellafaire, *Army Nurse Corps*, 7–8, 31; Weatherford, *American Women and World War II*, 19–21; Doris M. Sterner, *In and Out of Harm's Way: A History of the Navy Nurse Corps* (Seattle: Peanut Butter Publishing for Navy Nurse Corps Association, 1996), 208–09, 212.

30. Donahue, *Nursing, the Finest Art*, 421–6; Holm, *Women in the Military*, 149–50; Shields, *History of the Army Nurse Corps*, 33–5; Sterner, *In and Out*, 236; Gabriel and Metz, *From the Renaissance*, 257.

31. Sterner, *In and Out*, 230–5.

32. Eveline Kittilson McClean, LT, Navy Nurse Corps, Oral History Interview Tape Transcript, Self-interview, 4 July 1990, quoted ibid. 238.

33. Sterner, *In and Out*, 240–46.

34. Gabriel and Metz, *From the Renaissance*, 257; Donahue, *Nursing, the Finest Art*, 422, 426. E-mail correspondence with HQ USAF/SGI, 13 November 1997.

35. Shields, *History of the Army Nurse Corps*, 37, 40–41, 43; Feller and Moore, *Highlights*, 7, 14, 15; Donahue, *Nursing, the Finest Art*, 408.

36. Shields, *History of the Army Nurse Corps*, 41, 44–47, 51–52, 54; Holm, *Women in the Military*, 226; Feller and Moore, *Highlights*, 17–21, 25.

37. Dan Freedman and Jacqueline Rhoads, eds., *Nurses in Vietnam: The Forgotten Veterans* (Austin: Texas Monthly Press, 1987), 1–5; Holm, *Women in the Military*, 106, 225, 232–33; Donahue, *Nursing, the Finest Art*, 431.

38. Shields, *History of the Army Nurse Corps*, 41, 49, 55; Donahue, *Nursing, the Finest Art*, 427; Holm, *Women in the Military*, 226; Feller and Moore, *Highlights*, 20, 22, 24, 26.

39. Linda Grant Martin, "Angels of Viet Nam," *Today's Health* 45, no. 8 (August 1967): 17.

40. Sterner, *In and Out*, 258, 260, 310–15, 327.

41. Ibid., 318–54, *passim*.

42. Shields, *History of the Army Nurse Corps*, 41, 49, 55; Donahue, *Nursing, the Finest Art*, 427; Holm, *Women in the Military*, 226; Feller and Moore, *Highlights*, 20, 22, 24, 26; Martin, "Angels of Viet Nam," 19, 60–61; Sterner, *In and Out*, 301–2; E-mail correspondence with HQ USAF/SGI, 13 November 1997.

43. Katharine Drake, "Our Flying Nightingales in Vietnam," *Reader's Digest*, December 1967, 75–76, 78–79; Martin, "Angels of Viet Nam," 17; E-mail correspondence with HQ USAF/SGI, 13 November 1997.

44. Holm, *Women in the Military*, 227, 232–34; Donahue, *Nursing, the Finest Art*, 431; Gabriel and Metz, *From the Renaissance*, 259–60.

45. Holm, *Women in the Military*, 7, 228, 242; Shields, *History of the Army Nurse Corps*, 59, 62; Freedman and Rhoads, *Nurses in Vietnam*, 1; Feller and Moore, *Highlights*, 25–26; Joseph L. Galloway, "Another Vietnam Memorial," *U.S. News & World Report* 15 November 1993, 21.

46. Feller and Moore, *Highlights*, 21–26; Shields, *History of the Army Nurse Corps*, 51–53, 57–58.

47. Sterner, *In and Out*, 268–69, 278, 283, 287, 296, 306, 317, 337–38, 346, 352–53, 359, 361–62.

48. Amanda Maisels and Patricia M. Gormley, *Women in the Military: Where They Stand, A Women in the Military Project Report* (Washington, D.C.: Women's Research and Education Institute, 1994), 1; Sterner, *In and Out*, 365, 368–71, 380–1.

49. Feller and Moore, *Highlights*, 27–32.

50. Holm, *Women in the Military*, 404; Feller and Moore, *Highlights*, 28–36.

51. Feller and Moore, *Highlights*, 37.

52. U.S. General Accounting Office, *Women in the Persian Gulf War: Report to the Secretary of Defense*, GAO/NSIAD-93-93 (Washington, D.C.: U.S. General Accounting Office, July 1993).

53. Holm, *Women in the Military*, 442–43, 445, 450, 459.

54. Feller and Moore, *Highlights*, 37–38.

55. Sterner, *In and Out*, 385.

56. E-mail correspondence with HQ USAF/SGI, 13 November 1997.

57. *Defense Almanac 91* (Arlington, Va.: American Forces Information Service, September/October 1991), 25, 30.

58. Maisels and Gormley, *Where They Stand*, 7; *Defense Almanac 91*, 56–57.

59. Maisels and Gormley, *Where They Stand*, 1, 3; Feller and Moore, *Highlights*, 38–40.

60. Sterner, *In and Out*, 385; Feller and Moore, *Highlights*, 39; Maisels and Gormley, *Where They Stand*, 9.

61. Maisels and Gormley, *Where They Stand*, 1, 3; Faxed correspondence HQ USAF/SGWN, 12 November 1997.

62. Holm, *Women in the Military*, 367.

63. Sterner, *In and Out*, passim; Feller and Moore, *Highlights*, 38.

Autobiography
An Officer and a Feminist

Karen Johnson

During the blizzard of 1947, I began life as the first-born child of a young Negro couple in Jersey City, New Jersey. My birth was heralded by the world debut of the *Howdy Doody* show. Eleven months later, my brother was born. There was a twelve-year hiatus before my three sisters began making their entrances into this life.

During most of my childhood, our family lived in small apartments in a dangerous urban ghetto. Spending much time indoors, I became an avid reader and movie lover. At an early age, my brother and I began watching war movies on television. When I was about twelve, I read with horror about the Holocaust as newspapers covered the trial of Eichmann. As a teenager, my interest in the military grew as I read *Exodus, Failsafe, On the Beach,* and *The Green Berets.* However, I decided to work toward the more traditional goal of becoming a nurse, and I entered a registered nurse program at a medical center in Newark, New Jersey.

The war in Vietnam came to the forefront of my consciousness in 1965, when the United States sent 185,000 troops to fight in that country. Two years later, as a nineteen-year-old student nurse, I lay on the floor of my dormitory room listening to intermittent sniper fire and tanks rolling by in the street below during the Newark riots—my first combat-like experience. At age twenty, I became a registered nurse in charge of the evening shift in the emergency room at the medical center. In 1972, after seven years of watching news coverage of the Vietnam War filled with body counts and casualty figures, I joined the military. With three years of nursing experience in the emergency room, I wanted to put my skills to use in service to my country. The Air Force appealed to me because of its flight-nursing program. While I discussed my decision to join the military with my friends, I did not consult with my family. I was as confident of the correctness of my decision as I was of the disapproval of my mother. My mother feared for my safety and desired to have me nearby.

A Most Excellent Adventure

"A most excellent adventure" is the phrase I use to describe my twenty years in the military. My adventure began at Officers Basic Military Training School at Sheppard Air Force Base, Texas, in 1972, where I completed a two-week course on military customs, policies, and procedures. My first assignments were at Wilford Hall Medical Center, Lackland Air Force Base, Texas, and then at the 432nd USAF Hospital, Udorn Air Force Base, Thailand, followed by Torrejon Regional USAF Hospital, Torrejon Air Force Base, Spain. I was then allowed to complete my bachelor of science degree at Loretto Heights College, Denver, Colorado, under an Air Force–sponsored education program. After that, I returned to Wilford Hall Medical Center, Lackland Air Force Base, Texas. Next I completed my master of science degree at Yale University, in New Haven, Connecticut, again under an Air Force–sponsored education program. My final assignment was at Wright-Patterson USAF Medical Center, Wright-Patterson Air Force Base, Ohio.

In 1992, I retired as a lieutenant colonel with a chest full of ribbons, a head full of memories, and a heart full of gratitude for my "most excellent adventure" in the United States Air Force. Gone was the quiet, naive, nonpolitical idealist of the 1970s—I had "morphed" into an assertive feminist activist of the 1990s.

The Military Nurse

The Air Force was a fantastic place for professional growth and development. From the beginning of my time on active duty, I found that as I put maximum effort into nursing and strove to be a good military officer, my efforts were rewarded with opportunities to advance my nursing and military education. I entered the Air Force as a registered nurse with a diploma from a hospital school of nursing. Thanks to Air Force–sponsored education, I completed both my bachelor's and master's degrees while on active duty.

While much of my military education came through "on the job training" (OJT), I attended several formal military courses to advance my nursing and professional military education. In 1973, I graduated from the Flight Nursing Course and received the coveted flight nurse wings. In 1979 and 1980, I completed the Nursing Service Management Course and Squadron Officers School in residence. I completed other courses, such as Air Command and Staff College, in a seminar or by correspondence.

Military nursing truly allowed me to "aim high." I was and am impressed with the competency and professionalism of military nurses. My first supervisor, Captain Tommie Jean Hudson, had served as a flight nurse flying casualties from Vietnam. Thrown somewhat by her southern drawl (Captain Hudson was a native Alabaman), I quickly grew to admire and respect her nursing acumen. A no-nonsense, take-charge, compassionate, competent, and dedicated individual,

Captain Hudson was the epitome of the nurse officer and served as my role model.

Caring for the sick, injured, and wounded was a job that I loved. Thanks to the military, I was able to do that job in many places and in varying roles. As a clinical staff nurse, I worked on orthopedic pediatric, medical-surgical, and mental health units. As a nurse manager, I supervised mental health units, the operating room, the nursing quality-assurance program, and the entire nursing staff of the medical center. As a clinical nurse specialist, I served as consultant to the nurses, adviser to the nurse administrators, and staff developer.

Highlights of my twenty years of military nursing include chairing the planning committee of the first Nursing Red Flag course, an eighteen–hour didactic battlefield nursing course attended by more than 450 military nurses, and being selected as "Nurse of the Year" at the Air Force's largest medical center. Another highlight was presenting my master's research on the Air Force nurses' knowledge of caring for the patient with combat-related acute post-traumatic stress disorder at the Association of Military Surgeons of the United States conference in 1985. I also organized several daylong continuing education programs on nursing research as chair of the nursing research committee. In addition, I developed and taught numerous continuing education programs on such topics as mentoring, assertiveness training, stress management, coping with death and dying, conflict resolution, and quality assurance in nursing. Beyond that, I facilitated patient groups dealing with living with cancer, coping with being HIV positive, smoking cessation and bereavement.

While I rarely knew what it was to work just a forty-hour week during my twenty years of military service, I often experienced the pure joy of knowing I made a positive difference through my work. I am forever indebted to the military and particularly the United States Air Force Nurse Corps for a wondrous and professionally challenging career.

The Military Culture

On the other hand, the military culture and social milieu was less awe-inspiring than military nursing. Let me preface my remarks on the social milieu of the military by sharing that I joined the military as a nondrinking, nonsmoking, twenty-four-year-old sexually inexperienced black woman.

While the issues of sex and race were indeed central to the social aspects of my military experience, sex was the difference that seemed the focal point of my initial socialization into the military culture. When I attended the Officers Basic Military Training (OBMT) course at Sheppard Air Force Base, I noticed the paucity of women in military uniform. In 1972, about 1.6 percent of the active-duty Air Force was female, and most of the women were in medical or clerical fields. At Sheppard, we female attendees at OBMT were immediately and repeatedly informed by male officers that we were expected to attend daily happy hours at the officers club as part of our orientation to military life. Male officers came to the club to "hit on" the "new nurses." There were the obvious "meat-market" mentality and the strategy of plying us with alcohol in an effort to "get lucky." Married officers removed their wedding bands and became "geographical bachelors." Even twenty-five years later, in 1997, this "military tradition" of "welcoming" nurses to the Air Force continues.

In 1973, I was one of fourteen women stationed on a U.S. Air Force fighter-jet base with 3,000 men in northern Thailand; another 2,000 U.S. Army soldiers were housed about three miles away. There were 9,000 registered Thai prostitutes—many of whom were teenagers—to meet the "needs" of the U.S. servicemen. The services of a prostitute could be bought for $3–$5 a night, although often I witnessed airmen negotiating lower rates with the women. As a cost-saving measure, many men would rent a bungalow off base for $35 a month and then pay a "tealock" $1 a day to serve as a "temporary wife." Most of the married men were engaging in sex with Thai women, despite the regulations against adultery. Even though hospital personnel delivered condoms by the gross on a weekly basis to the local bars, every day twenty-five to thirty-five of our military men would be lined up outside our hospital's social-disease clinic.

In the officers club there were topless dancers and Thai women wearing low-cut red minidresses who would massage the chest and back of the officers for thirty minutes for twenty-five cents. The officers club had live bands and ten-cent drinks during happy hour. It was not unusual to observe a club filled with drunken officers who would fall to the floor simultaneously when a comrade yelled, "Dead bug." It was during this year, as I observed "men behaving badly" sans wives and family, that I consciously identified as a feminist.

During my military career, I was sexually harassed by military men on several occasions, and I was sexually assaulted once. Shortly after entering the Air Force, I encountered the first harasser, who was definitely a "wolf in sheep's clothing." This lieutenant colonel was a military chaplain and Catholic priest (my mom had warned me that all men were dogs). This "fifty-something" priest wanted to be my lover. With genuine horror, I explained to him that even though I was a Protestant, I believed in his vow of celibacy and didn't want to compete with God. On a couple of other occasions I was harassed by a captain and a colonel. While in civilian attire, I was exiting a disco in Spain when an enlisted sailor standing in a line of other sailors reached out and groped my genital area from behind—I had a few words with that sailor. The one time I reported being sexually harassed to the harasser's supervisor, I was told that I must have misinterpreted the officer's comments and behavior. So, like many other military women, I dealt with sexual harassment on my own.

Being a black female officer in the Air Force was about being conspicuous. At my duty assignments I was either "the one and only" or one of just a few black female officers. Soon I became used to stares and comments that came with my status. The stares came from all races and particularly the enlisted ranks. The comments were almost always from black military members, who expressed their pleasure at seeing a black female officer. Often I was told about another black nurse officer stationed somewhere else. The black nurses who had come before me and now were majors, lieutenant colonels, or colonels, soon took on the proportions of legend. Acutely aware that my behavior would reflect on other black Air Force members just because there were so few of us, I knew that I would be either a credit or a disgrace to my race.

Shortly after entering the military, I found a note in my military purse that said: "Nigger, we are watching you!" For the next twenty years, I always remembered that there were those watching who could only see my race and not my character.

Later in my military career, I learned that one of those "watchers" was the hospital commander. The commander was very distressed that his daughter was dating a black man. The daughter was also a casual acquaintance of mine. My supervisor, a white female, was instructed several times to downgrade my performance evaluation—eventually, she followed instructions. Several years after the evaluation, my supervisor informed me of what had happened and apologized for her lack of courage. Fortunately, that evaluation did not affect my promotion to major.

While encounters with sexism and racism in the military were distressing, those encounters served to increase my resolve to work to eliminate both of those "isms." My feminist activism was in direct response to the rampant sexism I witnessed in the military. In my third year in the military, I became a member of the National Organization for Women (NOW). In my eighth year, I walked for the passage of the Equal Rights Amendment, and in my fourteenth year, I became a national board member of NOW. One year after my retirement from the military, I was elected as a national vice president of NOW.

The majority of my encounters in military society were self-affirming as opposed to self-negating. As a nurse officer, my role was much more accepted by military men than women officers and enlisted women in nontraditional roles. There is still a great resistance, particularly within the "old guard," to seeing women as equally able to fulfill all duties of the "American fighting man." I believe that much of the sexual harassment and assault of women within the military by military men has to do with putting women in our place.

Yet in the military culture, I also felt a deeper sense of community, greater personal responsibility, and a larger commitment to others than I have experienced in the civilian culture. Over the years, military members extended many kindnesses to me just because I wore the uniform. Many of the friendships I developed in the military are becoming lifelong friendships.

In October 1997, I attended the dedication ceremony and festivities for the Women in the Military Service of America Memorial with about thirty thousand U.S. women veterans. I felt that I had come home. This was more than a dedication—it was a family reunion. This veteran of the Vietnam and Persian Gulf Wars hugged sister veterans of World War II and the Korean War. We laughed, shared "war stories," sang songs, and celebrated our history together. In the middle of this reunion, I encountered a group of female cadets from the Virginia Military Institute (VMI). These young women with buzz haircuts were the end of the 159-year-old all-male tradition at VMI. As a vice president of the National

Organization for Women, I had worked for the right of women to attend VMI, and here they were! The cadets were so thrilled to be among us women veterans that they had all decided that they would join the military after completing their VMI education. On my desk are two photos from the WIMSA dedication. One is a picture of me with my arms around two World War II Army nurses, one of whom served under General George S. Patton and earned five battle ribbons. Those two army nurses and I were standing among the graves of other military nurses in Arlington Cemetery. In my mind's eye, we represent the past. The other is a photo of me in the midst of the smiling VMI cadets. They and others like them are our future military leaders—awesome!

Two

From Women's Services to Servicewomen

Georgia Clark Sadler

Historically, military and political leaders in the United States did not want women in the armed forces, and certainly not in combat. Yet military requirements left America's leaders no choice: to cope with skill and personnel shortages, the military needed women. This chapter examines the changing roles of women in the U.S. armed forces: the Army, Navy, Marine Corps, and Air Force, which constitute the Department of Defense (DOD), and the Coast Guard, which is part of the Department of Transportation in peacetime but comes under the DOD during war. It assesses the progress of military women as they move from providing women's services to become servicewomen—that is, full and equal members of the armed forces.

Women Need Not Apply . . . Except As Needed

Women have been associated with the American military since the founding of the country. In colonial America, women cooked, sewed, and did laundry for soldiers (see chapter 6). During the American Revolution, General George Washington specified that nurses be women in order to free men for the battlefield. During the War of 1812, the wives of two sailors were nurses aboard the frigate *United States*, making them the first women to serve on an American warship.[1]

At the beginning of the Spanish-American War, the Army's Surgeon General was reluctant to have women nurses in the field with male soldiers and feared the Army might have to provide them with "luxuries," such as rocking chairs. Yet women did serve, though under contract with the Army, not in it. After the war, Army leaders realized they needed women nurses on a permanent basis: the Nurse Corps was created in 1901 as an auxiliary of the Army. Nurses, however, were not given military status, equal pay, or retirement or veterans benefits. Seven years later, the Navy Nurse Corps was formed (see chapter 1).

In World War I, the Army urgently needed personnel with clerical and telecommunications skills but refused to enlist women. Instead, it hired civilian women as clerks and telephone operators after determining that "with careful supervision, women employees may be permitted in camps without moral injury either to themselves or to the soldiers."[2] In contrast, the Secretary of the Navy decided to enlist women so "we will have the best clerical assistance the country can provide."[3] The Marine Corps and Coast Guard followed the Navy's lead and recruited women, albeit in small numbers. Importantly, women in World War I also showed they had, or could learn, nontraditional skills, such as those exercised by radio operators, translators, and camouflage designers.

At the start of World War II, attitudes generally had not changed; most military leaders did not want to recruit women. However, some had learned from the experiences of World War I. The Army Chief of Staff recognized that women had more training and experience in some noncombat skills than men and supported the formation of the Women's Army Auxiliary Corps (WAAC). Yet some members of Congress argued that women serving in the Army would be a humiliation to America's manhood, and one congressman worried about who would do "the cooking, the washing, the mending, the humble homey tasks to which every woman has devoted herself" if women went to war.[4]

Despite these objections, the WAAC was established, followed by the Navy's WAVES (Women Accepted for Volunteer Emergency Service), the Women Marines, and the Coast Guard SPARS (from the motto *Semper Paratus*). The descriptor Auxiliary was dropped from the WAAC title in mid-1943, and the WAAC became simply the Women's Army Corps (WAC). The WASP (Women Airforce Service Pilots) was a unit of civil service pilots who delivered supplies, personnel, and new aircraft to bases during part of the war. In 1947, when the Air Force was formed as a separate service, the WAF (Women in the Air Force) was established.

The different women's services had different policies regarding racial/ethnic minorities. The WAAC/WAC accepted African American women a year after its inception but segregated blacks and whites into separate units. Asian and Hispanic American women either passed as or were accepted as honorary whites or were assigned to "colored" units, depending upon a variety of factors, including post location and command.[5] The WAVES and SPARS excluded African American women until October 1944, when so few were admitted that segregation was not feasible. However, at least fourteen African American women had served in the Navy during World War I.[6] The first African American women integrated into the Marine Corps arrived at boot camp in September 1949.

The Army's policy of segregation surprised and angered many African Americans, especially those from integrated civilian communities. As former WAC Bernadine Flannagan recalls: "The whole military service was a shock to me because I had no idea it was segregated. . . . I just didn't think that way."[7] Job assignments of African American military women and men were also affected: many black women were assigned to cooking and cleaning duties, and many black men were manual laborers. African American personnel challenged such discrimination. Margaret Barnes Jones, a WAC officer, led 175 black women from boot camp to Camp Breckenridge, Kentucky, and upon their arrival found that they "were assigned as charwomen, and they had to work in the laundry. Now those WACs were skilled. One was a schoolteacher, they had done administrative work . . . they rebelled. . . ." Shortly thereafter, Brigadier General Don Faith, former commandant of the WAAC Training Center arrived at Breckenridge, and, according to Jones, the black WACs' "assignments were changed to jobs commensurate with their skills."[8]

Many African Americans believed that serving in the military would strengthen their claims for full rights as citizens in a society that continued to deny them equal access to education, housing, and employment. As Gladys Carter, a former WAC, put it: "We were going to do our duty. Despite all the bad things that happened in the country . . . there was a feeling of wanting to do your part."[9] They were also frustrated because, although black enlistment was limited to 10 percent of the force, proportionate to the presence of African Americans in the civilian population, the actual enlistment of African American women never exceeded 4 percent. Furthermore, few African American units were deployed overseas, where they felt they could prove themselves vital to the war effort. Only one black WAC unit, the 6888th Central Postal Battalion, was permitted to serve in Europe.[10]

Altogether, more than 350,000 women served during World War II. Women filled only noncombat jobs so men could be reassigned to fighting units. Many women pounded typewriters and operated telephones, but others packed parachutes, repaired radar gear, collected weather data, taught instrument flying, directed air traffic, and instructed men on antiaircraft weapons.

After the war, military leaders proposed that women become part of the permanent military force. Congress again resisted. House members were concerned about women being allowed to command men; senators worried that women would become disabled by menopause.[11] But the majority saw the need to keep some women on active duty to form a nucleus for women's mobilization in the event of another major conflict. Consequently, on 2 June 1948, Congress passed the Women's Armed Services Integration Act, which permitted women to become permanent members of the services in the Defense Department.[12]

Congress agreed to let women be part of the regular forces but restricted their numbers to 2 percent of personnel and limited the rank and duties of women officers: no women could be generals or admirals; only one woman in each service could be a colonel or captain; and women could command only female units. Women officers were promoted more slowly and had to retire earlier than men. Women had a higher enlistment age and were required to have more education to enlist.

The Integration Act also precluded some women from serving in certain combat assignments. The law forbade Navy and Marine Corps women from being assigned to any ship, other than hospital ships and transports. Women in the Navy, Marine Corps, and Air Force were prohibited from assignment to aircraft with a combat mission.[13] These restrictions would also apply to the Coast Guard in wartime. Because defining a ground-combat exclusion proved too difficult, Congress let the Army formulate its own assignment policy.

Additionally, the military was not a family-friendly employer for women. Married men automatically received special pay and benefits for their wives, but married women could receive them only if they could prove they were the "chief support" for their husbands. Women also had to leave the military if they became pregnant or if a child resided in their home for more than thirty days a year.

Essentially, military women were barely visible after passage of the Integration Act because their number stayed below the 2 percent ceiling. The Coast Guard discharged all SPARS after the war, although the law authorizing the Women's Reserves was still on the books, and some former SPARS volunteered for duty in the Korean War. The Defense Advisory Committee on Women in the Service (DACOWITS) was a civilian group established in 1951 to advise the Secretary of Defense on recruitment and retention of women. In 1967, under pressure from DACOWITS, Congress removed the ceiling on the number of women who could serve and modified the promotion system of women officers to make it similar to men's, including appointment to general and admiral. But the services were slow to implement the changes. Five years after the 2 percent ceiling was lifted, the nonnurse female proportion of the military still stood at only 1.7 percent.

A Time for Change: The All-Volunteer Force

Other than a small mobilization for the Korean War, the next time women were needed in substantial numbers turned out to be not a war but a *man*power crisis: the advent of the All Volunteer Force (AVF) in 1973 (see figure 2.1). With no draft, recruiting enough qualified men became difficult, so personnel managers looked to women to fill the gap. This included the Coast Guard, and in December 1973, Congress disestablished the Women's Reserves and authorized women to enter the regular Coast Guard. The number of military women increased rapidly, more than doubling from 45,033 in 1972 to 118,966 in 1977.[14]

Pressure to equalize the treatment of servicewomen was maintained by DACOWITS, and in 1974, Congress rescinded the higher enlistment age for women, and the services gradually began to equalize other standards. The Air Force, Navy, and Coast Guard integrated their basic training, but the Army vacillated— consolidating boot camp, then returning to gender-segregated training, then going back to mixed recruit training. The Marine Corps retained separate boot camps for men and women but increased weapons and combat-skills training for enlisted women.

Officer training and education also became gender integrated. By the 1980s, the services were training women officer candidates with their male counterparts. Even the Marine Corps sent women to its Basic School with men, but after charges that this was leading to a "softer" training, reverted to segregated officer training. In the late 1960s and early 1970s, women began to be admitted to the Reserve Officer Training Corps (ROTC) program, which trains future officers at civilian colleges. The most dramatic change in officer education came in 1976 with the admission of women to the military academies, detailed in chapter 3.

FIGURE 2.1

Department of Defense Female Active-Duty Military Personnel, Fiscal Years 1945 to 1997

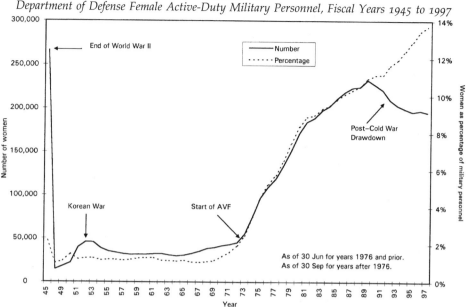

SOURCE: Adapted from U.S. Department of Defense, *Selected Manpower Statistics, Fiscal Year 1996*, DIOR/M01-96 (Washington, D.C.: Government Printing Office), 94–96; U.S. Department of Defense, Defense Manpower Data Center, *Distribution of Active Duty Forces by Service, Rank, Sex, and Ethnic Group*, DMDC-3035 (30 September 1997).

Family Policies Meet Reality

With more women being recruited and trained, the services also had to focus on keeping them. One major problem was family policies that encouraged married women to leave the military or mandated they do so. But since the military needed to retain as many individuals as possible, the services decided that marriage and motherhood were compatible with a military career and began to accommodate wives and mothers. Women were no longer expected to leave the service because they married. The services worked hard on assigning women with or near their husbands. In 1973, the Supreme Court struck down the different requirements for women to receive benefits for their spouses.[15]

In the 1970s, servicewomen raised court challenges to their automatic discharge when they became pregnant. Consequently, the services began granting waivers for new parents and pregnant women to remain in the service on an ad-hoc basis. In 1975, the Secretary of Defense told the services to make pregnancy separations voluntary and to end parenthood discharges. The services complied—except the Army, which continued to resist the change. In 1976, a federal court ruled that mandatory pregnancy discharges were unconstitutional.[16] In 1978, the Army finally capitulated and implemented a voluntary separation policy. In 1982, the Navy modified its policy to retain pregnant women with special skills and training, except in special circumstances. In 1995, the Secretary of the Navy said requests for discharge due to pregnancy would not normally be approved.

To date, the most innovative effort to help service personnel cope with pregnancy and parenthood is the Coast Guard's Care of Newborn Child Program. Under this policy, new parents—female and male—may leave the service for up to a year with the assurance that when they return, they will have the same rank and occupational specialty as when they left.

Women's Organizations Disband

As the number and proportion of women in the military expanded, the organizational structures that administered and supported servicewomen during and after World War II began to disappear. The office of the Director of the SPARS was eliminated in 1946, when most Coast Guard women were discharged. In 1972, the Director of the WAVES concluded that her office had outlived its usefulness, and it was closed in 1973.

In the early seventies, the head of Air Force personnel decided that women's issues should be integrated into the work of various personnel staff offices. This, coupled with a sharp reduction in its staff, led to the shutting down of the WAF Director's office in 1976. Similarly, in 1973, the Marine Corps Commandant directed that issues concerning women be handled the same as issues concerning male Marines, and in 1977, the office of the Director of Women Marines was dissolved.

The last organization to go was the WAC. Because it had been created by the Integration Act, congressional action was needed to eliminate it. Army leadership—including the WAC Director—sought to keep the WAC structure, but in 1975 a new WAC Director began to make plans to "self-destruct." In 1978, the DOD requested and Congress approved legislation formally abolishing the WAC, effective October 20, 1978.[17]

Not all servicewomen were happy about the changes. Many were concerned because men did not have a good track record on women's issues, and the changes were coming just as the expanding numbers and opportunities for women needed close monitoring. The services did, in fact, have difficulty integrating women's policy issues into the mainstream. The Navy, for example, eventually created the position of Special Assistant to the Chief of Naval Personnel for Women's Matters.

The Numbers Go Up

Resistance to the rising numbers of women in the services was strong, and some military leaders sought a return to the draft. But civilian leaders in the White House and Pentagon, intent on continuing the AVF, increased the number and opportunities for women. In 1977, the administration of Jimmy Carter ordered a review of the role of women in the military. The services gave rationales for capping the number of women, but independent analysis concluded women could fill many more positions without affecting combat readiness and that recruiting additional women would be cost-effective and result in a higher-quality force. Consequently, in May 1977, the Secretary of Defense directed the services to double the number of enlisted women by 1983.

When Ronald Reagan replaced Carter in 1981, many military leaders expected the draft would resume and hence all the services decreased their recruitment of women. However, the Reagan administration's planned buildup of U.S. forces relied on an all-volunteer force, and in July 1981, the Secretary of Defense made it clear he did not want a return to the draft. Six months later, he told the services to support actively an increased role for military women, and the recruiting slowdown ended.

The result was that during Reagan's two terms, the number of servicewomen increased by almost one-third. The upward trend continued during the administration of George Bush, peaking in 1989 at 232,823. Subsequently, the numbers began to drop because of the post-Cold War drawdown.[18] As of 30 September 1997, 198,851 women were on active duty in the military. Despite the decreasing numbers, the female percentage of the military continued to rise, reaching 13.6 percent in September 1997.[19]

A Shift in Race and Ethnicity

In addition to increasing the number of women, the AVF also brought a dramatic increase in the number and proportion of minorities—particularly African American women—in the armed forces. In 1972, the percentages of women and men who were minorities were identical: 16 percent (see figure 2.2).[20] By 1997, male-minority composition had risen to 30 percent, and women's to 43 percent. Numerically, the greatest expansion was in the Army, with a more than tenfold increase in the number of minority women. Proportionally, the most substantial rise was in the Navy, which saw minority women increase from 8 to 41 percent of servicewomen.

Variations were also evident by racial/ethnic group. In 1972, the proportion of military women who were black was 3 percent; by 1997, 31 percent. The rise of blacks among military men was not as large, increasing from 4 to 18 percent. Although the number of Hispanic servicewomen went up between 1972 and 1997, their proportion was cut in half, from 12 to 6 percent. This shift was true for all the services, except the Navy, which saw a rise in Hispanic women from 5 to 9 percent. Similarly, the proportion of Hispanic servicemen overall dropped from 11 to 7 percent, but in the Navy increased from 6 to 8 percent.

Compared to the U.S. female population, minority women are overrepresented in the military.[21] Of all American women, 27 percent are minorities; of military women, 43 percent. Minority men are only slightly overrepresented: they are 27 percent of American men and 30 percent of servicemen. Black women are significantly overrepresented in the military: they constitute about 13 percent of American women but 31 percent of servicewomen. Hispanic military women

FIGURE 2.2

Department of Defense Female and Male Minorities, Fiscal Years 1972 and 1997

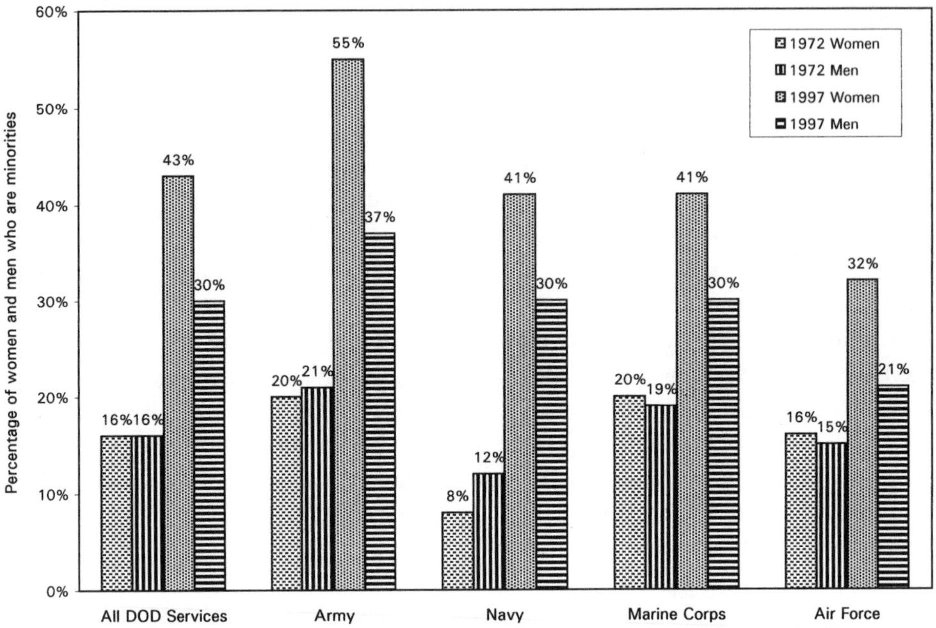

SOURCES: U.S. Department of Defense, Defense Manpower Data Center, *Distribution of Active Duty Forces by Service, Rank, Sex, and Ethnic Group*, DMDC-3035 (30 June 1972 and 30 September 1997).

are underrepresented: 10 percent of American women but 6 percent of military women.

Minority women, however, are underrepresented in the military when compared to the entire U.S. population. Minority females are 14 percent of Americans but only 6 percent of military personnel. Black women, who are 6 percent of the U.S. population, are only 4 percent of the military. Hispanic women, who are 5 percent of Americans, make up less than 1 percent of military personnel.

Sociologist Brenda Moore has suggested several possible reasons that minority women, especially blacks, have joined the AVF in large numbers. First, the military has actively recruited women and minorities. Second, it seems to provide an opportunity to excel, and, therefore, it attracts bright, ambitious blacks. Third, the unemployment rates of blacks have been substantially higher than those of whites.[22]

New Jobs Open

As more women entered the military in the 1970s and 1980s, pressure for the services to open new occupations and unit assignments increased. In early 1982, the Secretary of Defense told the services to ensure women were not discriminated against in career opportunities and to break down aggressively any barriers preventing the fullest utilization of women's capabilities.

Despite these urgings, women remained in support roles, but the breadth of those roles expanded substantially. In 1972, 67 percent of enlisted women were clerical personnel, 22 percent were in health care, and 10 percent worked in technical and other fields. By 1990, the proportion of enlisted women clerks had dropped to 38 percent, and health care givers had gone down to 15 percent. Enlisted women also filled technical (21 percent), craftsmen (11 percent), and combat-related jobs (4 percent).[23]

A major consequence of the expanded jobs was that women continued to edge closer to the battlefield. In the Army and Marine Corps, women were assigned to units that provide administrative, medical, and logistics support and generally operate well behind front lines. The assumption was that women assigned there would not see combat, but as the SCUD missile attack that killed three women during the Gulf War showed, these units were not out of harm's way. Women were also in units providing operational assistance to combat troops. Again, such assignments did not keep women out of combat; for example, a woman officer led her Army military police unit in a firefight during the 1989 Panama invasion.

Down to the Sea in Combat Ships

In 1978, the Navy had no ships to which women could be assigned, but it did have noncombat ships that lacked sufficient male crew members. Navy leaders therefore proposed to Congress that it open noncombat ships to women. Meanwhile, several Navy women successfully challenged the ship-exclusion policy in federal court.[24] In November 1978, Congress amended the law to permit the permanent assignment of women to hospital ships, naval transports, and support ships. Navy women immediately began to report for sea duty.

In the early 1990s, the Navy, facing the post–Cold War drawdown, needed women to fill out the crews of combat ships. Also, surveys by the Roper Organization in 1992 showed that two-thirds of the public and military supported the assignment of women to combat ships.[25] Consequently, the Navy requested, and Congress approved in December 1993, the repeal of the combat-ship-exclusion law. In March 1994, the first women reported for duty aboard the aircraft carrier USS *Eisenhower*. As of December 1997, 4,155 enlisted women were assigned to 61 combat ships, and 514 women officers were aboard 82 such vessels.[26]

Up, Up, and Away

On the aviation side, between 1973 and 1975 all of the services, except the Marine Corps, opened aviation training to women. Although women were legally barred from combat aviation, the Gulf War demonstrated that de facto they were in combat. Women helicopter pilots, for example, hauled Army troops and supplies fifty miles into Iraq, and Air Force women pilots refueled combat aircraft over Iraq. Because these aviators and other women in the combat theater had done

such an outstanding job and because the time seemed right politically, Congress-
women Patricia Schroeder (D, Colo.) and Beverly Byron (R, Md.) introduced
legislation to remove the combat-aviation exclusion. In November 1991, the law
was repealed, but Congress also created the Presidential Commission on the
Assignment of Women in the Armed Forces to review and make recommendations about what, if any, roles women should have in combat and other related
issues.

Although surveys conducted by the Roper Organization for the commission
found that about two-thirds of Americans and the military supported women's
being combat pilots,[27] and the commissioners agreed that "there are circumstances under which women might be assigned to combat positions,"[28] they still
recommended keeping combat aviation closed. However, by the time the commission's report was completed in November 1992, Bush had lost the election
and the incoming Clinton administration and Congress chose to ignore it. On
April 28, 1993, the Secretary of Defense directed the services to let women
compete for assignment in aircraft with combat missions. The services immediately opened combat aviation, and in November 1994, two women Navy F/A-18
pilots became the first women to fly combat missions as they patrolled the sky
over Iraq.

Stuck in the Mud

Although the Gulf War was a catalyst for change in aviation, ground combat
remained closed, even though Army and Marine women did an outstanding job
during the war. The Roper surveys showed weak support for change. Only 40
percent of Americans and a quarter of military personnel thought women should
be in the infantry.[29] The presidential commission voted overwhelmingly to recommend that direct ground combat remain closed. Subsequently, in 1994, the
Clinton administration established a policy that excluded women from ground-
combat units. However, it did open an additional 32,700 noncombat jobs in the
army and 48,000 in the Marine Corps, including assignments on combat ships.[30]

Today, although more than 90 percent of Army and Marine Corps *occupations*
are open to women, the major combat *units* of infantry, tanks, artillery, and
special forces remain closed. Yet the female proportion of troops in overseas
operations is increasing: women were 2 percent of the forces in Grenada (1983),
4 percent in Panama (1989),more than 8 percent in the Gulf War (1991). Over
time, the remnants of the combat-exclusion rule may erode as women continue
to move closer to the front battle lines.

The Ultimate Challenge: Military Culture

Undoubtedly, the military is still a predominantly male culture. It is argued by
some that war is man's work and that women are a distraction on the battlefield.

They contend that women are a weak link that has feminized our nation's defenders. They denounce the increasing role of military women as a result of radical feminist pressure and political correctness, not of an effort to improve combat readiness.

This hypermasculine ethos marginalizes military women. Women's performance has been scrutinized in numerous studies and, although study results generally were favorable for women, the fact that studies were done leaves the impression women are a problem. The view has been reinforced by sexual harassment and adultery scandals, gender discrimination, and women's being subjected to lesbian witch-hunts (see chapter 5).

Sexual Harassment

From the 1991 Navy Tailhook assaults to the 1997 accusations against the Sergeant Major of the Army, the military seems to have spent much of the 1990s struggling with the issue of sexual harassment. In a 1995 sexual harassment survey conducted by the Defense Manpower Data Center (DMDC), 55 percent of servicewomen said they had experienced one or more incidents of unwanted sexual behavior in the twelve months preceding the survey.[31] The Marine Corps had the highest incidence rate, while the Air Force had the lowest (see figure 2.3). In addition, black women reported slightly higher rates of harassment than did white women, and junior enlisted women reported more harassment than did senior enlisted women.

Sexual harassment ranged from 6 percent of women having been victims of sexual assault to 70 percent having experienced crude or offensive behavior. Thirteen percent of women had been subjected to sexual coercion, and 41 percent had received unwanted sexual attention. The DMDC survey also revealed that women do not have much faith in the system's ability to handle their complaints. Only 40 percent of harassed women had filed a report, with black women slightly less likely to make formal charges. Almost a quarter of the women said their complaint was not taken seriously, 12 percent indicated their supervisor was hostile, and 10 percent had been encouraged to drop their complaint. One in five women who had been harassed believed that "bad things" would happen if the harassment were reported. Only about half of the women felt the senior leadership of their service or command made an honest and reasonable effort to end harassment.

Although sexual harassment was still too prevalent, the 1995 survey did show the level had gone down since the previous survey in 1988, from 64 percent to 55 percent. Nonetheless, the survey gave warning signals to the Army. Less than half of Army women said that senior Army and installation leaders had tried to stop harassment. Army leaders should not have been surprised when sexual misconduct scandals began to break out at training commands, especially the Aberdeen Proving Grounds. In response, the Secretary of the Army appointed the Senior Review Panel on Sexual Harassment to review and make recommendations on the Army's sexual harassment policies and procedures.

FIGURE 2.3
Sexual Harassment of Military Women, 1988 and 1995

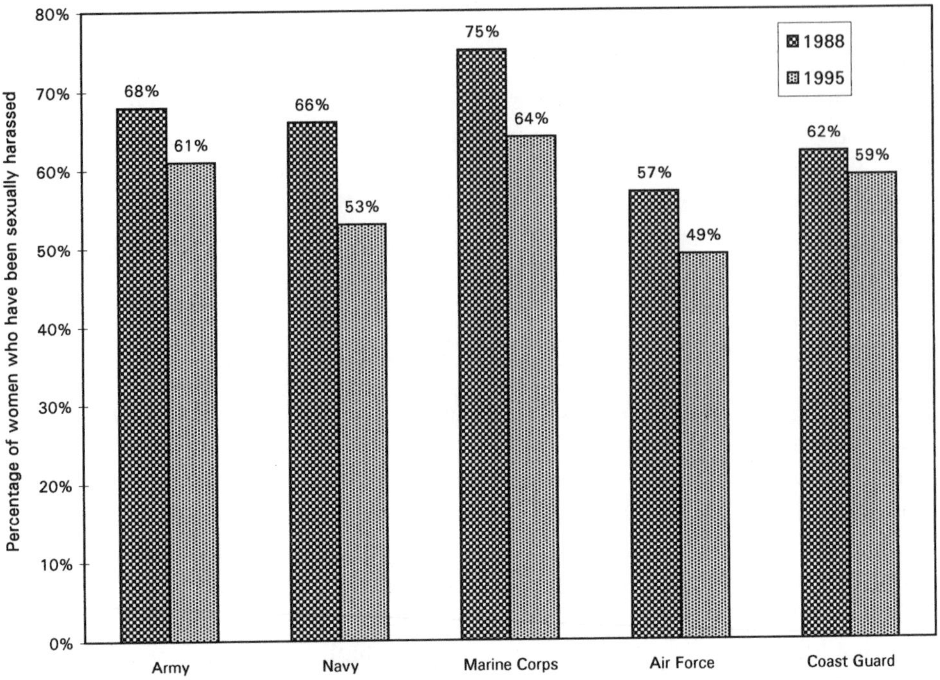

SOURCE: U.S. Department of Defense, Defense Manpower Data Center, *Department of Defense 1995 Sexual Harassment Survey*, DMDC 96-014 (December 1996), 10.

In the panel's survey, 84 percent of Army women said they had experienced inappropriate sexual behavior, but only 22 percent said they had been sexually harassed. The panel attributed the startling difference to two factors. First, women had low expectations of what constitutes acceptable behavior. Second, despite understanding the formal definitions of sexual harassment, the panel found that women tended "to apply a different, personal, informal working definition of sexual harassment in their personal experiences." Women considered themselves to be sexually harassed only when sexually coerced or assaulted.[32]

Adultery and Fraternization

Adultery came to the forefront with the highly publicized case of First Lieutenant Kelly Flinn, the Air Force's first woman bomber pilot. Historically, adultery has been handled quietly, but in the case of Flinn, who was accused of having an affair with a civilian, the Air Force decided to court-martial her. In May 1997, the Air Force accepted her resignation, but she was forced to accept a lower type of discharge. Men have also been affected. On 10 June 1997, Air Force General Joseph Ralston withdrew his name from consideration for the military's highest position, Chairman of the Joint Chiefs of Staff, because of an affair he had had with a classmate at a military college.

Closely linked to adultery is the issue of fraternization. Technically, *fraternization* refers to senior-subordinate relationships, but generally it is viewed as involving male-female relations. Policies have been promulgated by all of the services, but individuals find them confusing and often misunderstand them. Policies also lack consistency; an offense in one service may not be in another, and each service handles violations differently.

Gender Discrimination

Another form of discrimination that is prevalent in the military is sexism. In the 1995 DMDC survey, 63 percent of women said they had been subjected to sexist behavior: offensive actions and comments or condescending treatment based on their gender. The Marine Corps had the highest rate of sexist behavior (78 percent), followed by the Army (67 percent), Coast Guard (65 percent), Navy (62 percent), and Air Force (59 percent).[33] The survey also showed that gender discrimination was more widespread than sexual harassment in all the services.

The Army's Senior Review Panel on Sexual Harassment found that comments in its focus groups supported the statistical data. It reported that a group of women senior NCOs (noncommissioned officers) "spoke heatedly to Panel members about having no voice in meetings with male NCOs of their units. 'We speak, but it's as if we do not exist. They ignore us.' said one NCO." They also noted that although women believe their leaders have zero tolerance for racial discrimination, the same standard does not apply to sex discrimination. A woman soldier remarked: "You can't get away with saying blacks shouldn't be in the Army, but you can say women shouldn't be in the Army. . . . How can they [men] get away with that?"[34]

Similarly, the 1990 Navy Women's Study Group said that women lagged men in terms of mutual respect and equal access to training, recognition, rewards, promotions, and leadership roles.[35] In the 1990 Women in the Coast Guard Study, a select group of Coast Guard members said that the top barrier to increasing women's representation in the Coast Guard was "sexist attitudes and the lack of attention to this at the top."[36]

Polarization

Women have been subjected to discriminatory behavior, but men think women receive preferential treatment and benefit from dual standards. In the Army's 1997 survey, almost half of male soldiers thought female soldiers received more favorable treatment than men.[37] According to sociologist Laura Miller, "[S]ome Army men actually believe that women are the powerful gender within the military." The result is that tension and polarization between military men and women are rising. Miller found that "some men may even resort to covert gender harassment to express their disapproval of women's participation in the military."[38] A number of issues contribute to this feeling, but the predominant ones are physical-fitness standards, work assignments, pregnancy, and sexual harassment.

All services periodically test their personnel's general physical fitness. The tests are based on the physiological capabilities of different groups to perform various physical activities. As a result, physical-fitness tests are normed for both age and gender. Men willingly accept the differing age standards that affect them but loudly complain about the "lower" standards for women.

In the workplace, men see favoritism, saying women get the easier jobs, and they do the hard, dirty work. In the Army's 1997 survey, 81 percent of men said male soldiers "pull their load" in their company but only half thought female soldiers did.[39] No matter how well women perform their duties, the perception among some men is that women are not essential to a unit's successfully accomplishing its mission.

Servicemen also say that the policies for pregnancy adversely affect their units. Some accuse women of intentionally getting pregnant in order to avoid deployments. Men complain they must do more work because of the limitations doctors put on pregnant women and blame individual women personally rather than service policy. Men are more willing to accept absences caused by illness or injury than pregnancy.

Men express fear of being falsely accused of sexual harassment. They think their careers will be ruined by an allegation, even if it proves to be false. One way men avoid the problem is to avoid women. In talking with women, members of the Army's Senior Review Panel found that women were being isolated in their units by men who, in some cases, would not even speak to them.[40]

These issues have been difficult to address because they are based on erroneous perceptions, not reality. Service policies do not give women preferential treatment in work assignments. Women, including those who are pregnant, are available for duty about the same amount of time as men, who are more likely to be absent for disciplinary reasons. Physical standards for occupations are gender neutral. The basic problem is that some men blame the victims rather than examine the institutional climate men create in which women must function.

The Future

Tension and polarization undoubtedly exist in today's armed forces, but they should be kept in perspective. Women have made tremendous progress, and the number and proportion of women in the military has grown substantially over the past twenty-five years. Today, women have jobs, such as combat pilot, that were out of reach even a few years ago, and many combine career and family. And, most important, every day most military women and men go about their duties with little or no difficulty.

For the most part, however, this progress has been made in the areas easiest to change. Now women are entering the inner sanctum of the military: combat. For some men, this is a challenge to their masculinity and an intrusion into their private preserve. The issues being dealt with require a new attitude by many individual servicemen. It is one thing to assign a woman to a new type of unit; it is quite another for her to gain the acceptance of, and be valued by, her fellow male soldiers, sailors, airmen, or marines.

For progress to continue, some polices and procedures must be eliminated, most notably the direct ground-combat exclusion. But the key to women's becoming members of the first team is military leadership. From the service chief to the lowest NCO, leaders must set a positive example, and establish and enforce reasonable standards of behavior. The military culture, as it affects women, must change. This will continue to be a long, difficult, and erratic process, but is necessary to enhance the quality of our armed forces. The simple standard must be the best person for the job.

NOTES

1. Harold D. Langley, "Women in a Warship, 1813," in U.S. Naval Institute, *Proceedings* (January 1984), 124–25.

2. Quoted in Jeanne Holm, *Women in the Military: An Unfinished Revolution*, rev. ed. (Novato, Calif.: Presidio Press, 1992), 13.

3. Quoted in Joy Bright Hancock, *Lady in the Navy: A Personal Reminiscence* (Annapolis: U.S. Naval Institute Press, 1972), 22.

4. Quoted in Holm, *Women in the Military*, 24.

5. Bettye Collier-Thomas, "Recovering the Military History of Black Women," *MINERVA: Quarterly Report on Women and the Military* 1, no. 1 (spring 1983): 76–80.

6. Jean Ebbert and Marie-Beth Hall, *Crossed Currents: Navy Women from WWI to Tailhook*, 3d ed. (Washington, D.C.: Brassey's, forthcoming), 11.

7. Quoted in Brenda Moore, *To Serve My Country, To Serve My Race: The Story of the Only African American WACs Stationed Overseas During World War II* (New York: New York University Press, 1996), 58.

8. Ibid., 20–21.

9. Ibid., 18–19.

10. Brenda Moore, "African-American Women in the U.S. Military," *Armed Forces and Society* 17, no. 3 (1991): 367; Moore, *To Serve My Country*, passim.

11. Holm, *Women in the Military*, 115–19.

12. Public Law 80–625, 12 June 1948, ch. 449, §210, 62 Stat. 368.

13. 10 U.S.C. §6015, §8549.

14. U.S. Department of Defense (DOD), *Selected Manpower Statistics, Fiscal Year 1996*, DIOR/MO1-96 (Washington, D.C.: Government Printing Office, 1997), 95.

15. *Frontiero v Richardson*, 411 U.S. 677 (1973).

16. *Crawford v Cushman*, 531 F. 2d 114 (2d Cir., 1976).

17. Holm, *Women in the Military*, 279–87.

18. DOD, *Manpower Statistics*, 96.

19. U.S. Department of Defense, Defense Manpower Data Center, *Distribution of Active Duty Forces by Service, Rank, Sex, and Ethnic Group*, DMDC-3035 (30 September 1997).

20. Ibid. (for 30 June 1972 and 30 September 1997; numbers have been rounded).

21. U.S. population data are from the U.S. Bureau of Census, *Population Projections of the United States by Age, Sex, Race, and Hispanic Origin: 1995 to 2050* (1996) table 2.

22. Brenda L. Moore, "From Underrepresentaton to Overrepresentation: African American Women," in *It's Our Military Too! Women and the U.S. Military*, ed. Judith Hicks Stiehm (Philadelphia: Temple University Press, 1996), 123–29.

23. Martin Binkin, *Who Will Fight the Next War? The Changing Face of the American Military* (Washington, D.C.: Brookings Institute, 1993), 10.

24. *Owens v Brown*, 455 F. Supp. 291 (D.D.C. 1978).

25. Georgia Sadler, "The Polling Data," U.S. Naval Institute *Proceedings* (February 1993), 53.

26. U.S. Navy, Office of the Special Assistant to the Chief of Naval Personnel for Women's Matters, "Facts on Women in the Navy," 31 December 1997.

27. Sadler, "Polling Data," 53.

28. The Presidential Commission on the Assignment of Women in the Armed Forces, *Report to the President* (Washington, D.C.: Government Printing Office, 1992), 22.

29. Sadler, "Polling Data," 53.

30. U.S. Department of Defense, "Secretary of Defense Perry Approves Plans to Open New Jobs for Women in the Military," news release no. 449-94, 29 July 1994.

31. Data are from the U.S. Department of Defense, Defense Manpower Data Center (DMDC), *Department of Defense 1995 Sexual Harassment Survey*, DMDC-96-014 (December 1996).

32. U.S. Army, Office of the Secretary, *Senior Review Panel Report on Sexual Harassment*, vol. 1 (July 1997), 60–61.

33. DMDC, *Sexual Harassment Survey*, 12.

34. U.S. Army, *Senior Review Panel Report*, 61.

35. U.S. Navy, Navy Women's Study Group, *An Update Report on the Progress of Women in the Navy*, VI-2 (1991).

36. U.S. Coast Guard, *Women in the Coast Guard Study* (July 1990), C-1.

37. U.S. Army, *Senior Review Panel Report*, 64.

38. Laura Miller, "Not Just Weapons of the Weak: Gender Harassment as a Form of Protest for Army Men," *Social Psychology Quarterly* 60, no. 1 (1997): 32.

39. U.S. Army, *Senior Review Panel Report*, 64.

40. Ibid., 65–6.

Sources: Adapted from U.S. Department of Defense, *Selected Manpower Statistics, Fiscal Year, 1996*, DIOR/MO1–96 (Washington, D.C.: Government Printing Office, 1996), 94–96; U.S. Department of Defense, Defense Manpower Data Center, *Distribution of Active Duty Forces by Service, Rank, Sex, and Ethnic Group*, DMDC-3035 (30 September 1997).

Autobiography
Crossing the Line: NCO to Officer

Barbara A. Wilson

Armed with forged parental consent forms and admonishments from friends that "only queers and prostitutes join the service," on the 11th of October 1949, I raised my right hand and swore to uphold and defend the Constitution of the United States, as a buck private (the lowest enlisted rank) in the Air Force, for a whopping seventy-five dollars a month. My mother and father reluctantly took the afternoon off and witnessed the ceremony, even though they both totally disapproved of what was happening.

Their darling daughter was slated for West Chester State Teachers College on a partial art scholarship, after having finally made it through the prestigious Philadelphia High School for Girls: an all-academic, all-girls high school full of snobs and scholars and no fun. Or maybe become the next Madame Curie by virtue of my recent temporary job at Children's Heart Hospital blood lab—but I had been fired for making a milk shake in the centrifuge. Or perhaps they expected me to become a financial wizard from my brief stint with Dun & Bradstreet in the answered-ticket department—short-lived because I worked too fast and skewed the daily production record. My parents surrendered after the signing and swearing in, and willingly corrected the forged forms—you had to have parental consent if you were under twenty-one.

Basic training would take volumes to describe, but of all the glimmers that reconstructive memory offers, the thing I remember most is painted rocks.

For thirteen weeks, in the sweltering heat of San Antonio, Texas, we marched, we trained, we marched, we sang, we marched, and we painted rocks. We also made borders with the painted rocks, spelled out numbers with the painted rocks, and those who had the distinction of not knowing their left foot from their right got to carry a painted rock in their left hand.

Between marching, singing, and painting rocks, we experienced extensive training in everything from chemical and biological warfare to survival in the desert, survival in the jungle, and survival in the Arctic—which was difficult to absorb in 100-degree heat. We dug latrine trenches, shinnied up ropes, slid down ropes, and went through gas chambers (tear gas, not mustard). We carried packs, canteens (often filled with Coca Cola), and gas masks (a great place to stash candy bars), and in between we sat through hour upon hour of classes on everything from airplanes to venereal diseases.

By the time "Lights Out" was called and the loudspeaker blared out a bugle playing "Taps," we were exhausted and fell under our bunks moaning and groaning about everything from painted rocks to gruesome health movies. I say under the bunk because for some unknown reason the tradition of not sleeping on a perfectly made bed permeated our barracks, which resulted in great inspection reports but a lot of stiff backs.

But in spite of all the typical barracks bitching, we had fun. After dark, the dingy wooden building with its sterile lime-green walls became transformed into a giggling slumber-party atmosphere. We told jokes, sneaked smokes, and spit-shined our shoes by flashlight. On the down side, some of the girls did get homesick.

And then there was the unsolved mystery of a disappearing troop. Every morning, 5:00 A.M. to be specific, we had roll call, which consisted of lining up and shouting out our names and serial numbers. On more than one occasion, a particular troop would no longer be in line, and we were simply told to fill in the space. Later we found out that these women had been discharged for either "inadaptabilty" or "moral turpitude." Loosely translated, they couldn't cut it or they were considered lesbians. In retrospect, I can honestly say I never saw homosexual behavior in basic training and frankly wonder how anyone could pursue any type of sexual activity, given that we were kept occupied every minute of the day, including weekends, and were totally exhausted every night. That, coupled with the fact that there were no doors on anything from the toilets to the showers—the showers didn't even have curtains.

With basic over and graduation a memory of a parade and a trip to the Alamo, the next stop was technical school, now with one stripe on my arm as Private First Class, or PFC, Wilson. In typical military fashion, my assignment to tech school was based on aptitude testing. I scored high on academics and low on mechanical. Therefore I was sent to Teletype Maintenance School for six months in Cheyenne, Wyoming. From 100-degree heat to six-foot snowdrifts.

As was typical at the time, the women's barracks were in an isolated corner of Warren Air Force Base (AFB), accessible only by shuttle bus or private auto, which only the officers and a few sergeants owned. The WAF squadron area (WAF stood for Women in the Air Force but was often misstated as Women's Air Force) was self-contained in that it had a dining hall, an Orderly Room—the administrative hub of any squadron—and a Dayroom—a kind of recreation room, with "comfortable" chairs, magazines that nobody read, the ever-present Coke machine, and a jukebox that played incessantly. Television sets were not yet standard Dayroom equipment.

The week that our group arrived at Warren, one of the young women in the WAF squadron had been brutally beaten and raped at a remote service club on the main base. She was barely alive and the base was in turmoil, trying to deal with a public relations nightmare and to protect the rest of the women in the squadron. We were restricted to the area, military police were assigned to guard the exterior of the barracks, and the dreaded OSI (Office of Special Investigations) agents were everywhere, asking questions and taking copious notes. We all had to attend lectures, briefings, commanders' calls, and classes on everything from self-defense to sexually transmitted diseases. To say the situation was tense is an understatement.

Fortunately, the victim recovered, although she had to undergo extensive plastic surgery and psychotherapy, and was subsequently discharged for medical reasons. And fortunately, they caught the creep, who, according to the base grapevine, suffered several arm- and leg-breaking falls every time he was transported to and from his cell and to his pending courts-martial.

When the furor died down and school started up again, we went about the business of learning how to repair Teletype machines, which for some reason I could not comprehend. At the end of practically every day I went home to the barracks with leftover bolts, screws, and machine parts in my ugly fatigues pants pockets. I aced the academics and passed every written test, and could explain voltage, electricity, pull-bar-bearing-rollers, and platens on paper. I just couldn't make the damn machines work.

Except for having to shovel a lot of snow, and a lot of coal because the barracks were heated by coal burners and stoking them was one of our many details, the rest of technical school was uneventful. Unless you count almost getting busted for crossing the state line and drinking underage in an off-limits bar on graduation night. I'm still not sure how I got out of that one except that I had a very understanding WAF squadron commander. One remembers understanding commanders. I also remember the wicked ones, and, in my next assignment, I was about to encounter a few of each.

Hamilton AFB in Marin County north of San Francisco, California, was about as plush a tour of duty one could get on a first enlistment. And I had two years of plush mixed with sex, lies, and strange happenings. The WAF squadron was large, and as usual self-contained. We had our own mess hall where we all had to pull KP, or kitchen police—why police I'll never know, nor did anyone else. There was nothing resembling police work about being knee-deep in a grease pit or washing pots and pans the size of bathtubs.

My Teletype maintenance career ended when I succeeded in shorting out the entire communications center by dropping a screw driver into a rectifier, but not before I had been promoted to corporal. I was transferred to a radar detachment and made a "scope dope," which means sitting in front of a small, circular, green screen for hours watching nothing, as a dial winds around and mesmerizes you. This career move came to an abrupt halt when one day, after seeing what I thought was a flight of unidentified aircraft on my screen, I picked up the red phone and scrambled the base fighter squadron. When the "enemy aircraft" turned out to be a flight of migrating ducks, my days in radar were summarily ended, and I darn near lost my corporal stripes.

For reasons still unknown to me, while stationed at Hamilton, I acquired a mysterious benefactor; to this day I can only speculate on her identity. I was hastily reassigned to the Base Information Office and put on the staff of the base newspaper. The staff was excellent, and the guys taught me everything there was to know about journalism, public relations, and news gathering. It was a dream assignment on a plush base, and I was promoted to sergeant. But sadly the "witch-hunt of the year" brought it all crashing down.

When you're nineteen or twenty, three thousand miles away from home, and earning your own paycheck, you're pretty much in the "girls-just-wanna-have-fun" mode, no matter what decade it happens to be. And we did just that. We went to the base clubs at the beginning of the month and partied in the barracks at the end of the month when our meager pay ran out. We dated, we went sight-seeing, we pulled pranks on the officers, and we also did our jobs, marched in parades, stood inspections, and played sports. And we gossiped.

One day the barracks grapevine started buzzing about the OSI calling women in for interrogation. And believe me, it was nothing less than interrogation because I was the next one hauled in.

Here I was, about to be promoted to staff sergeant, thus becoming the youngest noncommissioned officer (NCO) in the squadron, and those clowns dragged me off to a remote building and started hammering at me about lesbians in the barracks and prostitutes using the base taxi for a call-girl ring. They questioned me for hours, and, believe me, I was scared. Not because I was a lesbian or a call girl but because they were naming young women who were not homosexuals or prostitutes. These jokers were about to have fine young women kicked out of the service—maybe even me. Then they went too far.

One of the agents told me that he knew I was queer because he had my letters from another woman signed "Love, Madge." The OSI had gone through our mail, and I was furious. I know that memory is selective and we re-create it, but I remember that day well. First I told the agents that Madge was my sister and of course she would sign her letters with *love*. Second, they had no right to go through my mail, and I was reporting it immediately to several of my mother's close personal friends: two senators, Congressman Hugh Scott, columnist Walter Winchell, commentator Drew Pearson, and I threw in another celebrity or two. And third, if they ever talked to me like that again, or went through my mail, I would have my father call his old Navy buddy, the vice president. The last threat was pure bluff in that my father and Richard Nixon were not in the Navy at the same time. But my mother really did know all those people, and Madge was my sister—we simply had different last names because she was married.

I stormed out and left three startled agents with their mouths hanging open. And, again apparently due to my mysterious benefactor, within a few weeks I was sent to Norton AFB in southern California. I was promoted to staff sergeant before I left. And sadly, after I left, many fine young women were discharged from the service as a result of the witch-hunt.

Norton was a desert hellhole that I choose not to remember, so from there, I wangled an assignment to Ent AFB in Colorado, which was totally uneventful.

By 1954, bitter, disillusioned, bored, and thinking that I needed some motivation, education, and new horizons, I got out of the Air Force. After eight months in Mexico on the G.I. Bill attending college, I returned to the mundane suburbs of Philadelphia, followed by a menial job as a desk clerk in the Pocono Mountains. Not exactly a scintillating lifestyle for a twenty-three-year-old. Luckily, when I separated from the Air Force, I said "yes" to staying in the inactive reserve. The AF Reserve decided to offer me voluntary recall, so after a year off I was back on active duty as a staff sergeant and on my way to Mitchel AFB, New York.

My assignment was to be the first sergeant of the WAF Squadron, which didn't mean first in anything because this particular women's squadron was being deactivated. Essentially, I had the grand and glorious job of shipping everyone out and breaking up the squadron. But turning in all squadron supplies and equipment was a problem, and I became a female Sergeant Bilko practically overnight, scrounging bits of linen and blankets, trading them at the Linen Exchange for new ones, and turning them in to credit the squadron linen account. Knocking the metal beds apart with hammers was fun, but convincing the supply guys to count a headboard as a whole bed, and its footboard as the next whole bed, was a real challenge.

The unit was officially closed. There were only four of us left: two hospital WAF, one recruiter, and me—a first sergeant with no squadron. I had applied for recruiting when I first heard that the squadron was being disbanded. Just as I was about to be shipped out to who knows where, the application was approved, and the absolute best tour anyone could ask for in the military began in 1955 and lasted until 1960.

Recruiting was a glamour assignment: custom uniforms, three-inch heels, regular beauty parlor appointments, speechmaking at career days, radio and television appearances, more speechmaking, and incidentally interviewing and processing female recruits. The assignment was a blast except for the sexual harassment—an unknown term in those days.

When you cross the first line, moving from the lower ranks, like airman or private, to the esteemed NCO grades, like sergeant or staff sergeant, you suddenly become more visible. Not because of the additional stripes on your arm but perhaps because you have lasted long enough, or reenlisted, and been promoted. With this new visibility, your sexuality becomes a major point of interest and topic of curiosity and conversation for the men with whom you work. Recruiting duty was no exception.

Long Island, New York, from Montauk Point to the Brooklyn Bridge, was my turf, with a weekly trip to the Manhattan office for meetings, reports, and supplies. Processing for the women who enlisted took place in lower Manhattan, in a combined enlistment center for all of the services on Whitehall Street, which required additional trips to the city. Side trips to the USO for free movie, theater, and sports tickets were SOP (standard operating procedure).

I learned fast that doing the hated paperwork for the recruiters would earn their gratitude and get them off my case about dating. Not that I wasn't interested in dating. I was seriously trying to do my job and worked tons of overtime doing other people's work. One of my supervisors was a really nice guy, and the other was a real jerk. The fact that the nice guy could neither read nor write beyond about third-grade level became a bonanza for me. In return for doing all of his letters, budget reports, inspection-visit summaries, press releases, and performance evaluations, he ran interference for me with the goon-squad boys. He made sure that on any trips we had to take, I went with the "married gentlemen" of the outfit and not the party boys. He also got me my own Air Force staff car, and recommended approval of my application to go to college at night.

We had a program then called "Operation Bootstrap" whereby enlisted personnel could attend college, with all expenses paid by the Air Force, and you were given time off to go to school full time. Bootstrap was my goal and to get there I had to have ninety semester hours of credit. At the time I had about twelve from Mexico City College.

For three years, I worked eight to ten hours a day, six days a week, and broke all recruiting records for the area by exceeding quotas. I went to school four nights a week from six to ten, maintained an A average, and still managed to see every Broadway show and two World Series, appear on every major television program game show, and have a few lighthearted affairs. New York was my fast lane, recruiting was my race car, and I was headed for burnout on the steepest curve.

Fortunately, the college registrar, Frances Smith Patterson, became my mentor. Thanks to her wise counseling, I settled down and concentrated exclusively on school.

With the required ninety semester hours completed, I applied for "Operation Bootstrap" and was promptly turned down by our newly arrived detachment commander. This lieutenant colonel did not believe in higher education for women, and certainly not for enlisted personnel. Luckily for me, a female Lieutenant Colonel thought differently and overrode his disapproval. The Air Force gave me six months off to complete college. In January of 1960, I was graduated cum laude from Mitchel College of Long Island University, with a B.A. in psychology—the first woman in the Air Force to accomplish this!

I promptly applied for Officer Training School (OTS). While the application bogged down in the endless murk of military red tape, I got my orders for the next duty assignment—the first of two "low blows."

There I was, a college graduate, coming off a five-year tour in glamour and public relations, and I was reassigned to the military training center to be— wonder of all wonders—a drill instructor! And to add insult to injury, I had to go to school first to learn how to do this monumental task.

While I was marching around drill pads in 90-degree heat, in fatigues, at Lackland AFB, Texas, my application for OTS was denied. The official reasons for the rejection were couched in terms that only a Ph.D. in bureaucratic bilge could translate. One reason given was that I was too old. At the time I was twenty-nine. A friend in the Pentagon told me the unofficial reason for the rejection was that I had been enlisted too long—eleven years—and that the unknown "they" did not think I should "cross the line" into the officer ranks. I remember saying at the time, "Nobody ever told me I should have been taking medicine for this rare condition."

Furious at this invisible wall that had been thrown up against me and, in my eyes, against every enlisted woman who would follow, I immediately reapplied, requested an age waiver, and sent everything back through formal military channels. Then I began a full-fledged campaign in other channels, too. Call these channels the "underground channel," the "grapevine," the "friends-of-friends channel." I even used the political-influence channel. You would probably call it networking today. Well, whatever you call it, something worked. I think I know who pushed the final button that reversed the decision. She is no longer with us, but I will be eternally grateful to her.

In May of 1960 I entered Officer Training School, the first technical sergeant, male or female, to do so. And in August of 1960 I was commissioned a second lieutenant in the United States Air Force: the first WAF, the first NCO, the first enlisted woman to complete OTS and become a commissioned officer.

I had crossed the line.

The Commissioned Years

From Officer Training School my first assignment was to the Strategic Air Command (SAC), then the most elite command in the Air Force, according to SAC. The base was Lockbourne AFB, south of Columbus, Ohio; the job was Family Services Officer; the surprise was that I was one of only two women officers on the entire base, and the other one would be my boss. Fortunately, we got along rather well, and she taught me every aspect of the job while grooming me to be her successor as Personal Affairs Officer.

The title "Personal Affairs Officer" was the subject of a lot of jokes, but the job was pretty intense. The not-so-much-fun part of it was the casualty side—dealing with death and survivors—and on more than one occasion having to be on-site at plane crashes and help with body bags. The up side of the job was working with the two hundred volunteers in the Family Services Center: wives of officers and NCOs whose contributions were astounding. Those ladies, whether by choice or to enhance their husbands' careers, gave a tremendous amount of hours to the center, helping during disasters, aiding newcomers, and caring for the Air Force family.

In spite of moving up to become head of the division and being promoted to first lieutenant, after three years, I was bored with the job, the base, and the city of Columbus. But the unwritten code was tightly in place: you can't get out of SAC unless you die or retire—neither of which I was ready to do in Ohio. As always there was a loophole. The Air Force had a program called AFIT, the Air Force Institute of Technology, and one facet of it offered graduate school to qualified junior officers.

I was selected for AFIT and sent to George Washington University Graduate School. At the risk of sounding like a recruiting propagandist, it was a wonderful opportunity: all expenses paid, housing and subsistence allowance, and two years in the nation's capital. It was great, and I loved, and seriously appreciated, every minute of it. Sadly, just as I was about to finish, my father became seriously ill and died, and I had to go to Philadelphia on extended emergency leave. His death left my mother alone in a deteriorating neighborhood, so I requested reassignment to a base near her.

In February of 1965, with new silver captain's bars on my shoulders, I reported to McGuire AFB in New Jersey, about thirty-five miles from my home in Philadelphia. At first I was to be a personnel officer, but there was a large WAF squadron at McGuire and the commander was leaving for another assignment. Her designated replacement announced her pregnancy and plans to separate, and I got the job as squadron commander—literally a dream come true. And, I might add, the ultimate challenge for a former enlisted person.

To some NCOs I was considered a traitor for crossing the line, yet to others I was a heroine for having the guts to fight to get commissioned. This new situation was no longer one of crossing lines but, rather, of maintaining a fine line between me and my troops. It was not easy. But then maintaining discipline while caring about the welfare of two hundred women is never easy. I had to become a mother, teacher, psychologist, marriage counselor, sex therapist, mind reader, social director, morale booster, cleanliness inspector, and arbitrator, all rolled into one. The mix of backgrounds in the unit ran the gamut from girls who had never worn shoes to upper-class debutantes and from immature youngsters to irritable menopausal women. The problems ranged from missing underwear to attempted suicides, interracial dating, and senior officers harassing enlisted women.

We had to fight with the base engineers to get bathtubs. We got the general to stop making the women march in New York City when antimilitary demonstrations were rampant, and we got the women out of having to pull KP at the Officers Club. We got permission for the young men to be in the dayrooms and patio area, and we got the medics to issue birth control pills. We got a patio area built for the barracks and got celebrities to visit our fashion shows. Lastly, we attained the reputation of being one of the finest WAF squadrons in the Air Force.

My troops called me "the bitch on wheels," "the old lady" (I was all of thirty-six), "the female mustang" (a Navy term for one who crosses from enlisted to officer), and, my favorite, "the iron hand in the velvet glove." My five years as WAF squadron commander were, without a doubt, the most challenging, gratifying, difficult, rewarding years of my career. I was proud to be the commander of such remarkable women.

In 1970 I was ready to move on, had orders in hand for a promotion to major and a brief trip to Vietnam, and at least another ten years to enjoy as an Air Force officer, when destiny dealt a blow that only I could deal with. My seventy-five-year-old mother developed Alzheimer's disease, and my being the single daughter somehow meant that Mother was my responsibility.

To the rest of the family, my mother became a pariah. To me, she became my child. Faced with the most difficult decision of my life, I agonized for days and finally chose my mother over the rest of my Air Force career. I declined the promotion and reluctantly submitted an application for retirement. It was not what I really wanted to do.

So there you have it. An abrupt end to a brilliant career and fourteen years of caring for an Alzheimer's victim while teaching at a local college. But through the years, my consolation has been untold thanks from the many young women and men who did not have to battle to cross the line from enlisted to officer.

Three

Lessons on Gender Integration from the Military Academies

D'Ann Campbell with Francine D'Amico

The Citadel and Virginia Military Institute (VMI) have been in the news as they begin the integration of women into their previously all-male academies. Although fewer than one-third of Citadel graduates and only one-fifth of VMI graduates actually choose military careers, the Citadel and VMI military education programs are in many ways modeled on those of the federal military service academies: the U.S. Air Force Academy at Colorado Springs, the U.S. Army Academy at West Point, and the U.S. Naval Academy at Annapolis. This chapter analyzes the twenty years of gender integration at these military academies to see what lessons the Citadel and VMI should—and should not—learn from these experiences. I examine the four areas of military education: academics, military leadership training, physical training, and the social/cultural environment at each academy. I focus on three *snapshots* or time periods in the process of gender integration of the academies: the first four years, a decade later, and two decades later (the present). I conclude that the current programs and plans for gender integration show that VMI has a better understanding of this history than does the Citadel.

The U.S. Merchant Marine Academy and the U.S. Coast Guard Academy admitted women before the Army, Navy, and Air Force academies did and moved quickly to classes of at least 20 percent women, whereas the other academies have not reached that goal yet. (The Merchant Marine Academy currently has a class composed of one-third women, two-thirds men.) This puts them in a different stage of integration, for sociologists have demonstrated that acceptance of minority groups increases dramatically as their numbers approach 20 percent.[1] Thus the two academies' experiences of gender integration are different, even unique, and will not be examined here.

Academics

All three service academies emphasize math, engineering, and science courses, and all require a hefty number of these courses regardless of the ultimate major of the cadet. Twenty years ago, women were just beginning to enter engineering and science-oriented programs. Today, the number of women in scientific fields has jumped from 1 percent to 15 to 40 percent, depending on the discipline. For example, more women pursue biology degrees than physics degrees, and women now constitute two-fifths to one-half of the entering classes in medical schools.

The women admitted to the service academies for the past twenty years have not withdrawn from the academies for academic reasons more often than have the men.[2] Indeed, women come to higher education and to the academies with slightly higher grade point averages than the men. They score slightly higher than their male colleagues on the verbal portion of the SAT or ACT exams but slightly lower on the quantitative portion of these exams. It is not surprising, then, that as cadets they will earn higher grades than the men in English and foreign language courses and slightly lower grades (in their first few years) in science, engineering, and math courses.[3]

Although female cadets bring to their collegiate experience higher GPAs, their grades are slightly lower than those of their male counterparts during their first year or two at the academies. By their junior or senior year, women's GPAs are comparable to men's. One possible explanation is that the service academies' emphasis on science and math courses explains these differences in the overall collegiate-level grades. A second explanation might be that the other parts of the equation—military, physical, social/cultural environment—exact more of a drain on female than on male cadets. In other words, women may take longer to learn how to balance the various parts of their military education.

The one accommodation tried by Annapolis, and later on a short-term basis by West Point, was to schedule each woman's classes so that she was not the only woman in a class. Annapolis assigned several women to a section of fifteen midshipmen, so that the women would constitute a critical mass and could serve as support for one another.[4] Consequently, these women would be less likely to be viewed as representing all women. Of course, this arrangement meant that there would remain some all-male sections. However, the experiment did not seem to have a measurable effect.

In sum, none of the service academies have made major alterations to their curriculum or academic standards to retain women cadets. Neither men nor women leave the service academies in large numbers for academic reasons, and women are even slightly less likely to leave for academic reasons than are men. As more and more women become better prepared than ten or twenty years ago in science and math courses, the service academies should have less difficulty each year in recruiting women students with the necessary academic credentials. Indeed, each of the academies has now had a woman graduate as the top academic student, and each has had a woman serve as the overall cadet leader.

Military Leadership Training

After attending classes all day—demerits are handed out for missing any class without a written excuse—the cadets rush to physical activities and military training courses. New physical fitness courses were developed with the advent of women in the academies. Indeed, all the surveys and interviews with top cadets and administrators at the academies in 1975 reflected a clear message: women were not wanted at these academies, which train officers to be combatants. Because women could not serve in combat roles until recently, they were seen as taking precious slots away from those who could be combatants. In reality, as the Air Force Academy reminds entering cadets today, only a fraction of cadets become fighter pilots. In the past few years, each of the academies has tried to tone down the emphasis on combatants. The Air Force Academy's curriculum discusses the range of options open to officers, and the USMA has renamed what used to be infantry, armor, and artillery weeks Cadet Field Training. However, even to the casual observer, the hierarchy is clear: training for combat arms is the primary, if not the only, mission of the academies. Indeed, the motto "Bring Me Men" is one of the most eye-catching features at the Air Force Academy. These words seem to be literally and figuratively cast in stone.[5]

All of the academies have struggled to develop physical and military leadership training programs and curriculum that will help make each cadet become "all he or she can be." During the first few years, the programs on women seemed to be simply tacked on, and workshops on proper professional relationships between men and women as peers and as leaders/subordinates bored the men and angered many of the women. By the end of the first decade, all the academies were revamping their military programs to add more palatable contents *and* to downplay the focus on women and to stress leadership training to motivate all cadets. Within a decade of gender integration, women complained bitterly about always being singled out for study and reevaluation. They felt that they had proven themselves and should be seen as simply cadets who must develop as leaders.

A comparison of early ratings illustrates that male cadets—peers and upperclassmen—rated females much lower on military leadership tests than did male or female officers.[6] One possible explanation is that the male cadets give physical prowess a disproportionate weight in the overall evaluation of potential leaders. By this criterion, women, on average not as fast or as strong as men, would not appear to make the best leaders in a mixed-gender military.

In addition, the first female officers assigned as AOC (air officer commanding) and TAC (tactical) officers to supervise cadet military training and discipline and to serve as role models for the female cadets were not well regarded by either male or female students. Indeed, many of the women who were senior enough to be captains and majors had come into the military while the women's corps were still separate. Therefore, physical requirements were clearly different for male and female officers, and few females would shine in the physical arena. In addition, these women were not academy graduates—a strike against a male officer but a fatal flaw for a female officer trying to achieve credibility. A decade after gender integration, the first female officers who had been cadets or midshipmen were assigned to the service academies and were taken more seriously. In addition, in the academic areas, more women were assigned to teach at the service academies, and ten years after women first arrived, the first women senior professors were recruited. These professors were majors and even lieutenant colonels; West Point now has its first female full colonel outside the Army Nurse Corps.

After women had been attending the academies for almost a decade and a half, a group of cadets came up with a second bedrock value, "Consideration of Others," which was designed to work in tandem with "Honor." "Consideration of Others" is a brilliant way to focus on the entire issue of diversity and internationalism without limiting the scope to issues of gender or allowing gender issues to be blown out of proportion. Behavior from basic civility to sexual and racial harassment can then be seen as part of the same continuum. The most effective programs to sensitize cadets to the problems women face are done without focusing on women.

Another outgrowth of the integration of women into the academies and the new emphasis on "Consideration of Others," was a new leadership style. First classmen (graduating seniors) now had to motivate each person in a squad, platoon, company, squadron or wing or brigade to develop to his or her very best. The traditional ways of leading fourth classmen included depriving them of sleep, and food, and yelling at them at them were downplayed or forbidden. With the introduction of women, academy leaders began worrying about physical and mental hazing, which could lead to charges of sexual harassment. Although this was not the only reason the academies moved away from physical and extreme mental punishment/hazing, critics told the cadets that the integration of women was "softening" the previously rigorous training. By implication, the cadets who were "exposed" to women for only a year or two—the classes of 1978 and 1979—were "tougher" than those who followed. Women became a convenient scapegoat for the frustrations of these "softer" men.[7]

When I was at West Point, I was told how much "harder" the training had been by colonels who talked about not being allowed to go home for spring vacation, even for Christmas, while they were plebes. Even the majors and captains reminisced about the "good old days" when physical hazing and pinging all corners was a way of life. Yet the changes have benefited men as well as women. While I was there, the mandatory dinner meal was abolished so that cadets would have a more flexible schedule for their sports activities. A result of this new order was that plebes were able to eat one square meal a day. One upperclassman told me he had lost twenty pounds his first year because he had been hazed so much at every meal that he always left the table hungry and had to sneak candy bars to keep up his strength for his rigorous athletic routine.

The advent of optional supper, the inability to resort to physical punishment, and the encouragement to lead without mental hazing may be some of the best revisions the academies made in the training of future leaders who could lead inside and outside the military. The leadership programs at the academies began to resemble the leadership training done in the business world. Japanese business leaders have honed the skills of collaborative efforts to a fine point. However, in the United States, the characteristics of nurturing, of building up instead of destroying, have been eschewed as "feminine."

The academies will vehemently deny any connection, but the same atmosphere that pushed for gender integration also produced the Cadet Leadership Development System (CLDS). CLDS insists that it is not just the obligation of firsties to learn to be leaders and doolies/plebes to be led but, rather, that leadership should be a four-year program with members of each year given more responsibility and accountability each year. Such a system worked to the advantage of gender integration: all cadets/midshipmen had to learn to lead and be led by women. As a result, the differences between the peer and cadet evaluations of women cadets and those of the officers have diminished significantly.

Physical Training

The physical arena has proven the most perplexing and the most difficult for gender integration.[8] The service academies have learned to accommodate the physiological differences of men and women, but this has not led to women's acceptance by male cadets/midshipmen.

When the first class of women came to the service academies, there was little data on what women athletes in top shape should be able to do. Even today, with much higher standards demanded of the women, the female cadets/midshipmen develop their physical abilities to a greater extent than do the males during four years at the academies. In 1976, West Point set an initial standard higher than Annapolis, and its program administrators argued that women should be stretched to, but not past, their limits, and that some women, like some men, would fail the physical tests. The Naval Academy physical education instructors set a lower standard, which would allow more women to pass the initial tests and then gain confidence as the standards were increased each year they were at the academy, and increased with each entering class. Both approaches proved problematic.

All of the academies failed to convince the male midshipmen/cadets that the standards set for women required the same effort/ability by women that the standards set for men required of men. In other words, from the perspective of a midshipman, a woman could receive an A for running at a speed that would be judged an F for men. The concept of *equal effort* is still not accepted by most male cadets/midshipmen, and because physical prowess is given great weight in the formula for success as a leader, women—even outstanding athletes—seldom can compete with the majority of men. Midshipmen point to women weight lifters, bench pressers, or Olympic-quality runners who can "make it" in this man's military. But the overwhelming majority of women are, by these standards, inferior.

Fortunately, the academy administrators have begun to articulate the difference between strength and fitness/wellness and are now connecting physical standards to requirements for a particular billet or occupational specialization. In other words, if a particular job requires lifting one hundred pounds of ammunition, then few women can or should hold that job. However, if a job requires superior mental ability and a highly fit person, then women can and should be allowed to compete for it.

If the military would reexamine its requirements and recognize that running, push-ups, and sit-ups are not the best measures of an overall physically fit person, then perhaps this major barrier to gender integration can start to be eroded. West Point took a step in the right direction when it required a faster time for the male cadets to "max" the two-mile run but required more sit-ups for female cadets to "max" sit-ups. It is also true that the minimum standards have risen—justifiably—for servicewomen. If fitness/wellness is a goal, then aerobic and anaerobic tests should be added to strength tests; this will level the playing field for men and women. For example, when male officers at West Point came to the female officers' aerobics class, they almost died before the class was officially over for the day. The academies are dividing runners into sections now so that most women are not seen as always bringing up the rear in a group run. Women run with men or with other women who have similar times and can then work on gradual improvement of their running time instead of always looking ahead at runners who leave them in the dust.

Deciding what *equal effort* is and educating all cadets on the differences between strength and fitness/wellness and job requirements remains a major challenge at all of the academies and in the military in general.[9] Until women can be seen as competitive in the physical arena, they will never be seen as equals. Because more women enter the service academies each year with varsity athletic experiences, the minimum standards for women will continue to climb. However, there will always be a marked difference between men's and women's physical abilities in the tests as they are currently constructed.

One reflection of the emphasis the academies and their cadets place on physical achievement is the higher for women than men attrition rate after the summer between the fourth and third class system. Some have hypothesized that males and females bond as fourth classmen because they are both under scrutiny and stress but then when they finish the most rigorous developing period, men and women drift apart. What the cadets see daily in Cadet Field Training (their summer training camp) is that on the official physical tests, most women just can't compete. In addition, in the earliest years, some women learned for the first time that they were not eligible for most combat roles but must learn combat support roles. I watched some of the male cadets begin to sense and act as if they were superior to women because they could participate in combat. Slowly but consistently, the males began to distance themselves from their female counterparts.

Retired Marine Colonel and Naval Academy professor Paul Roush takes on this superiority attitude, challenging James Webb's famous article "Women Can't Fight," which still circulates among the midshipmen and has been revised and reinforced by Admiral Webb in a 1997 article entitled "The War on the Military Culture." Roush argues that " 'Women Can't Fight' has been the single greatest purveyor of degradation and humiliation on the basis of gender that academy women have had to endure." Because physical beatings and high degrees of stress supposedly prepare cadets to be effective warriors, Roush suggests that "every women graduate thereby is more prepared to be a warrior than all of her male counterparts." Roush explains that if a mixed-gender Naval Academy precludes the development of warriors, then the U.S. Marine Corps is in trouble, because the majority of its officers are trained in ROTC units with women and missed out on the brutality and physical abuse of academy upperclassmen. Roush continues: "The unwarranted litany of half-truths with regard to alleged double standards creates—and, in my judgement, is calculated to create—resentment among the men."[10]

Another challenge for the military, which was flagged as a problem when the women's corps were formed during World War II but remains a problem, is women's uniforms. Women's uniforms do not fit well. The inability to find boots that will fit women has caused some of the academies to have all cadets do their physical fitness tests in running shoes. Women have been four times as likely to suffer from shin splits and other leg ailments due to extensive running. Women's uniforms also accent a woman's hips, which emphasizes further the difference between the sexes and suggests that even highly fit and trim athletes are "fat."

The issue of body fat and "overweight" cadets was not tackled head-on by the academies until a decade after civilian college officials were focusing on these issues. Women cadets who are excellent athletes in terrific shape can still fail the height/weight chart if they are petite. That means that they can be singled out to sit at special remedial "weight-control" tables and must pass a body-fat test. If a woman is even one-half of 1 percent above the academy or military-wide standard, she can be put on probation unless she rectifies the situation before the next physical training tests. One civilian physical-fitness visiting professor at West Point observed that the method used by the Army to measure body fat is accurate to within 1 percent for men but accurate only within 5 percent for women, thus making finer gradations meaningless.[11]

By focusing on weight and body fat, the service academies have added to an already major problem of college-age women, the inclination toward eating disorders such as bulimia or anorexia nervosa. I personally watched young women athletes starve for a week or two before the PT test to lose weight. They were susceptible to dizziness and fainting and were not learning anything about long-term wellness. Not until 1992 was material on bulimia and anorexia widely introduced to cadets and some effective proactive action taken by service officials.

Social/Cultural Environment

Because of the combination of academic, military, and physical components of the service academy educational program, gender integration cannot be easily compared to civilian colleges and universities.[12] In a civilian setting, students can retreat, even hide, drop out, and reenter after a few days. The midshipmen and cadets cannot escape from or easily change their environment. As a result, the social/cultural dynamics of the service academies may be unique. According to a four-year study of the first classes at Colorado Springs, young men coming to the Air Force Academy are seen as very traditional in attitudes and background, more traditional than their civilian counterparts. In contrast, women coming to the academy are seen as nontraditional because they wanted to participate in and excel in a "man's world." As sociologist Lois B. DeFleur explained, mixing nontraditional women and traditional men may prove a recipe for nonacceptance by both women and men.[13] For example, women beginning the academies were less likely to plan on marriage than women in a civilian setting. Perhaps many assumed that they could not combine a career and marriage and had to choose—twenty years ago that was not a far-fetched assumption. Moreover, these women often did not date while in college. Male cadets teased and ridiculed men who dated a female cadet. The men were treated to visiting busloads of women from nearby areas. A similar arrangement for the women cadets was not well received.

Second, the service academies have found that male cadets believe that their experiences make them more masculine, whereas female cadets report that their experiences have made them more masculine in some ways, more feminine in others. Maintaining *feminine* women has been a constant concern of the military since World War II. When a senior official at West Point saw female cadets dancing with male cadets and both were wearing slacks, he ordered that women wear skirts to all dances. Indeed, just as in World War II, servicewomen are constantly fighting the stereotypes of being either prostitutes or lesbians. The first classes of women at the Air Force Academy separated men and women for some training and brought in makeup consultants to work with the women. Since women cannot wear much makeup or even jewelry—even for the fanciest occasions and none during field training—one wonders how useful such instruction was. Makeup classes also reemphasized the differences between the sexes.

Gradually, the motivation for women to attend a service academy has shifted closer to the motivation for men. The first few classes contained women who wanted to be pioneers, wanted to prove something to themselves, their families, and society. The profile began to shift when the novelty started wearing off—about the classes of 1983 and 1984. At that point, more women came to the academies because of family lineage—their brothers or fathers were alumni. More women came in knowing the hierarchy and not saluting postal carriers and airplane pilots or waving to the academy superintendent.

Third, the most important volatile issue in the social/cultural environment is sexual harassment. The first few classes at each of the academies faced weekly if not daily overt and covert forms of sexual harassment, ranging from whistles and catcalls to unwanted touching. There are still cases reported yearly involving male cadets' entering female cadets' quarters and touching them, but the number has dropped considerably. However, with one in ten women still reporting unwanted touching according to a recent survey, these occurrences are more frequent than service academies officials would like. While upperclass women are still likely to be addressed as "Sir" by fumbling and groggy doolies or plebes, "Ma'am" is becoming a commonly heard salutation.[14]

Although intense training can reduce sexual harassment, as the Naval Academy has been proving, sexual harassment will never be eliminated from the military if leaders condone it, laugh it off, or allow whistle-blowers to be themselves harassed. Naval Academy professor James Barry identified a serious morale problem at the academy due to hypocritical leaders who "tolerate sexual harassment, favoritism, and the covering up of problems." He discovered that most women do not report sexual harassment incidents because of fear of retaliation.[15] As the Army recently discovered at its training post at Aberdeen, many young women tolerated sexual harassment, even sexual assault, because they feared retaliation or assumed that their complaints would not be taken seriously. What is critical is how sexual harassment is treated when it is reported *and* how to encourage its reporting.

Administrators at the Naval Academy provided a classic example of how *not* to react to sexual harassment in 1989 when a female midshipman was chained to a urinal. School officials downplayed the incident as routine hazing and part of "academy culture" until national media attention forced a more serious response. The incident demonstrated that the captains and admirals could not control their own ship. West Point's prompt and decisive response to the groping of female cadets during a pep rally/football cordon is an example of how to react.[16] The solution to the problem of sexual harassment must involve decisive leadership, especially swift and clear action on the part of academy officials to enforce a policy of "Zero Tolerance." Unfortunately, this message has to be reinforced by education and by severe consequences to those who choose to engage in sexual harassment, assault, and misconduct. The penalty for inaction, as many senior officers have discovered, can be loss of promotion or the ruin of a career.

The Citadel and VMI: Lessons Learned?

The Citadel, more formally the Military College of South Carolina, has apparently not learned many of the lessons on gender integration offered by the national military academies—nor has the Citadel learned from its own history. A major difference between the Citadel, located in Charleston, and the federal military academies at West Point, Annapolis, and Colorado Springs, is that "the Citadel is South Carolina's military college, not the nation's," chartered to train state militia leaders: "The day a Citadel cadet undoes his brass buttons, he is a civilian—and of course he was a civilian all along."[17] Unlike federal academy cadets and midshipmen who are Army, Navy, Marine Corps, and Air Force officers-in-training and who have military commitments after graduation, only about 30 percent of Citadel graduates enter military service.

One woman, Shannon Faulkner, was admitted to the Citadel under court order in fall 1995. Harassed and isolated, with no support in the institution, Faulkner resigned shortly thereafter.[18] Four more women were admitted in fall 1996. Before the term was over, two of the women alleged harassment, including being splashed with nail polish remover and set afire and being physically and verbally abused. Their complaints were initially silenced by upperclassmen. School authorities learned of the abuse, suspended several of the alleged abusers pending investigation, then reinstated and disciplined them with extra marching tours, confinement to campus, and demerits in their records. Dissatisfied with the school's response and fearful for their safety, the two women withdrew. Subsequently, two of the alleged abusers resigned, and one was dismissed; the state prosecutor decided not to pursue criminal charges.[19]

The Citadel's own history illustrates its intransigence in the face of change. Consider the experience of an earlier Citadel cadet: Charles DeLesline Foster, the first African American to join the Corps of Cadets in 1966. The harassment, intimidation, and abuse Foster experienced are illustrated in a fictionalized account by a classmate.[20] Unlike the women cadets, Foster's entry into the Citadel received less media coverage and little public attention, but Foster did find some sympathetic white cadets to support him.[21] Twenty years later, in fall 1986, the hazing of another African American cadet, Kevin Nesmith, would become infamous as "the incident," in which five white cadets dressed Klan-style in white linens entered Nesmith's room, chanted, and burned a paper cross. The five cadets were disciplined but not expelled, and Nesmith resigned in protest.[22] According to Vietnam Navy veteran and former Citadel president Admiral James Stockdale, the fault lies with the Citadel's discipline system, which is run almost completely by upperclassmen unsupervised by college authorities. Stockdale, a former POW, condemned the excesses of the discipline system as psychological torture.[23] Since the system had not changed substantially since "the incident," the women's recent experiences are not surprising.

Apparently, administrators at the Virginia Military Institute (VMI) have been paying more attention to the history of gender integration of military education than have Citadel officials. Located in Lexington, VMI—which some call "the Holy City"—is a public, state-funded military college like the Citadel. An even smaller proportion of VMI graduates—only about 20 percent, compared to the Citadel's 30 percent—pursue military careers. In response to a court challenge brought by the U.S. Justice Department in 1990, VMI refused to admit women and instead implemented a military training program for women at nearby Mary Baldwin College. The separate but purportedly equal program, the Virginia Women's Institute for Leadership (VWIL), was challenged, and on 26 June 1996, the Supreme Court ruled that VMI's men-only admission policy was unconstitutional.[24]

In fall 1997, 430 men and 30 women arrived at VMI. General Josiah Bunting 3d, a VMI alumnus initially opposed to women's admission, vowed as the new

VMI president to make gender integration work. Bunting said that the number of women admitted was deliberately high to establish a "genuine cohort" of women cadets "to form a support system" for one another. He explicitly stated that this decision was based on previous integration experiences: "It's a little like having someone cross a minefield a hundred yards ahead of you—you learn what to avoid."[25] Only three women (and thirty-seven men) had resigned by midterm, and VMI's admissions office reported that of 13,600 inquiries for admission in 1998–99, 3,500 were from women.[26]

To help the women cadets assimilate, VMI implemented a mentor program, moving women into administrative and staff positions, and initiated training about what constitutes sexual harassment. In addition, VMI required the same physical standards, and even the same uniforms and haircuts, for the women cadets as for the men. Most women cadets favored this policy, hoping this would make the men see them as equals.[27] The Citadel, on the other hand, required different—more feminine—haircuts for women, and disciplined the first class of women for cutting their hair shorter, like the men's. Also, female Citadel cadets may wear cosmetics; female VMI cadets may not. The Citadel's only accommodation to the presence of the first class of women was to install door latches on their rooms (at a cost to each cadet) and to post guards outside their restrooms; after two women resigned, alarm buttons were installed in the other women's rooms.[28]

But Citadel officials seem to be catching on. Twenty-seven women were admitted in fall 1997 (seventeen of those that began in the second class completed the year), and the Citadel recently announced plans to increase the proportion of women in the corps to 5 percent within two years, or 85 of 1,700 cadets, and gradually to 12 percent. Administrators also planned to increase adult supervision in the barracks, to hire an ombudsman to address hazing and other issues confidentially, and to add a female assistant commandant. These changes were brought about in part by the new commandant, Emory Mace, whose daughter is one of the two women in their second year at the Citadel.[29]

NOTES

1. Rosabeth Moss Kanter, *Men and Women in the Corporation* (New York: Basic Books, 1977).

2. Many thanks to Colonel Robert Toffler (USMA) for his research assistance. See Project Athena data in "United States Military Academy Report on the Integration and Performance of Women at West Point" (February 1992).

3. "Integration of Women at the U.S. Air Force Academy: Preliminary Findings," 17 March 1989; "Superintendent's Survey Team" (U.S. Air Force Academy, 1984).

4. Navy Women's Study Group, "An Update Report on the Progress of Women in the Navy," unpublished report (U.S. Navy, 1990).

5. Judith Hicks Stiehm, *Bring Me Men and Women: Mandated Change at the U.S. Air Force Academy* (Berkeley: University of California Press, 1981).

6. Robert F. Priest, Howard T. Prince, and Alan G. Vitters, "The First Coed Class at

West Point, Performance and Attitudes," *Youth and Society* 10, no. 2 (December 1978): 205–24; Robert W. Rice, Jan Yoder, Jerome Adams, Robert F. Priest, and Howard T. Prince II, "Leadership Ratings for Male and Female Military Cadets," *Sex Roles* 10, nos. 11/12 (1984): 885–901.

7. James Webb, "Women Can't Fight," *Washingtonian,* November 1979, 144–48, 273–82; Brian Mitchell, *Weak Link: The Feminization of the American Military* (New York: Regnery, 1989).

8. Jane E. Good and Karl M. Klein, "Women in the Military Academies: U.S. Navy (Part 1)," 99–106, and "Women in the Military Academies: U.S. Air Force Academy (Part 2)," *Physician and Sportsmedicine,* February 1989, 99–106, 133–142; Michael J. Welch, "Women in the Military Academies: U.S. Army (Part 3)," *Physician and Sportsmedicine,* April 1989, 89–96. See also Maureen Keenan Leboeuf, "Effectiveness of the Physical Education Curriculum at the United States Military Academy in Preparing Its Women Graduates" (Ph.D. diss., University of Georgia, 1994).

9. *Presidential Commission on the Assignment of Women in the Armed Forces* (Washington, D.C.: Government Printing Office 1992).

10. Paul E. Roush, "A Tangled Webb," in U.S. Naval Institute, *Proceedings* (August 1997), 43–44.

11. Personal communication.

12. Robert F. Priest, Alan G. Vitters, and Howard T. Prince, "Coeducation at West Point," *Armed Forces and Society* 4, no. 4 (August 1978): 589–606.

13. Lois B. DeFleur, Frank Wood, Dickie Harris, David Gillman, and William Marshak, "Four Years of Sex Integration at the United States Air Force Academy: Problems and Issues," report for the U.S. Air Force Academy, August 1985; Lois B. DeFleur, "Sex Integration of the U.S. Air Force Academy," *Armed Forces and Society* 4, no. 4 (August 1978): 607–22.

14. "Equal Opportunity: DOD Studies on Discrimination in the Military," GAO/NSIAD-95-103 (Washington, D.C.: U.S. General Accounting Office, 7 April 1995); Carol Barkalow, with Andrea Raab, *In the Men's House: An Inside Account of Life in the Army* (New York: Poseidon Press, 1990).

15. James Barry, "Adrift in Annapolis," *Washington Post,* 31 March 1996, C1, C3.

16. D'Ann Campbell, "Servicewomen and the Academies," *MINERVA: Quarterly Report on Women and the Military* 13, no. 1 (spring 1995): 1–14.

17. Mark F. Bernstein, "The Pride of Charleston," *American Spectator,* May 1996, 58–59.

18. "Woman Registers at Citadel, Then Is Barred," *New York Times,* 13 January 1994, A12; Catherine S. Manegold, " 'Save the Males' Becomes Battle Cry in Citadel's Defense Against Woman," *Finger Lakes Times,* (Geneva, N.Y.) 23 May 1994, A10; Kevin Sack, "A Woman Reports for Duty as a Cadet at the Citadel," *New York Times,* 13 August 1995, 14.

19. "Father: 'Terrorized' Cadet May Leave Citadel," *Finger Lakes Times,* (Geneva, N.Y.) 16 December 1996, 2; "Citadel Suspends Second Cadet in the Inquiry on Hazing Women," *New York Times,* 18 December 1996, A23; "Citing Abuse by Fellow Cadets, Two Women Leave Citadel," *New York Times,* 13 January 1997, A10; Adam Nossiter, "Early Reports of Abuse Cited in Citadel Inquiry," *New York Times,* 22 January 1997, A10; Adam Nossiter, "Woman Who Left the Citadel Tells of Brutal Hazing Ordeal," *New York Times,* 18 February 1997, A1, A16; Adam Nossiter, "A Cadet Is Dismissed and 9 Are Disciplined for Citadel Harassment," *New York Times,* 11 March 1997, A15; Kevin Sack, "Citadel Cadets Won't Face Charges in Women's Hazing," *New York Times,* 21 August 1997, A14.

20. Pat Conroy, *The Lords of Discipline* (New York: Bantam, 1987).

21. Linda L. Megget, "Citadel of Trauma: The Untold Story of the Citadel's First Black Cadet," *Black Issues in Higher Education,* 9 January 1997, 22–25.

22. Michael W. Hirschorn, "The Citadel, Trying to Shed Old-South Image, Set Back by 'the Incident,'" *Chronicle of Higher Education,* 4 February 1987, 24–26.

23. Stockdale cited in ibid., 26.

24. *United States of America v Commonwealth of Virginia (Virginia Military Institute),* 113 Sup. Ct. 2431 (1993) and 116 Sup. Ct. 2264 (1996); William A. De Van, "Toward a New Standard in Gender Discrimination: The Case of Virginia Military Institute," *William and Mary Law Review* 33 (winter 1992): 489–542; Rosemary C. Salomone, "The VMI Case: Affirmation of Equal Educational Opportunity for Women," *Trial* 32 (October 1996): 67–70; Jennifer R. Cowan, "Distinguishing Private Women's Colleges from the VMI Decision," *Columbia Journal of Law and Social Problems* 30 (winter 1997): 137–83; Abigail E. Adams, "The 'Military Academy': Metaphors of Family for Pedagogy and Public Life," in *Wives and Warriors: Women and the Military in the United States and Canada,* ed. Laurie Weinstein and Christie White (Westport, Conn.: Bergin and Garvey, 1997).

25. Quoted in William H. Honan, "The Man with the Plan," *New York Times,* Education Life Supplement, 6 April 1997, 27, 33.

26. "VMI's Women Cadets May Help Recruit More," *Finger Lakes Times,* (Geneva, N.Y.) 20 October 1997, 7.

27. "All Eyes on VMI," *Finger Lakes Times,* (Geneva, N.Y.) 18 August 1997, 1; Eric Schmitt, "A Mean Season at Military Colleges: Beleaguered, Embarrassed, Marching On," *New York Times,* Education Life Supplement, 6 April 1997, 24–26, 28, 30–31, 38.

28. "Citadel Suspends Second Cadet in the Inquiry on Hazing Women," *New York Times,* 18 December 1996, A23; Mike Allen, "Women at the Citadel Get Shorter Hair, and in Trouble," *New York Times,* 9 November 1996, 9; Catherine S. Manegold, "Citadel Adopts Positive View of Its Female Cadets," *New York Times,* 24 August 1996, 7; "What to Wear, What to Touch, What to Say, What to Tuck (Citadel Etiquette)," *New York Times,* 11 August 1996, 9.

29. "Citadel Offers Detailed Plan for Women," *New York Times,* 23 May 1997, A21.

Autobiography
Too Bad She's a Girl . . .

Lillian A. Pfluke

When he was ten and I was twelve, my brother John and I were the biggest football fans in the world. We carried a pigskin with us everywhere we went so we could run pass patterns whenever we had a few moments to do so. Pass patterns were especially fun when we could talk Dad into playing quarterback. Dad could throw a lot farther than either one of us, so running a deep fly pattern when Dad put it up there was the ultimate thrill.

One fall, Dad's boyhood friend Jerry and his wife were visiting us for a few days, and we were showing them around the city. On these tours, when John and I got back to the car before the rest of the family did, we would get the football out and toss it around. Dad and Jerry started throwing the ball around with us as we waited. As the rest of the family caught up and came toward us in the parking lot, Dad let loose with one last bomb. I could tell with a glance that it was long . . . way long. Nonetheless, I took off to try to run under it. With visions of Gene Washington running under a John Brodie pass, I strained to get every bit of speed out of my young legs. I could sense that even a quick look over my shoulder would slow me down too much to make the catch, so at what seemed like the right moment I stretched out my arms and watched with tremendous satisfaction as the ball came down right onto my fingertips. In more than twenty-six years of playing on various athletic teams since then, this still ranks as one of my very best catches ever.

I jogged back toward the car, breathless and grinning from ear to ear. Dad and Jerry were whooping and hollering and slapping each other on the back. John was dumbstruck. As I casually flipped Dad the ball and got in the back seat of the station wagon, I overheard Jerry say something that I didn't think much of at the time but that has come to haunt me recently: "What a waste of talent—too bad she's a girl!"

I guess you can tell that I was a tomboy. I was also a great leader from an early age, being the oldest of five children. I've had someone to lead around since I was fourteen months old and my sister Teresa came along, so I have a knack for getting people to do things they may not otherwise want to do. In fact, if you talk to people who knew me in my youth, they'd all tell you the same thing: great student, great athlete, great leader.

One other thing really characterizes me: I hate being told I can't do something because I'm a girl. When my brother John got a paper route I wanted one, too. Unfortunately, the paper didn't want a papergirl. So, I used my then four-year-old brother Paul's name to get the route. I was amused when two years after I started the route, the newspaper finally changed its policy and allowed paper-girls. They wrote an article about me as the first new papergirl. I never told them I had had the route all along.

I swam competitively from when I was eight years old. When I got to high school, I wanted to swim for the school. There was no girls team in those days, so along with a few buddies I became one of the first girls on the boys team. I won the junior varsity city championship in the butterfly and freestyle sprint events that first year. There were more write-ups in the paper, but again I never understood what the fuss was all about. Of course girls could compete with boys. Why not?

When I was a senior in high school, a West Point recruiter came around to the swim team looking for smart, athletic girls to be in the first class of women. I had never heard of West Point. In my nonmilitary family way out in California, it just never came up. I was definitely intrigued. Shooting guns and jumping out of airplanes sounded like a lot more fun than just studying engineering at the University of California. The further I got through the application process, the more I became convinced that this was for me. I love challenges, and this sounded like a great one.

I was accepted and entered the U.S. Military Academy in the first class of women on 7 July 1976. My family was very proud and supportive because they understood me and my need to do something like this. In fact, the whole family (parents, five kids, and a dog) drove from San Francisco to New York in our van to drop me off.

It certainly was a challenge—and I loved every minute. Pushing myself to physical exhaustion, withstanding all the mental and emotional pressures, inspiring others to push themselves as hard as they could; it was all very fulfilling.

All, that is, except for the fact that I never seemed to get a fair shake. Sure, everyone expects to get harassed as a plebe, but we women all seemed to get more than our share. It's no secret that we were regularly called bitch, whore, and worse; that we were accused of sexual promiscuity or lesbianism; that we were subjected to such inappropriate "pranks" as shaving cream filled condoms in our bed or semen in our underwear drawer. What most people don't realize is the toll that juvenile and hateful treatment takes on a person after a while. The constant barrage of insults, harassment, and inequities made even the strongest among us harbor self-doubts. We all felt very isolated and defensive as a result of never being accepted as contributing members of the institution, and we became extraordinarily sensitive to all issues of prejudice.

During my four years at West Point, I found that infantry training gave me the most personal satisfaction and seemed to be what I was best at. I relished the unique combination of mental and physical toughness required and sought out all of the infantry training experiences available to me, including the Jungle Operations Training Course in Panama, and the Airborne school at Fort Benning. And as an instructor of the challenging Recondo Course at West Point. I loved the intense physical demands, being outside, braving the elements, carrying everything I needed on my back, and finding my way in the woods. I especially enjoyed pushing myself to my personal physical limits. I enjoy risk, challenge, and adventure, and that is what the infantry offers.

In December of 1979, I wrote a letter to Secretary of the Army John O. Marsh requesting an exception to the combat-exclusion policy and expressing my desire to choose infantry as a branch. I was denied, of course, but went into the Army convinced that if I consistently showed my physical, mental, and emotional competence, the barrier against women in combat would fall, as had other barriers for me. I did have a court action lined up with the American Civil Liberties Union Women's Rights Project, but that fizzled when the male-only draft registration legislation passed at the same time as my graduation.

I went into the Ordnance Corps for two reasons. First, it was where I could best use my mechanical engineering education. Second, it was always close to the action. After my four years at West Point, I spent six of my fifteen years in the Army in troop units running maintenance facilities where we fixed tanks, trucks, howitzers, guns, and everything else necessary for a combat division. Army life was fun! It's a real thrill to lead soldiers. To be part of a trained and smoothly functioning team is very fulfilling, especially when it is so because of your efforts.

All throughout those fifteen years, though, my goal was still to prove my competence to get into the infantry: to become an Airborne Ranger and an Infantry battalion commander. Unrealistic expectations? I didn't think so. The entire West Point experience and subsequent socialization into the Army stressed my goals as laudable and important milestones to a successful Army career. After all, for years every single role model I was exposed to in key senior leadership positions wore combat arms brass, airborne wings, and a Ranger tab. Every jody sung started with "I wanna be an Airborne Ranger . . ." I didn't set out to be a maverick; I merely bought into the system and the institutional values as presented.

So, prove my competence I did. I was a physically fit and mentally tough leader of soldiers. I was the National Military Triathlon Champion, the two-time National Military Cycling Champion, the two-time Interservice European Ski Champion. I played rugby. I achieved a maximum score on every Army PT test taken in fifteen years of service. I achieved a First Class score on the U.S. Marine Corps men's PT test. I got a master's degree in mechanical engineering, and years of perfect efficiency reports. I made almost two hundred freefall parachute jumps. I was physical, aggressive, and very competitive. I was a leader who could inspire people to their own personal bests by providing a powerful example and through my genuine infectious enthusiasm for adventure and challenge. Men followed me, bonded with me, respected me, and we fought as a team.

I was also absolutely consistent and outspoken about my views on women in the Army and their lack of opportunity. It was such a gnawing frustration for me to see wonderfully competent women not get taken seriously because of the restrictions on our utilization. We were a separate class of soldier, able to endure all the risks and hardships of Army life but unable to reap the benefits. So, I wrote about these inequities, and talked about them, and confronted my senior leaders about them. I quickly became an "expert," but, more important, an active-duty soldier willing to speak out on the record—a rarity in the Army because a strong part of the institutional culture is to be a team player and not "rock the boat." I wrote opinion pieces and did radio, television, and print interviews. Whenever the subject of Army women was in the news, so was my name.

Because of my notoriety, I was very close to the action as the Army leadership once again debated what to do about "the woman problem" in 1993-1995. The actions and attitudes of the senior Army leadership in that time frame regarding the Army's women's-assignment policy were extraordinarily disheartening and deeply personally disappointing to me. I had invested nineteen years proving my competence in the organization and suddenly realized that it was *not* a matter of competence. The Army was content to choose less qualified men over more qualified women for its key leadership positions because of politics and deeply entrenched and dated attitudes. In fact, it was fighting desperately for the ability to continue to do so.

As I approached consideration for lieutenant colonel, I realized that my personal ambitions of being an Airborne Ranger and an Infantry battalion commander had slipped away. Since my hope for the institution was stalemated and my personal goals were unrealizable, I reluctantly concluded that with them went my reasons for staying in the Army. I wanted to play on the varsity team and be a contributing member of the first string. I did not want to be tucked away in some support role. I retired on 30 September 1995.

My transition to civilian life went smoothly. With two sons (then three and five years old) and an overseas move when my husband was assigned to France, I had no time to dwell on my disappointment. I started teaching at the French War College, traveled all over Europe, spent more time with my kids, and stayed in great shape. My boys think everyone's mother can do nineteen pull-ups, run faster than Dad, and jump out of airplanes on weekends.

I am still actively engaged in the cause of women in the Army and find that I can speak much more freely about Army women's issues now than I could while in uniform. As I look back on the twenty years since I entered West Point, I take tremendous pride in knowing that I played a role in the vast strides that Army women have made in that time frame. I am confident that the current fusses involving military women (pregnancy rates, sexual harassment, fraternization, deployment issues, and so on) are all just growing pains and transitional problems that will get better as more and more women rise through the ranks. I am convinced, however, that the issues will never go away until the Army adopts one simple policy: The best soldier for the job.

Four

Women Veterans' Issues

Joan A. Furey

Editor's note: The following passages are excerpted from the ''Proceedings'' of the National Summit on Women Veterans' Issues, held 25–27 September 1996 at the White House Conference Center in Washington, D.C., cosponsored by the Department of Veterans Affairs' Center for Women Veterans, the White House Office for Women's Initiatives and Outreach, and American Veterans of World War II, Korea, and Vietnam (AMVETS). The ''Proceedings'' were provided to us by Joan A. Furey, Director of the Center for Women Veterans.

In his keynote address to the summit participants, Secretary of Veterans Affairs Jesse Brown noted:

For too long, the role women played in the military has been ignored.

Women have been there for the nation; the nation must be there for them.

Today there are more than 1.2 million women veterans. We need to help them gain the recognition they deserve and the benefits and health care they have earned.[1]

Secretary Brown went on to observe that in 1995 the Veterans Administration (VA) had 130 clinics, 8 Comprehensive Health Care Centers, and 4 stress-disorder treatment teams for women veterans, as well as a women veterans division at the VA's National Center for Post-Traumatic Stress Disorder in Boston. Brown further noted that the VA had adopted policies ''to ensure that gender-specific care is available at all VA health care facilities.''[2]

In her introduction to the summit ''Proceedings,'' Joan Furey, Director of the VA's Center for Women Veterans and herself an Army Nurse Corps veteran, wrote that women veterans, who in 1995 were 4 percent of the U.S. veteran population, are projected to become 10 percent of that population by 2010. She continued:

Over the last few years, we have begun to recognize that both the services required of these women and the issues they face as they return to civilian life are different from those of male veterans. The changing demographics of the veteran population will have a significant impact on all agencies and organizations providing services to women veterans. The Center for Women Veterans is committed to assuring that the services women veterans require will be there for them.

The first *National Summit on Women Veterans' Issues* was organized to provide an opportunity for veteran service providers, federal and state agency representatives, women veteran activists, and other individuals concerned about women veterans to come together, discuss their concerns, and develop recommendations to address them.[3]

She concluded her introduction by observing:

Tremendous progress has been made in improving services for women veterans, but more needs to be done. To give us an opportunity to review our progress, I hope we will have a second summit in 1998–99. Using this report as a working document, together we can evaluate where we are, where we need to go, and how we would like to get there. It is our hope that as we enter the twenty-first century, women who have served their country will be able to access the services we provide with comfort and ease, secure in the knowledge that the nation is grateful for their service and sacrifice.[4]

The "Executive Summary" of the "Proceedings" detailed the background of recent legislation relating to women veterans:

Recognizing that some veterans failed to use the health services and readjustment benefits to which they were entitled led to the enactment of Public Law 102–218 in December 1991. This legislation created the position of Chief Minority Affairs Officer (CMAO) within VA. That statute defined minority group members as individuals who are Asian American, Black, Hispanic, Native American, Pacific Islander, or female.

In December 1993, Jesse Brown, Secretary of Veterans Affairs, separated the CMAO responsibilities by creating a Women Veterans' Program Office and a Minority Veterans' Program Office under the Office of the Assistant Secretary for Policy and Planning.

In 1995, Congress passed Public Law 104–446 establishing the Center for Women Veterans (CWV) and the Center for Minority Veterans (CMV). These program offices were reorganized to the Office of the Secretary to reflect the intent of Congress.

During the summit, speakers briefed the participants on government initiatives relevant to women on active duty and women veterans, including women-centered VA health care, sexual trauma, specialized personnel, claims processing, outreach, coordination of services, transition from military to civilian life, and the demographics of women veterans. Representatives from two advisory groups, the Defense Advisory Committee on Women in the Services (DACOWITS), a civilian organization established in 1951, and the Advisory Committee on Women Veterans, an internal advisory committee established within the VA in 1983, also addressed participants.

The more than one hundred summit participants also met in six working groups to focus on key issues of concern. The six group topics were benefits, health care, economics and employment, homelessness, minority, and active duty. The Summit participants generated 160 recommendations, which are detailed in the "Proceedings." Briefly, the recommendations offer ways to improve women veterans' access to benefits and services, as well as the quality of those services, by increasing "attention to, education about, and sensitivity toward issues affecting women veterans." For example, the working groups recommended eliminating the one-year limitation on provision of care for victims of sexual trauma; extending VA counseling assistance to reservist and National Guard members who experience sexual assault during drill periods; ensuring greater privacy for women at VA medical facilities, and including minority women veterans in all veteran-survey activities, focus groups, and health research.[5]

The appendices included a profile of women veterans based on 1990 data indicating that of the total veteran population of 27,183,662, 1,093,921 were women. Of these, 312,937 had served during World War II; 81,738 served during the Korean conflict; 217,293 during the Vietnam era; and 368,494 post-Vietnam. Somewhat more than one-third of women veterans are older than sixty-five; 27 percent are younger than thirty-five. Eighty-four percent of women veterans are white; 12 percent are African American; 1.2 percent are Asian-Pacific Islanders; 1 percent are Native American.[6]

Women veterans have a high degree of educational attainment: 60 percent had attended some college, obtained a college degree, or received an advanced degree. Yet the median personal income of female veterans reported was $12,598. Although the overall rate of unemployment among women veterans is low—6.8 percent—the rate differs among racial/ethnic groups, such that only 5.8 percent of white veterans were unemployed, compared to 8.9 percent of Hispanic veterans and 11.1 percent of African American veterans.[7]

NOTES

1. Jesse Brown, "Keynote Address," in National Summit on Women Veterans' Issues Proceedings, 25–27 September 1996, 1 (cited hereafter as Proceedings).

2. Ibid.

3. Joan A. Furey, introduction to Proceedings, I.

4. Ibid.

5. "IV. Key Issues," in Proceedings, 13–15.

6. "Appendix H: Profile of Women Veterans from 1990 Census Data," in Proceedings, 78.

7. Ibid.

Veterans' Voices
Autobiography: Warriors without Weapons

Donna M. Dean

*Editor's note: In the following two essays, we hear the voices of two veterans of different ranks, services, and eras. The first voice is that of Native American Donna Dean, whose Cherokee name is Running Black Wolf, an eighteen-year Navy veteran and former mental health therapist. In her new book, "*Warriors without Weapons: The Victimization of Military Women,*" Dr. Dean documents the hostility and psychological and sexual abuse women experience in military service, and she argues that this abuse contributes to the prevalence of post-traumatic stress disorder (PTSD) among women veterans. In the passage reproduced here, she describes her coming to terms with her own experience of military service beginning at a 1983 conference for women veterans and culminating with publication of her book.[1]*

I had been out of the Navy for several years and was not doing well at all. I didn't have a clue about *why*, but I did know that my life was miserable. I was a professional mental health counselor with a master's degree from a prestigious university and years of experience in middle and top management, yet I could not get or hold down a job. There were days I could not even get out of bed, and I thought of committing suicide all the time, if I could muster up the energy to do it.

I did think it was rather odd that I couldn't stand going over to the Navy base with my husband, an officer in the Naval Reserves, much less carry on a conversation with his colleagues, considering that I had spent most of my adult life as one of them. Now they terrify me. I was overwhelmed with a need to run as far away from them and all their rank and power as I could get. I didn't know why. I thought I must be crazy.

The Conference

In 1983 Julia Perez, an Army veteran, was working as the coordinator for the women veterans' program within the Veterans Center at the University of Massachusetts in Boston. She invited me to speak at the first conference on women veterans of which I had ever heard. Julia tracked me down through the Viet Nam Era Veteran's Intertribal Association. She asked me if I would come to Boston and participate on a panel of women veterans of color.[2] I reluctantly agreed, not knowing what to expect but not expecting much.

How little did I know! How little did any of us know, the two hundred women vets at the conference. There were women who had served in all branches of the service, in almost all the wars of the previous half century, and in all the "peacetime" periods. Even frail Gurtha Lee Clark was there, a veteran of the famous all-black unit of women postal clerks who had been sent to Europe during World War II.

Those of us on the opening panel, women veterans of color, sat nervously in our chairs at the front of the auditorium. African American, Native American, Jewish American, Chinese American, Japanese American, Mexican American/ Hispanic—we started out by introducing ourselves to the crowd. Name, branch of service, era—I don't remember just how things really got started, but they did. Emotions began to break through our flat voices, and we began to talk. Really talk. We began to talk about things that had happened to us and what it had been like. I don't remember who was the first one needing to choke back the tears; it doesn't matter. Eventually tears flowed freely all around us.

At first the World War II women said very little. When they spoke, they tended to have smiling faces as they recalled the sweet American boys so far away from home and so glad to see American women that they treated them "like queens," according to one woman veteran of the era. It was those of us from Vietnam, Korea, and the Cold War who talked, gaining courage to tell what had happened to us as, one by one, we told secrets we had kept so long. Then, all at once, the World War II veterans began to talk, too.

I don't know exactly when it happened—quickly, though—but the audience began to interact with us on a personal level. They began to interject with stories of their own. Very soon we were one large group of women veterans sharing our stories, not a panel and an audience. The preset conference schedule was put aside, and we continued to share our experiences and to pull aside the thick curtain of shame and isolation covering our shattered spirits.

Jessica cried inconsolably as she tried to get through the story of her dear friend in Europe during the 1940s who had been raped by the most popular, attractive young officer on the base. The friend, Sue, became pregnant as a result of the attack and was frantic to avoid the shame of being found out and immediately discharged. Until 1972, women were summarily discharged as the inevitable result of pregnancy, no matter how it happened. If you were unmarried, disgrace and a ruined future were the only options. A sympathetic friend told Sue how to find a backstreet abortionist, and she was too desperate to do anything else. In a filthy kitchen he injected her with something and sent her back to her barracks to await the miscarriage. It took all the endless, dark hours of the night to take effect. Jessica held a pillow over her dear friend's contorted face to muffle the agonizing screams while the poison in Sue's body took hold. Somehow, they got through the night, but Sue committed suicide shortly afterward.

One of the women—a World War II marine, I think—wore the little hat of the veterans' organization she represented. This organization had been exclusively male until it was forced by court order in the early 1970s to admit women. This woman was enraged at what she was hearing: all this whining and complaining! She spitefully spat at us, "Remember, you all volunteered! None of you were drafted!" We listened and were too polite to correct her. None of us had volunteered for rape, violence, and dehumanization.

Everything got talked about at the conference. Secrets and shame and the freeing flow of tears accompanied the stories of long-hidden pain. The stories came from all the generations, all the veterans, young and old. Even the camera crews, all male veterans attending from various veterans' programs, and those in the audience merely because they were interested in the topic were crying, too, as these frozen and almost-forgotten nuggets of grief were dug up and exposed to the heat and light of day for the first time. It was a healing experience, too.

I began to realize that I was not alone in the destruction of my life and that there might be a reason for what I was experiencing, for the way my life was not working. Maybe, *maybe* it had something to do with what had happened to me in all those years in the Navy. Maybe being a woman veteran had some bearing on my own situation.

I Remember

When I entered the Naval Reserves in 1963 at Treasure Island, California, Navy women were known as WAVES, Women Accepted for Voluntary Emergency Service, which would remain our proud sobriquet until 1972. The women in the leadership were mainly veterans of World War II. These were the women who "raised me" to be a WAVE, who shaped and molded me in the ways of the "Old Navy."

My Commanding Officer, then-Lieutenant Commander Emanuela Catena (Tena), my Leading Chief, Chief Draftsman Elizabeth Conley (Chiefie), and my Leading Petty Officer, Dispersing Clerk Second Class Beverley Humphrey (Bev), are some of my dearest friends more than thirty long, hard years later. They taught me well. I think they are proud of me still. I know I am proud of them, and no matter what befell me later, I continued to remember them. I remembered their complete dedication to the Navy and their pride in the traditions they passed down to the high-spirited young women we were as we learned to be WAVES under their guiding hands.

I did serve for eighteen years with honor and pride in the way I lived out their legacy. I never forgot the lessons I learned from them: never disgrace your uniform, don't lie when the going gets rough, and never forget who you are and what your uniform represents.

In 1967 I reported to my first active duty station after Officer Candidate

School. In San Diego everyone referred to the senior WAVES as "old war horses," and the medals they wore attested to the lives they had selected in the military. My immediate boss was the rarest of beings, a WAVE full Commander. I had seen only one other woman with that exalted rank, commanding the WAVE Officer Candidate School and "sitting at the right hand of God."

Since I was the Women's Representative (WR) for the enlisted women in my command, as well as in two other commands that had no female officers, I was responsible for a large number of enlisted Navy women. In those days, Navy women had a separate and direct Chain of Command to the Pentagon, which resulted in a de facto separate Navy. Station Commanding Officers generally relied upon this separate hierarchy to deal with virtually any and all issues arising with female military personnel. The Director of the WAVES, Captain Rita Lenihan, was a formidable woman we called Saint Rita. She obsessively insisted on our practicing the utmost in outmoded "ladylike" behavior at all times. We never went outside without gloves and hats, we never played baseball, and we never swore. We always wore girdles and firmly engineered brassieres so there would be no unseemly jiggle. Pantyhose were believed to herald the beginning of the end of morality and right thinking, as there were no seams to keep straight. This would lead straight to a loosening of discipline and good order.

The older women were a close-mouthed lot, and they were not inclined to discuss their experiences with new, untried Ensigns. But I watched them. I "knew" them through the mandatory WAVE meetings, luncheons, and other functions in which all women officers stationed in the area took part. It was obvious they lived lives severely circumscribed by who and what they were: "lady officers."

Their conduct in public was invariably impeccable, and I never saw them "let their hair down." I did, however, see them drink. They drank with a quiet competency that amazed me, never becoming obviously drunk, never disorderly, never even rowdy. Their drinking seemed to be motivated more by a need to numb than a desire to foster pleasure. Even then, I absorbed the silent lessons implicit in their lives: women in the Navy did not live in a friendly world. Later in that tour, I reinforced that lesson with experience.

I was left pretty much to my own devices to figure out how to fulfill my many duties. Like all Ensigns, I had my primary job, Personnel Officer, plus myriad collateral duties.

I watched the Commander and the other senior women, and I learned. Eventually I discovered why the Commander took so little notice of me beyond making me do my paperwork over and over until I learned "The Navy Way." She had troubles of her own.

Our Commanding Officer was an Admiral who apparently was a genuine misogynist. One of my superiors warned me that he was dedicated to removing as many women as possible from "his" Navy.

In November 1967, however, the seas parted, the heavens roiled, and lightning struck the Pentagon. President Johnson signed Public Law 90–130, removing the restrictions preventing women in the armed services from reaching higher ranks.

Suddenly, all the WAVE Commanders were to be considered *en masse* for the few Captain slots. Those who failed of selection would see their careers abruptly terminated. Commanding Officers were directed to write updated Fitness Reports for consideration.

Our Commander waited, breath caught, with her Commander sisters. The Admiral wrote a slyly worded, less-than-perfect Fitness Report on her. With twenty-six years of absolute perfect fitness reports stretching out behind her, the Commander was now doomed. Her career was over. No appeal. No more Navy.

Not long after, I was sitting in her office one day, trying not to cry. The Admiral had changed the perfect Fitness Report she had written on me and which the Captain over both of us had approved. The Admiral had altered all the marks downward because "no Ensign is perfect" and "Ensigns need something to strive for."

We both knew that I, too, was doomed. Not now; I would almost certainly make it to Lieutenant, probably Lieutenant Commander, but I would never make Commander. The Commander told me that I was the best Ensign she had ever seen in all her years of service. I left that command some months later, with that time bomb ticking in my record. There was no question in my mind why old war horses drank with such tight-lipped determination.

There were no other WAVES at my next command, and by the time I reported to my third command in 1971, almost all the World War II women were gone. After twenty, thirty, or even more years, they had retired from the service that had been their only life and their only family. Few had ever married. Marriage and children were not an option, and they had lived, breathed, and slept the Navy for so long that the edges blurred where the uniform ended and they began.

I had served with the last of them.

Because I Cannot Forget

I have been out of the military since 1981. Sixteen years. It has been a long and difficult time, and I have felt the need to lay some ghosts to rest.

As a survivor [of gender hostility, emotional and sexual harassment, and rape], I found myself stitching pieces of myself and my story together and weaving in the stories and pieces of other women veterans like me—women veterans who have paid their dues in pain and grief and who deserve to be heard—women veterans with all the scars of the battle, all the horrors if "battle fatigue," "shell shock," and "post-traumatic stress disorder," or PTSD, in the current lexicon. We may never have been at the front. We may never have been anywhere near Vietnam or Korea or anyplace else in active combat. Yet we have lived every day of our lives in a secret, hidden combat. We have been wounded, and the scars are not always from gunshots and napalm.

Sometimes it seems nobody can see our scars.
So I wrote a book.

NOTES

1. Donna M. Dean, *Warriors without Weapons: The Victimization of Military Women* (Pasadena, Md.: MINERVA Center, 1997), xii–xix.
2. Ibid.

Autobiography
Women Are Veterans, Too; or, No One Should Experience This

Anne Black (pseudonym)

Editor's note: Next we hear from an Army enlistee who has adopted the pseudonym Anne Black to protect her identity. Like many women veterans, Anne was neither a careerist nor an officer; she served only one enlistment tour and shares her reasons for enlisting and for leaving the service is this original essay.

My parents divorced when I was thirteen, and Mom, my little brother, and I had been destitute since then. I spent my days working as a flag girl for a construction company that was installing water lines, my evenings cleaning charter fishing boats, and my nights getting my high school education. I was in love with learning and wanted so strongly to go to college. We could barely afford the gas for me to drive to school, much less tuition. With my difficult life experiences, I had destroyed my perfect grades and no longer qualified for a scholarship.

I was at the very wise age of seventeen and about to graduate from high school when I received a postcard from the military inviting me to join the American armed forces.

When I found the flyer in the mail, I started thinking of the possibilities for a future I hadn't considered before. I approached the subject with my mother, and she was extremely positive about the idea, believing I would have a secure financial future and a serious profession. Had she been more concerned with my mental health instead of seeing only a steady job and education for me, she might have been more cautious.

I was born in Bethesda, Maryland, on January 7, 1965, number six out of seven kids and the first female in the family to join the military. The males on the paternal side of the family have had at least one family member fight in every war the United States has been involved in.

I grew up in a small town in Maryland—population 300 and that included the cows. When my parents divorced, we moved to Rockville. My little brother and I spent much time moving between our parents' homes until the abuse got so bad at both homes I ran away, at age fourteen, and lived with a friend of the family, quit school, and worked full-time at McDonald's as a cashier. Since then I have worked at dozens of jobs and lived all over the United States and France. I've had as many jobs as I've had moves, and almost all of the jobs were in the male traditional realm. I guess being raised on a farm with four brothers didn't make me the kind of person to sit behind a desk or to take being told, "You can't do that, you're a girl."

In the summer of 1982, the summer I got the postcard from the military, I took time from my construction job and interviewed for the military. All the promises, possibilities, and options the recruiter described didn't leave a young, uninitiated farm girl like myself much escape. It sounded like paradise.

I took the required tests and did so well they asked me to be an officer. I didn't know what an officer was and it was too scary to find out, so I refused. Boy, do I regret that!

Because I was only seventeen, my parents had to sign papers stating I could join the United States Army. My father had some concerns about my joining the military, probably because he had spent a few years in the Army during World War II. Finally, after much deliberation, the deed was done—I was now the proud owner of a four-year enlistment as a Morse Code interceptor, with a $10,000 enlistment bonus, in the Army.

In October of that fall, shortly after I received my adult education certificate from the high school, the recruiter drove me from my home to the train in Miami, Florida. I was so nervous and stressed about going into the Army, because it was such an alien concept, that I had my period for an entire eight weeks. Then I didn't have another period for three months (which made boot camp that much easier).

I spent two of the best months of my military career in boot camp at Fort Dix, New Jersey: aka Fort Sand. I got to do what I'd always loved doing as a child: I crawled through the mud and sand—only now it was with a M16 rifle, under barbwire, in the dark, while blank tracer bullets were shot at me. What an incredible high for me. I couldn't understand the sissy women around me who could only whine and cry.

Right before I finished boot camp, I was told I did not get my top-secret security clearance and I was being transferred, against my will, into photography. I cried and screamed and attempted to file a legal suit. I fought the transfer hard and eventually lost. Then I discovered my $10,000 enlistment bonus was also taken from me because I was no longer going to be a Morse Code interceptor. I got my security clearance three months later and remained an angry photographer for the next four years.

I was sent to Lowry Air Force Base in Denver, Colorado, for six months of photography training because the Army doesn't teach photography. I hated photography, and I hated the military for transferring me into it on a bogus excuse. I developed a real attitude and made my own life hell during training. I finally accepted the fact that since I had three years and three months of time left in the military, I might as well make the best of it.

After training, I was permanently assigned to Fort Ord, California, one of the

Army's largest infantry bases. As a youngster, I had dreamed of living in sunny California, so I was very happy about my transfer. While off duty, I enjoyed every minute of friendship and sunshine I could squeeze in, but on duty I was very unhappy.

My two male bosses thought of me as a rookie to be relegated to the back room processing film and prints. One of the bosses was more of a father figure to me; the other one did not like me from the moment he met me and did his best to make my life miserable. After a few months, the fatherly boss retired, leaving the other one in charge of the photo lab.

He accused me of sabotaging the processing equipment. He told me how intolerable a photographer I was, and he found fault with me in every way. I was given the rottenest assignments and working hours. My work life was extremely difficult, especially since I was young, naive, and female. I had grown up in such a bizarre, deviant, sick household that I just didn't have the emotional tools necessary to deal with this behavior. After a few months, I could not tolerate the stress, so I began to complain to the chain of command. The complaint only got *me* transferred to a secretarial job, and nothing happened to him.

I applied for an assignment in Korea and was shipped to Italy. I had already been to Europe and didn't want to go back, especially to live there for two years.

My civilian counterpart at the photo lab was an elderly Italian man who refused to suffer an eighteen-year-old girl for a boss. Some days he would literally barricade me from the photo lab by pushing the desk across the door. One time he threw a jar of chemicals at me, missed, and the jar broke on the floor. Often he would "lose" my completed assignments.

My boss was short on her time and felt no compulsion to interfere. When my new boss arrived, he immediately demanded sex in exchange for fixing my problems. When I refused his advances, he insulted my character in front of command. I became so ostracized that I had a major nervous breakdown.

In 1986, the military began downsizing because of the Gramm-Rudman Act. I was not asked to reenlist, and I was able to leave the military two months early. I couldn't wait to get out!

I had developed such a dislike for the military, I would never have stayed even if I could have reenlisted. In retrospect, I'm not sorry I joined the military because it was an emotional and work experience I needed to have in order to grow into who I am today. It was neither pleasant nor rewarding, nor would I do it again, but it did give me many useful lessons I live by today.

Some of the lessons I've learned are not to trust anyone, to have faith in myself, and to believe my instincts. I've gained an intimate understanding of the male hierarchal games and rules, and now I can not only survive but thrive in the male traditional workforce. Experiencing a nervous breakdown led me to acknowledge the problems in my family and myself, and that caused me to go into therapy.

It has taken me years and lots of therapy to recuperate from the damage the military has done to me emotionally. I basically had a four-year trial in torment and harassment.

After I outprocessed from the Army at Fort Dix, I moved to Panama City, Florida, and signed up at the local community college in a premed curriculum. The only job I could find was as a waitress at Shoney's restaurant and selling Rainbow vacuum cleaners. Neither of the jobs paid enough to live on, and I soon ran out of money.

It took far too long for my military college money to be processed, and I had to place everything in storage and get home to family in Maryland before I ended up on the street. Out of need, I asked the military to reimburse me the $2500 I had given it as my share of the college benefits. As a result, I lost all college benefits I had with the military.

I spent a few years puttering around with a job in home improvements and finally decided I wanted a career that didn't beat up my body everyday and was financially stable. I always knew I wanted to work in the public service field, but didn't know in what capacity.

I was lunching with my father, a lawyer, and one of his associates asked me if I'd ever thought about becoming a police officer. I had never thought about the police department before and promptly sent in applications to all the local and state police departments. Almost immediately I received a response from the Maryland State Police, and within a few months I was in its six-month, live-in training academy. I later discovered the state hires prior military personnel because it gets some financial reward.

It didn't take long for me to realize I did not want to be a police officer for the next twenty-four years of my life. The judicial system, even though it is the best in the world, was so frustrating. I felt I was risking my life by doing my job, and the system was just letting the criminals return to the street. While on duty as a police officer, I would stop at the firehouse and use its facilities. After a few months, the firefighters began to ask me when I was going to quit whining about my career choice and become a firefighter. Oh!

I resigned from the Maryland State Police and went back to home improvements while I waited for my application with the fire department to be processed.

On 26 February 1990, I was enrolled in the Department of Fire and Rescue's Training Academy. I knew from the first day that I had finally made the right choice. This career has all the essential ingredients I need to receive satisfaction. I am such a people person, and the fire department is team-oriented and provides structure. I get to help people in a way that is appreciated and valued. And finally, saving lives is a reward all of its own.

When I got out of the military, I swore I would never take a job where I had to wear a uniform, pin my hair up, or couldn't quit. Well, I got one out of three with the fire department.

Five

Lesbian Exclusion

Laurie Weinstein and Francine D'Amico
with Lynn Meola (pseudonym)

> There are so many gays and lesbians serving in the
> military the ban is ridiculous. We often joked if every
> gay man and woman were to turn a light on at a
> predetermined time at night, we would light up Man-
> hattan.
> —Capt. Lynn Meola (pseudonym) 8 February 1998

Historically, some of the most invisible servicewomen have been lesbians because they have been forced to hide their sexual identity or risk discharge and even prison. Captain Lynn Meola, an active-duty officer who provided material for this chapter, cannot use her real name. Until recently, the military tried to exclude gays and lesbians by asking recruits about their sexual orientation and by investigating personnel suspected or rumored to be gay or lesbian. The Clinton administration ordered the Department of Defense to replace this exclusion policy with a new policy, "Don't Ask, Don't Tell, Don't Pursue, Don't Harass," which in simplest terms said that a person's sexuality should be private: recruits and military members could no longer be asked about their sexual identity (Don't Ask), people in service should keep their orientation to themselves (Don't Tell), military bosses should not investigate their workers' private lives (Don't Pursue), and harassment of servicemembers based on sexuality is prohibited and punishable conduct (Don't Harass).

How well has the military adhered to this policy? Not very well, according to the Servicemembers Legal Defense Network (SLDN), a watchdog organization that provides legal aid for those targeted under the new policy. For the past four years, SLDN has issued an annual report documenting violations of the "Don't Ask, Don't Tell, Don't Pursue" policy. These reports examine how the military has tried to deal with the "problem" of homosexuality—a problem the military itself has created because of its narrow construction of gender norms. SLDN's 1998 report finds:

Command violations of "Don't Ask, Don't Tell, Don't Pursue" increased for the fourth year in a row. Command violations include instances where commands asked, pursued and harassed service members in direct violation of the limits to gay investigations under current policy. Servicemembers Legal Defense Network documented 563 command violations in 1997, up from 443 reported violations in 1996. SLDN documented increased asking, increased pursuits and increased harassment in 1997. The Navy was the worst in . . . compliance; the Air Force was a close second.[1]

SLDN's 1997 report detailed the history of the "Don't Ask, Don't Tell, Don't Pursue" policy and recent discharges:

Four years ago, President Clinton assumed office and announced that he would issue an Executive Order to prohibit the mandatory discharge of gay personal honorably serving their country. Congress opposed President Clinton's efforts and codified into law the same rules that had been in effect since 1981—that servicemembers would be discharged from military service if they stated that they were gay, engaged in handholding, hugging or other affectional or sexual conduct with a person of the same gender, or attempted to marry someone of the same gender.

President Clinton, Congress and the Pentagon, however, agreed to end the affirmative efforts to ferret out suspected gay members. They agreed to stop asking servicemembers about their sexual orientation, end witch hunts and prevent anti-gay harassment. They agreed to implement the law with due regard for the privacy of servicemembers. They agreed to treat servicemembers in an even-handed manner in the criminal system, by stopping the criminal investigation and persecution of servicemembers for allegations of gay consensual relationships when the services would not normally proceed in the same fashion regarding allegations of heterosexual conduct. The law became known as "Don't Ask, Don't Tell, Don't Pursue" to signify the new limits on gay investigations. While the law did not mark an end to treating lesbian, gay and bisexual servicemembers differently than their heterosexual counterparts for saying and doing the same things, it did mark what was to be a more humane policy of coexistence. The Department of Defense promulgated regulations implementing the current law on February 28, 1994.

[T]he reality of "Don't Ask, Don't Tell, Don't Pursue" has been anything but humane as many commanders have continued to ask, pursue and harass suspected gay servicemembers with impunity. One result is that, according to the Department of Defense's own figures, gay discharges have soared to 850 in fiscal year 1996, a five-year high, and up 42% since 1994. The rate of gay discharges is at its highest level since 1987.[2]

The Department of Defense's statistics on gay discharges for 1997 have not yet been released.

In its 1998 report, SLDN notes that although civilian officials have reiterated that the policy must be enforced, violations continue:

The "Don't Ask" regulations state that "commanders or appointed inquiry officials shall not ask, and members shall not be required, to reveal their sexual orientation." Secretary of Defense William Cohen reaffirmed the rule last year, stating that asking is "a clear violation of the law." SLDN documented 124 "Don't Ask" violations in the past year. That is up 39% from 1996 when SLDN reported 89 "Don't Ask" violations.[3]

SLDN's 1997 report documented the following types of violations of the "Don't Ask" part of the regulation:

> SLDN has found, for example, that the armed forces continue to use a January 1989 recruiting form which asks recruits: "(a) Are you a homosexual or a bisexual? and (b) Do you intend to engage in homosexual acts?" While recruiters are supposed to line through this section, some do not. One recruiter even circled the forbidden questions as ones that had to be answered. The complaints SLDN has received to date on this issue focus primarily on East Coast Coast Guard recruiting stations.[4]

Last year, SLDN documented several cases where inquiry officers used "homosexual/bisexual questionnaires" to pry into servicemembers' private lives. Even roommates of suspected gay/lesbian servicemembers were asked about their own sexual orientation. SLDN's 1997 report explains:

> "Don't Tell" requires gay, though not heterosexual, servicemembers to keep their sexual orientation a "personal and private" matter. "Don't Tell," however, does not prohibit all statements about sexual orientation. Indeed, the current regulations specifically permit statements to lawyers, chaplains, and security clearance personnel.[5]

SLDN's 1998 report found that the number of "Don't Tell" violations has dropped significantly since 1997, but the news is not all good:

> In both the Army and Navy, the violations have dropped by approximately fifty percent, while Air Force violations have dropped approximately twenty percent. SLDN documented 22 "Don't Tell" violations in the past year, down 29% from 31 in the previous year. Despite these developments, "Don't Tell" violations continue to be a problem, especially given the intrusive nature of these violations. Psychotherapists and other health providers continue to report to SLDN that they have been ordered to turn in gay service members who confide in them during private counseling sessions. Service members continue to report that their military psychotherapists have violated their trust, usually resulting in the service member's discharge.[6]

SLDN's 1997 report found that the "Don't Pursue" part of the policy was not enforced:

> In the words of General Colin Powell, "Don't Pursue" means that "We won't witch hunt. We won't chase. We will not seek to learn orientation." The current regulations and guidelines echo General Powell's words. Witch hunts are prohibited: commanders cannot expand investigations beyond the instant allegations by (1) asking servicemembers to identify suspected gays and lesbians or (2) fishing for information about a servicemember to see what they can turn up. Commanders must have "credible information" of a statement, act or marriage before launching an inquiry or investigation. Not all information is deemed credible, including rumors, speculation and reports from unreliable individuals. Lastly, commanders are not to use the criminal system against suspected gay servicemembers for consensual,

adult sexual activities when they would not investigate or prefer criminal charges against heterosexuals for the same activities. These clear limits on investigations and criminal prosecutions were intended to prohibit the far-ranging, punitive and heavy-handed investigations that have characterized prior policies. These limits have been roundly ignored.[7]

The pattern of ignoring limits on investigating sexuality held true in 1998:

"Don't Pursue" violations rank as the worst problem. SLDN documented 235 "Don't Pursue" violations, up 23% from last year's figure of 191. The Air Force led the services with 90 'Don't Pursue' violations.[8]

Another disturbing trend among all services is the "prove you're gay" phenomenon. In the "prove you're gay" cases, inquiry officers conduct wide-ranging fishing expeditions in an effort to dig up additional information about a service member who has already made a statement that he or she is gay.[9]

SLDN's 1997 report found the following types of violations of "Don't Harass":

The "Don't Harass" portion of the new regulations makes explicit that "the Armed Forces don not tolerate harassment or violence against any servicemember, for any reason." Violations of "Don't Harass" include physical abuse and threats (including death threats), verbal harassment, and hostile command climates marked by constant anti-gay slurs. Violations also include sexual harassment of women through lesbian-baiting, the practice of pressuring and harassing women by calling, or threatening to call them, lesbians. Women frequently are accused as lesbians in retaliation for rebuffing sexual advances by men or reporting sexual abuse.[10]

SLDN's 1997 report further observed that the policy has had a disproportionate effect on women:

Violations of "Don't Ask" also include lesbian-baiting, a form of sexual harassment. Women, straight and gay, are accused as lesbians when they rebuff advances by men or report sexual abuse. Women who are top performers in nontraditional fields also face perpetual speculation and rumors that they are lesbians. Too often, commanders respond by investigating the women under the guise of enforcing "Don't Ask, Don't Tell, Don't Pursue" rather than disciplining men who start such rumors or who perpetrate sexual abuse. As a result, many women do not report sexual harassment or assault out of fear that they will be accused as lesbians, investigated and discharged. Other women report that they give in to sexual demands specifically to avoid being rumored to be a lesbian.

The toll lesbian-baiting takes on women is evident in DOD's own statistics for 1996. Though women comprise only thirteen percent of the active duty force, they constitute twenty-nine percent of those kicked out under "Don't Ask, Don't Tell, Don't Pursue." In the Army, women comprise forty-one percent of those discharged under the gay policy, an astounding figure that is three times women's presence in this service.[11]

SLDN's 1998 report found that reported "Don't Harass" violations increased 38 percent from 132 reported incidents in 1996 to 182 in 1997, including death threats and physical assaults.[12] Civilian officials have attempted to enforce this rule, but military commanders are not cooperating:

> The "Don't Harass" regulations clearly state that the "Armed Forces do not tolerate harassment or violence against any servicemember for any reason." In a major development in 1997, the Department of Defense issued guidance clarifying that commanders should respond to anti-gay harassment and lesbian-baiting by investigating the harassment itself, not the servicemembers who report it (the "Dorn memo"). The services, however, have failed to distribute the Dorn memo to the field. No commander, attorney, inquiry officer, investigator or other service member asked by SLDN in the course of assisting service members last year had ever heard of the Dorn memo, much less read it.[13]

SLDN's 1998 report further states:

> In May 1997, the Senate Armed Services Committee also addressed this form of harassment for the first time, in Senate Report 105–29 supporting the DOD Authorization Bill. The committee report "urges the Department of Defense and leaders at all levels" to "ensure that no individual experience the need to submit to unwanted sexual advances or harassment for any reason" and to permit individuals to report inappropriate activities without fear of retaliation.[14]

The recent case of Senior Chief Petty Officer Tim McVeigh is one clear violation of the "Don't Ask, Don't Tell" policy. Without McVeigh's knowledge or even a legal warrant, Navy investigators obtained personal information about him from America On Line (AOL). The Navy then began to prepare McVeigh's discharge on the basis of his assumed sexual orientation. McVeigh is suing the secretaries of defense and the navy for violating the "Don't Ask, Don't Tell" policy and the Electronic Communications Privacy Act.[15]

Whether or not McVeigh is gay, homosexuality is a problem for the military because it threatens the status quo of the hypermasculine, heterosexual, all-male military. The military is where one goes to "become a man" as the stereotypical Marine Corps recruiting posters illustrated with the slogan "We're Looking for a Few Good Men." The irony of the situation is that gays and lesbians have always served in the military.[16]

For lesbians, the problem of sexual orientation makes them doubly damned because they are women *and* lesbians. Quite cleverly, military regulations against homosexuality have helped keep many women—straight and lesbian—out of the military. Many military women are assumed to be gay unless proven otherwise. After all, why would women want to serve and do "a man's job" unless they were either "looking for a man or for a woman?"[17]

In her research about how lesbians try to "pass" as heterosexuals and how heterosexuals try to avoid being labeled as lesbians, Melissa Herbert was told that "nice girls don't join the Army."[18] Such comments echo the words Francine D'Amico's father said to her when she told him she was thinking of enlisting. "Passing" and avoidance strategies include wearing makeup, skirts, and pumps; not associating with groups of other women; and even acquiring boyfriends, discussing boyfriends, and getting married. Many women try to prove themselves by having sex with men, which encourages sexual harassment because women "who don't acquiesce [to men] are routinely accused of being a lesbian."[19] Yet, despite these strategies to avoid being labeled as a lesbian, many more women than men are discharged because of suspected homosexuality, as noted by the SLDN report. Sometimes, routing out lesbians is a chief objective: "In 1990, Vice Admiral Joseph S. Donnell directed officers on 240 ship and shore installations to discharge any woman thought to be a lesbian. He worried that his directive might not be enforced because lesbians were hard-working, conscientious, top-performers."[20]

Lynn Meola argues that the military uses the Criminal Investigative Division (CID) to pry into women's lives. Butch women are especially suspect. She talks about some memorable evenings spent at gay bars and the "persistent rumors that CID agents were in the bar from time to time hunting for lesbians stationed at the fort nearby." Although she was never targeted, she knows of witch hunts in which suspected women had their phone lines tapped and private discussions between lovers were taped. The CID would then call the women in, replay the tape and demand confessions as well as information about other lesbians. Lesbian enlisted women were not as concerned as the officers about possible CID investigations. The enlisted women tended to be more careless about their affairs than the female officers. They had less at stake—many were not career military. Officers, however, had more to lose if they were booted out as lesbians, and many developed their own means of communicating who was and was not "safe" (that is, a lesbian).

Meola further suggests that lesbians in the military attempt to don the gender camouflage of the androgynous "keep-your-mind-on-your-own-affairs, be a good soldier." If you are too feminine, "no one takes you seriously, and the guys try to take advantage of you." If you are too masculine, you are "too dykey and you run the risk of being discovered by the CID." Her comments reflect the great conundrum mentioned in the introduction of this book. Should women attempt to be one of the guys? one of the girls? the gender-neutral "soldier"? Or should they directly challenge the military system? Regardless of the strategy and whether or not women wear pumps or hang out with the guys, women can't win. As Georgia Sadler discusses in chapter 2, women are still excluded from most combat-related jobs in the military, which helps preserve male authority. Herbert notes that keeping some areas "for men only" means that there is a "preferred gender ideology," and women just don't fit in.[21] Even talented women who could compete with men for particular posts are excluded from male-only posts. And as for women who do infringe on male turf (combat), their accomplishments are minimized and/or completely negated, as the stories of Kara Hultgreen and Linda Bray demonstrate, as noted in the introduction.

Captain Meola is confident that the U.S. military will eventually relax the restrictions on gays and lesbians. "If the military were to lift the ban on gays in the military I don't think it would be such a big deal since most gay folks in the service are discreet, conservative, and not impressed with flamboyant displays of affection." This seemingly small step to end the ban, however, appears to be more like a step across the Grand Canyon. Because sexuality is so closely tied to preferred gender norms and because targeting lesbians is used as a means of eliminating women who claim sexual harassment, the military is not likely to eliminate such an effective promasculine status quo tool any time soon.

NOTES

1. C. Dixon Osburn and Michelle M. Benecke, with Kirk Childress, Kelly Corbett, Travis Elliott, and Jeff Cleghorn, *Conduct Unbecoming: The Fourth Annual Report on "Don't Ask, Don't Tell, Don't Pursue"* (Washington, D.C.: Servicemembers Legal Defense Network, 1998), 3. Cited hereafter as SLDN 1998.

2. C. Dixon Osburn and Michelle M. Benecke, *Conduct Unbecoming: The Third Annual Report on "Don't Ask, Don't Tell, Don't Pursue"* (Washington, D.C.: Servicemembers Legal Defense Network, 1997), 1–2. Cited hereafter as SLDN 1997.

3. SLDN 1998, 4.

4. SLDN 1997, 3.

5. Ibid., 5.

6. SLDN 1998, 9.

7. SLDN 1997, 8.

8. SLDN 1998, 1.

9. Ibid., 19.

10. SLDN 1997, 16.

11. Ibid., 22.

12. SLDN 1998, 1.

13. Ibid., 25–26.

14. Ibid., 30–31.

15. "Last Gasp Reprieve for McVeigh," *News Planet* electronic news service, 15 January 1998.

16. Randy Shilts, *Conduct Unbecoming: Gays and Lesbians in the U.S. Military, Vietnam to the Persian Gulf* (New York: Fawcett Columbine, 1994); see also Craig A. Rimmerman, ed., *Gay Rights, Military Wrongs: Political Perspectives on Gays and Lesbians in the Military* (New York: Garland, 1996).

17. Melissa S. Herbert, "Guarding the Nation, Guarding Ourselves: The Management of Hetero/Homo/Sexuality among Women in the Military," *MINERVA: Quarterly Report on Women and the Military* 15 (summer 1997): 2.

18. Ibid., 70.

19. Shilts, *Conduct Unbecoming*, 5.

20. Herbert, "Guarding the Nation," 61.

21. Ibid., 71.

Autobiography
I Wish I Could Use My Own Name

Winni S. Webber (pseudonym)

Editor's note: The "Don't Ask, Don't Tell" policy affects many servicewomen and men, both straight and gay. Here is one woman's story, excerpted with permission from her book, "Lesbians in the Military Speak Out" (1993), which includes the stories of thirty-one other women, both active-duty and veterans.[1]

I wish I could use my own name, but as a member of the military on active-duty status, I can't. . . . I didn't write this story to discredit or malign the military. I love the military—it is my life. I don't want to lose my place in it.

I am proud to serve my country, but I am not proud of a system that openly sanctions discrimination, harassment, and persecution of homosexuals. Discrimination, whether based on gender, race, rank, or sexual orientation is still too prevalent in all the armed forces. Discrimination of any kind is often based on ignorance. Part of the answer to ending discrimination against homosexuals is education. I hope this story will help educate.

It was probably inevitable that I would join the military. I grew up with hearing my dad express his regret at having left it. He had been drafted in World War II and had gone from a private to a major in less than seven years. When I was a kid, his pictures and medals (several Bronze Stars) from World War II fascinated me. I would question Dad about his war experiences and usually the response I got was something like, "There's no glory in fighting a war and killing folks who don't share your point of view." Dad had left the service as soon as he could. His regret at not staying in the military was purely financial. He calculated he could have retired with twice the pension, in half the time, and with a third of the effort if he had stayed in the military. My sisters and I remind him that he is assuming he would have survived the Korean War and possibly Vietnam.

I graduated from high school and went to college. I had developed a rather serious relationship with one of my high school sweethearts. I really admired John and trusted him. He was intelligent, and I thought he would make a good husband and father. I don't think I loved him, but I figured that would come with time. When I was about to graduate college I still felt the same way about John. I liked him, admired him, but the spark just wasn't there. He was headed to law school and I to graduate school when I decided to enlist in the Army.

I showed up at Fort Jackson, South Carolina, on a hot July afternoon. I was older that most of the recruits. I remember hearing sobs in the bays of the reception station that first night as new recruits cried their distress. I was every bit as distressed, but it was during basic training that I fell in love for the first time. The woman I fell in love with was a Bette Midler type, funny, intelligent, and entertaining. Karen was divorced and in her thirties. We were the Abbott and Costello of basic training who paired up every chance we could. We were always in trouble.

Basic training ended too soon as far as I was concerned. Karen and I went to AIT together although we weren't in the same class. We did everything together, but our relationship wasn't sexual. We never mentioned sex, although the energy flowing between us was incredible. I had never felt so alive. We went our separate ways after AIT, and I regretted that I never shared my feelings with Karen. We corresponded for years afterward. When I finally came out to her, I told her that she had been my first love. Her letters stopped.

My sexual awakening occurred when I had been released from the Army to attend medical school. It was then that I realized that I was gay. I fell head over heels for a medical student. We were opposites in every way. Laura was a Democrat, I a Republican. She was a hippie from California, I was a conservative from the South. She wore baggy pants and Birkenstocks. I wore tailored clothes and Bass Weejuns. She smoked dope, I didn't. She despised the military, I loved it. She spoke her mind and wasn't afraid to confront people. I was raised to sugarcoat my demands so as not to "offend" anyone.

We met by chance. The only thing we did have in common was that we both needed money. In an effort to raise funds, each of us had donated her body to science—so to speak. Each of us had volunteered to be a research subject.

Our friendship was launched. We talked nonstop about books we read, about our values, our goals. We had such entertaining discussions, that the night nurses would come in on their breaks just to join in.

One night while we were at a symphony she took my hand, squeezed it and said, "Okay, let's try it."

We "tried" it for eight years. They were wonderful years. Laura was an outspoken activist, I was a shy do-it-by-the-book type. I wasn't used to making waves, so it was a shock when Laura informed me that "we were going to make a statement" at a medical school function. Laura was an honors student and had just received a rather important scholastic award. She was asked to sit at the head table during a formal banquet where she would receive her award. Laura was told she should bring a guest, so she brought me. I sat there and no one blinked an eye. That's not true—I blinked a lot and my stomach was doing back flips from nervousness, but I survived.

There was never any doubt in my mind that I would go back into the military as an officer when I graduated from medical school. It was in my blood. I have since been told by people who know me that I "bleed green"—meaning I'm military through and through.

In the end, it was the military that broke us up. Laura told me that she thought my personal values conflicted with those of the Army. I valued people, the Army valued production. Part of my integrity was due to the fact that I was what she called "alarmingly honest" and being in the military put a damper on that honesty in many ways. I had to stay in the closet. I also learned that professional honesty often is not appreciated in the military. I saw officers who had promising careers passed over for promotion or further training because they spoke their mind to their boss. Their performance reviews characterized them as not being "team players," sealing their fates.

Although the separation was amicable, it was very painful and to this day I am not sure if I did the right thing in choosing my career over a relationship. We are still close friends and get together at least once a year to ski, hike, or just hang out.

Most of the years since that choice have been devoted to my career as a medical officer in the Army.

I was fortunate to work in the medical field both as an enlisted soldier and officer. The servicemen and women in medicine generally tend to be a little more liberal in their opinions and politics. They also tend to be more highly educated—although education alone is not an inoculation against bigotry.

On the whole, my experience as a woman in the military has been positive. That isn't to say I have not been sexually harassed. I have. I think we tend to ignore or accept it as the norm after awhile. Most of the time the harassment was verbal. For a long time it was the norm for male surgeons to make crude jokes in the operating room—at least they seemed to go out of their way to do it when women were present. The behavior seems to be declining, but it still takes place.

The military has been hell on my personal life. Three times transfers have ended relationships that I didn't want ended. I was once told by a lover who was older, wiser, and had been in the military for twenty years, "Honey, you had better get used to *serial monogamy* because it's the only way you're going to survive in the military."

I also worry that [the] military has cost my soul something. I don't have a problem with being ordered to go to war—even if it is a war I oppose. I'm not paid to make policy, I'm paid to carry out orders. But I try to make my area in the military a little more compassionate, a little more humane, a little more liberal in its interpretation of policies.

NOTE

1. Winni S. Webber, *Lesbians in the Military Speak Out* (Northboro, Mass.: Madwoman Press, 1993), ii, 123–32.

Part II

At the Margins
Women *with* the Military

Six

Military Wives
Breaking the Silence

Doreen Drewry Lehr

To learn to speak in a unique and authentic voice, women must "jump outside" the frames and systems authorities provide and create their own frame.
—Mary Field Belenky et al.,
Women's Ways of Knowing

The gendered pattern of U.S. military culture has institutionalized the wives of military personnel to provide services essential to military readiness. Despite the centrality of these services, these women have been absent from academic literature, marginal in military policy, and invisible to the American public. Indeed, the collective designation of these women as *military wives* suggests that the women marry not only the man but also the institution that employs him. This chapter analyzes the causes and consequences of the invisibility and silence of military wives, as well as their efforts to organize for change.

As contemporary U.S. military forces face some of the most unprecedented changes in history, they have also been subjected to unparalleled scrutiny and public discussion about military gender policies: women in combat, the Navy's Tailhook incident, gays and lesbians in the military, prostitution in Asia, fraternization, sexual assaults during the Gulf War, sexual harassment at the service academies, and the Army's 1996 sexual scandal involving female recruits at Aberdeen Proving Grounds. Although these unusual revelations have provided a public lens on some aspects of military culture, the lives of women married to military men remain firmly locked behind closed doors.

The civilian community has knowingly or unknowingly colluded with the military to keep military wives silent and invisible. Anti-Vietnam feminist activists viewed military wives as collaborators of the military and ignored them. Contemporary feminist researchers have excluded the voices of military wives from their conferences and their literature, seeing these women only in their adjunct position as mothers of future military troops or supporters of their military husbands. This exclusion and neglect has reinforced wives' supportive roles both to their husbands and to the military.

The women we call military wives are individual and diverse, and their experiences in this extremely gendered society are shaped by many variables, such as husband's branch of service, his rank and/or position, the woman's nationality/race/ethnicity, command of the language, age, and educational background. Even so, many women married to men throughout the ranks and the services share similar experiences, including military control over their lives and dependence on husband's rank for all privileges, including housing, club membership, and even choice of friends. Some military wives are now challenging this control by breaking the silence about their experiences.

Camp Followers

Women who followed European armies, even legal wives, were called *camp followers*, a term synonymous with *whore*.[1] Eighteenth-century American armies realized the value of the women's unpaid or low-paid work and did not use the term *camp follower* as a derogatory label.[2] In 1777, some 20,000 women and their children followed the first Continental Army. Although displeased by the number of camp followers, General Washington recognized that if he got rid of the women, many men would desert. Further, he saw that the services of the camp followers—caring for the sick and dying, sewing and washing clothing, and gathering, preparing, and serving food and drink—were essential to the welfare of his troops.[3]

When individuals were *pressed* (forced) into the army or volunteered for service in those early years, many families lost their major source of income. Because camp followers who provided services to the military received half rations for themselves and quarter rations for their children, women chose to accompany their husbands to war rather than face starvation. Officers' wives, who usually could afford to support themselves in their husbands' absence, often traveled with them, not merely for companionship. Regardless of status, all women had to work for the war effort.[4] Martha Washington, who said she heard the first and last gun of every campaign of the war, traveled from her home at Mount Vernon to bring supplies to General Washington.[5] She also served as the honorary adviser and president of the Association, the first military wives club, established during the Revolutionary War. Members of the Association raised large sums of money to supply necessary items that the government did not provide for the troops.[6] The good works of Martha Washington set a high standard of volunteer activities against which all future military wives would be measured.

Throughout the generations, military wives' services to armies included combat, injury, and sometimes death. The women's collective memory survives under the generic name "Molly Pitcher," believed to have been the sobriquet of a military wife called Margaret Corbin. When Corbin's husband was killed, she took over his small cannon; she was also wounded and remained an invalid. For her service to her country, "Captain Molly" was awarded half a military pension, and her story "was recorded through oral tradition."[7] Many other women took on military tasks, among them, Lydia Lane, who was left in charge of Fort Fillmore in 1861 by her colonel husband "with authority over the sergeant and the ten-man garrison and possession of post funds."[8]

Women were similarly an integral part of the enemy forces. When British troops left England to participate in the Revolutionary War, many officers' wives traveled with them. Baroness Frederika von Riedesel, the young wife of the German general who commanded Britain's mercenary troops, kept exceptional diaries of her experiences. "Red Azel," or "Mrs. General" as she was dubbed by the Cockney soldiers, joined her husband in Canada and followed the campaign as "an eyewitness to the Battle of Saratoga" and through Bennington and New York State. General von Riedesel and the Baroness were captured and sent as "prisoners of the Convention" to Cambridge, Massachusetts, and later to Charlottesville, Virginia, where on a cold winter march the Baroness was said to have faced the challenge of starvation with "amazing aplomb."[9]

For every one hundred British troops, six women, usually the wives of enlisted men, accompanied them to provide services as laundresses, nurses, and sutlers (vendors who followed armies to sell food and drink to soldiers). When a husband was killed, his widow seldom wasted many days before remarrying, a safeguard in an uncertain and dangerous environment. In the Continental Army, remarriage was so prevalent that some chaplains were specifically assigned to find mates for army widows.[10]

Collectively, these women set a precedent for generations of their successors, who, with increased United States military involvement, would follow their husbands around the world, supplying ever-changing but necessary labor for the military institution.

The Military "Dependent"

Military commanders exerted total control over the first military wives. For example, commanders established the rate at which laundresses were paid and could discipline "unruly" wives, who, in severe cases, were flogged and/or banished from the post.[11] Although the control of today's military commanders may differ in degree, they still dictate the expected behavior of wives, have families removed from housing, base, or country, and decide whether a wife or child is a victim of abuse and in need of protection.

The early camp followers were grateful to be provided their basic needs and learned to deal with extreme adversity; after World War II, the U.S. military professed to provide for military families "from the cradle to the grave." Each military installation is like a welfare state, supplying military families with hospitals for free family medical care, schools for their children, stores with reduced prices, theaters for their entertainment, and churches for their worship. The inhabitants of these military bases can live for months, as many do at overseas locations, without leaving the base. Particularly on isolated installations, separated from family and friends, the women become dependent on the military for their survival. A military husband's signature is required to renew a wife's identity card, to join the wives club, or to become a member of the library. As Nattaya Leuenberger told me in a 1996 interview, "When my husband signed up, I lost my rights."

The military system is built on hierarchy, and the officer ranks are forbidden by military regulation from fraternizing with the enlisted corps. These factors also affect the women's relationships and create what Coffman called "a sharp line of demarcation" between officers' wives and the wives of enlisted personnel.[12] In a 1996 interview, Penny, a foreign-born Air Force captain's wife, explained that her sister was married to an Air Force sergeant and lived on the same base. However, the sisters, living thousands of miles from family and friends, were isolated from each other by the enlisted husband, who used the fraternization rule to deny his wife the company of her sister. Julie, the wife of an Army sergeant, noted in a 1997 interview: "I don't know what will happen when I become a lawyer; at present I am only allowed (by the military) to associate socially with the wives of enlisted personnel." This is yet another example of how the lives of military wives are impacted by military regulations.

Over time, the term *camp follower* was replaced with the term *dependent* to identify family members of military personnel. This term reflected the subordinate role assigned to wives in military culture. Military wives were expected to bear full responsibility for the problems of daily life in order to leave their husbands free to concentrate on their military mission. Further, the isolation of the bases and the mobility of the military lifestyle restricted military wives' ability to find work. The military had a captive audience to perform its volunteer requirements—a situation of considerable benefit for the services but not necessarily for the women.

In 1982, the U.S. Defense Department officially terminated use of the word *dependent* from the military lexicon, and replaced it with *family member*. Yet even high-ranking officers and official government documents continue to use the term. As the 1997 *Handbook for Military Families* explains: "The word 'dependent' is no longer officially acceptable in everyday military speech. The term 'family member,' used in this handbook, is considered preferable." Despite this admonition, the word *dependent* is used throughout the handbook.[13]

By way of contrast, when the military was ordered to end racial segregation in 1948 and to stop the official use of racist language, the penalties for disobeying such directives forced military personnel to comply, at least in the public forum. Addressing minority members of the services in derogatory terms quickly became unacceptable. According to retired General Colin Powell, by the 1950s, "less discrimination, a truer merit system and leveler playing fields existed inside the gates of our military posts than in any Southern city hall or Northern corporation."[14] Efforts to change the labeling of the civilian wives of military personnel as *dependents* have been less successful.

The Married Military Force

Organizers of the U.S. Army considered it against the interest of the military for men to be married, particularly in the enlisted ranks. In the late 1800s, the Army became known as the Army of deserters because of the poor conditions of frontier life and the 1847 federal law that stated, "No man with a wife or a child may enlist."[15] At the time of World War I, the Defense Department permitted some military marriages "in the public interest" but argued that the efficiency of the service had to be the first consideration.[16] This discouragement of military marriage is reflected in the well-known aphorism: "If the Army wanted you to have a wife, they would have issued you one."

During World War II, more than sixteen million U.S. personnel enlisted, and a large percentage of those who were drafted were already married. The military changed from being a single service to a married force. The change brought the need for family programs, and, in response, the Army Emergency Relief Program began in 1942. In 1954, Operation Gyroscope was established to retain quality personnel and help military families adjust to living as occupation forces in Japan and Germany, as well as other areas of Europe. This program was the forerunner of on-post/base housing and Medicare.[17] By the 1960s, military family members began to outnumber serving members. In 1972, when the draft ended, 42 percent of military personnel were married; by 1995, the figure was 61 percent.[18] The DOD reported that in 1994 "61.4 percent of the force has family; 60 percent of the force is married, 78,463 are single parents, and 96,261 are dual military parents."[19]

In the 1950s and 1960s, U.S. military social services "included assistance in mate selection." Military members serving overseas, regardless of age, had to obtain their commanding officer's consent to marry. Permission was given only after a background check of the future spouse's "moral and political background."[20]

With the exception of the lowest-ranking enlisted members, the contemporary military has made it more desirable to be married than to be single. Married military members are given extra pay for spouses and children. Senior Airman Maurice Milstead III, a married aircraft structural mechanic at Moody Air Force base, said in 1995 that the extra pay was not the reason he got married, "but it helped the decision." Former Navy commander Lee Mairs complained that "subsidizing marriage has caused the military to become an increasingly married force," but military sociologist David Segal has pointed out that "studies show that married service members are more stable and cause fewer disciplinary problems than single service members."[21]

Single officers rarely made promotions to senior commander without a wife to carry her share of military responsibilities. Conversely, this "two-for-one" expectation meant that the wives of married officers had to participate in ostensibly volunteer base activities or their husbands would not be promoted. In 1987, Judy Croxton and Nattaya Leuenberger, two Air Force colonels' wives, stated that they had been told by their husbands' commander to give up their jobs, the better to support their military husbands, or the men would not be promoted. The Blue Ribbon Panel on Spouse Issues convened by the Department of Defense to examine the role of the military spouse confirmed that the Air Force–wife role had indeed become "institutionalized" and recommended that, particularly the role of the commander's spouse, be "de-institutionalized." The Department of the Air Force issued AF Regulation 30–51 in 1988 that in part stated:

> It is Air Force policy that the choice of a spouse to pursue employment, to be a homemaker, to attend school, or to serve as a volunteer in Air Force or local community activities is a private matter and solely the decision of the individual concerned. No commander, supervisor, or other Air Force official will directly or indirectly impede or otherwise interfere with this decision.[22]

The Department of Defense issued similar regulations to all the services. Although many commanders gave the appearance of complying with the regulation, they neglected to do so in practice; thus, on many installations, the status quo remained.

Military Wives' Support

In 1969, a group of military wives and widows established the National Military Family (formerly Wives) Association (NMFA) to advocate financial security for survivors of military personnel and retirees. NMFA's mission is to educate policymakers about quality-of-life factors, to keep military families informed about issues that affect their lives, and to serve as a source of support for individuals from all services and ranks (see appendix).

One of the most important actions to focus attention on military wives' issues was the advent, in 1977, of the grassroots organization Family Action Council (FAC), initiated by a group of Army wives. In 1980, the group presented the first Army Family Symposium, an unusual event that was not organized, funded, or sponsored by the military. The FAC group and its actions brought military-family issues to the attention of the military, as indicated in a statement by General Edward C. Meyer, then Army Chief of Staff, who said, "We recruit soldiers; but we retain families."[23]

As a result of the heightened emphasis on military families, the different services established Army Community Centers, Air Force Family Support Centers, Navy and the Marines Family Service Centers, and Coast Guard Work-Life Centers. There are now 218 centers, on bases and posts worldwide, designed to alleviate the stresses of military life. The centers offer financial, relocation, career, mental health, outreach, and education services at no charge. However, these programs lack consistency across and within the different service branches.

At Aviano Air Force Base in Italy, a team of social workers has created a program called Home-based Opportunities Make Everyone Successful (HOMES). The team comprises a social worker, a nurse, and an administrator who go into military families' homes to help individuals deal with their problems. An AF official at the Aviano base, however, cautioned that families would be hesitant to use the program because it is connected with the Family Advocacy Program (FAC), which is viewed as "an investigative unit that exposes maltreated families."[24]

In the mid-1980s, the Military Spouses Business and Professional Association (MSBPA) was founded by military wives, one in Washington, D.C., and another in San Diego, to help women find jobs when they relocated. Initially, the wives in the Washington area attempted to join forces with the military wives clubs already in existence, but the MSBPA inclusion of wives of all ranks did not meet with military approval, and the idea was rejected. According to Paddy Wells, an MSBPA spokesperson, in the Washington area, the organization has integrated with the military job-placement agency to help provide networking and assistance to military wives in their job searches at their new locations.

In addition to these programs organized to "take care of the military family," the National Military Family Resource Center was established in the mid-1980s to assist professional and paraprofessionals to learn more about military culture and its effect on those who live within its environs (see appendix).

Living Room Wars

Cynthia Enloe contends that "without women to objectify, men's military service would be less confirming of their manhood, perhaps even of their citizenship," and that what she names "militarized masculinity" depends in large measure on esteem derived from men's sense of manliness.[25] With the increase in the number of women entering the military, the myth of male superiority is hard to maintain when military men are obliged to work equally alongside, or for, military females. It is officially mandated that men cannot display their frustration in the workplace, but no such restrictions apply to home life.

Even though incidents of domestic violence are prevalent throughout all branches and ranks of the services, they receive little attention inside or outside the military community. A Department of Defense (DOD) Child and Spouse Abuse Report stated that there were 38,298 complaints of military abuse in 1988, a figure that increased to 46,450 in 1994. Despite these figures, military domestic abuse receives little attention in the civilian community, even for the military wives whose homes are as dangerous as the battlefield. The deaths of military wives at the hands of their military husbands are seldom reported by the national media; therefore, the general public may be unaware, for instance, that: "a soldier in Washington state killed his wife, packed her body into a suitcase, and threw it off a bridge. In Southern California, a Marine, who was a hero in the Persian Gulf War, shot and killed his newly divorced wife and their five year old daughter. In North Carolina, an airman hacked his wife to pieces, wrapped her remains in plastic garbage bags, and stored them in the refrigerator."[26]

Despite such incidents, in 1993 Pentagon officials continued to insist that military wives had few problems because there were programs in place that addressed the issues faced by military families.[27] Yet in May 1994, *Time* magazine leaked the results of a confidential and unprecedented Army-initiated survey on domestic abuse. The report concluded that one in every three families of the 55,000 soldiers interviewed at forty-seven bases had "suffered some kind of domestic violence from slapping to murder," and the statistics suggested that military abuse was double that of a comparable civilian population.[28] A subsequent 1995 DOD report about military-spouse abuse acknowledged that the women still feared that if they reported domestic violence "they would ruin their husband's careers." The majority of abused women said they were more afraid of the consequences of reporting the abuse than the abuse itself. Alternatively, military wives who worked outside the home were less likely to fear negative consequences, presumably because they could support themselves and their children in the event of separation or divorce.[29]

The women's fears were justified when those in the military system either ignored their complaints, blamed the women, dishonorably discharged their husbands, or in some instances, promoted them. Cindy Zamora, the wife of an Army enlisted man, went to a shelter for battered women in Kileen, Texas, when her husband bit her, beat her, and said if he didn't get promoted she "was going to get hurt." Zamora said, "There's a lot of women in here married to soldiers whose sergeants protect them if they're good soldiers."[30]

Peter Neidig, whose firm Behavioral Science Associates, conducted the Army survey, stated that military abuse is not confined to the enlisted corps. In 1997, I interviewed Joyce, an Army lieutenant colonel's wife, who said that from the mid-1980s to the early 1990s, she sought help for injuries inflicted by her husband. No action was taken against the high-ranking service member because his commander said he was "a good officer." Rather, Joyce was asked what she "had done to instigate the beatings."

Why is spouse abuse so prevalent in the military, and why has the prevalence of domestic violence in the military increased?

Although military authorities deny any connection between military occupations and spouse abuse, a 1979 study by the University of New Hampshire found a correlation between combat jobs and domestic violence. Murray Straus, an expert on family violence and one of the researchers on the study, stated, "There's a spill-over from what one does in one sphere of life in one role to what one does in other roles. If you're in an occupation whose business is killing, it legitimizes violence."[31] In addition, the military's downsizing from 2.2 million troops in 1987 to 1.5 million in 1997 has increased work pressures and more frequent deployments that have exacerbated the stresses of military life.

In his study of wife abuse, *What Troubles I Have Seen*, David del Mar argues that the increased independence of women since the 1960s has been attributed to men's uncertainty about the definition of masculinity.[32] The author concludes that for some men, this has resulted in more violence against women. In the military context, this suggests that the larger numbers of women in military service and particularly their entry into traditionally masculine jobs undermine men's vision of militarized masculinity and provokes greater violence.

Lenore Walker, a feminist psychologist and expert on the subject of battered women, states that violence has flourished because the support system of the extended family, which previously relieved some of the pressures and stresses of the nuclear family, has eroded. She writes that "even the presence of one extended family member in the home reduces the amount of violence immediately."[33] For the majority of military families, there is no extended family nearby. Military families move as often as every one, two, or three years, which requires wives to develop new friendships and support systems at each location.

Furthermore, it is difficult for the spouses of military members to assert themselves against domestic violence in an environment where many aspects of their lives are controlled by their husbands' employer. In a June 1997 interview, Sidney Hickey, assistant director for government relations at the National Military Families Association, stated that although there are a few combined wives clubs, the majority continue to be divided into officers'-wives clubs and enlisted men's wives clubs. Hickey believes this separation, based on husband rank, has a definite effect on the women's self-esteem. Research suggests that by making healthy connections outside the battering relationship, women become empowered to overcome the societal restrictions and institutional barriers to lead violence-free lives.[34]

The increased media attention to domestic abuse and the programs that support its victims have given some women the courage to speak out against family violence. Also, Congress has instituted financial assistance for the abused spouses of military personnel to help them relocate and find a job. However, to define what constitutes "abuse" still remains the prerogative of the military commander.

A Military Double Standard

The public's lack of knowledge about military culture allowed the military to maintain the traditional role of the military wife well beyond the time when women in the larger society were expanding their professional horizons. From the 1960s to the 1990s, while their civilian sisters were renegotiating their gender roles, relationships, and boundaries, military wives were providing volunteer labor for the benefit of the military, frequently against their will. Military wives continued to raise considerable funds to benefit the military community. For example, in 1987, the Ramstein Air Force Officers' Wives Club annual bazaar raised $1.5 million.[35] Further, military wives were still expected to be unofficial hostesses, representing the military at home and abroad, taking care of their families, and, if officers' wives, the families of subordinates.

The double standard of gender, so familiar in American society, is exacerbated in the military world. Maleness has traditionally been based on sexual prowess and military-sanctioned promiscuity. Cartloads of women were brought in to provide pleasure for soldiers during the Civil War; the men of the Indian Fighting Army formed liaisons with Indian women; and World War II troops were entertained in Hawaii's Hotel Street by prostitutes shipped in from the mainland.[36] According to Saundra Sturdevant and Brenda Stoltzfus in *Let the Good Times Roll*, "Although prostitution is illegal in the Philippines, Olongapo, and the two small neighboring towns Barrio Barretto and Subic City, have an estimated 15,000 to 17,000 'hospitality women,' " and approximately 9,000 of these women were registered by the local authority and the U.S. Navy for the entertainment of U.S. servicemen.[37] Brothels have always been located in close proximity to bases in the United States and around the world. Most military wives knew about sanctioned promiscuity, yet the subject was seldom discussed. And, although the military turned a blind eye to male infidelity, any sexual misconduct on the part of the wives was deemed unacceptable.

Breaking the Silence

In the 1880s, Elizabeth Custer, the wife of General George A. Custer, complained, "It seemed very strange to me that with all the value that is set on the presence of women of an officer's family at the frontier posts, the book of army regulations makes no provision for them, but in fact ignores them entirely!"[38] In the late 1880s, Martha Summerhayes's captain husband, Jack, reiterated the same point when he said: "Why Martha, did you not know that women are not reckoned at all at the War Department?"[39] Jane, the wife of an army major I interviewed in 1997, said, "The military does not care about the needs of wives, only for their value to influence retention and the military mission."

The published stories about military wives have been left by the more-educated "officers' ladies," who in diaries and books recounted, primarily, their own lives. The women described the hardships of military life, the lack of food, housing, and education. Many wrote that when they married, they had "enlisted in the army" and were as much a soldier as their military partner. These military wives addressed the difficulties of communication between their isolated outposts and the outside world, and the loneliness of their existence. There are even fewer accounts of enlisted "women," who were invisible to their own sex and were seldom mentioned unless they caused a problem or had some peculiarity. Because the personal and professional lives of the military are closely aligned, the women found it almost impossible to write about themselves as separate from the military and their husbands.[40]

A plethora of military etiquette books in the 1950s and 1960s influenced the role of military wives, stressed their subordinate position, and suggested that even if wives had knowledge about their husband's work they "should keep it to [themselves]." These and other texts were updated throughout the years to ensure that the behavior of the military wife complied with the role the military had set for her.[41]

In the 1960s and 1970s during the Vietnam conflict, the U.S. military discouraged the wives of prisoners of war (POWs) from speaking out, advising them to avoid the press in order to protect their husbands. But some, like Sybil Stockdale, wife of Vietnam POW Navy Captain Jim Stockdale, insisted that their stories be heard. Because she refused to be silent, when Sybil Stockdale met with the Viet Cong representatives in Paris, they knew her name and her work on behalf of POWs and their families. Many believe that the publicity these women gave to the plight of their POW husbands played a significant role in the men's survival.[42]

During the Gulf War, military wives were interviewed by the news media; however, the questions were usually about families' problems rather than more substantive topics. Military wives were not asked to give their opinions on such controversial questions as "Do you believe that your husbands should be sent to fight in Saudi Arabia?" or "Should Saudi Arabia and Kuwait use their own armed forces to protect the area?" Such weighty issues were reserved for the myriad of primarily male military analysts.

Military parents received much media attention, especially some dual-career military couples who had no suitable child-care arrangements when both parents were deployed to the Gulf. Some couples were unprepared because one member was on active duty and the other was a member of the reserves and did not expect to be called up. Equal publicity was not given to the majority of couples who had made the necessary provision for their children.[43]

When troops deployed from a southern base to the Gulf, the enforced silence of military wives was demonstrated when an armed marine rebuffed the attempts of a reporter to interview young women who had previously agreed to speak with him. Air Force wives I interviewed on three bases in Europe during their husbands' deployment to Saudi Arabia agreed with Lisa, a lieutenant colonel's wife, who said, "Even if we do have opinions, no one listens, they never have."

Recent interviews with military wives across the services indicate that today they are more inclined to believe that they can speak out. First, in the late 1970s military studies concluded that wives' satisfaction with military life had a direct influence on their husbands' retention and readiness, acknowledging that wives were indeed important to the military mission.[44] Second, more military wives are employed, and, although their numbers are fewer than those of their civilian peers, this gives the women both financial stability and the self-esteem to stand against military pressure. Working spouses do not have the same need, or time, to socialize with other military wives and are more apt to form civilian relationships. Also, the increased numbers of military women married to military men—rendering them both wives and warriors—are in positions of authority where their voices are heard.[45]

Third, the Family Support Centers have taken over as a clearinghouse for volunteers, which was one of the functions of the wives clubs. The volunteer responsibilities, with some exceptions, have been divided more equitably throughout the bases.

Fourth, greater networking has been established through women's associations and on line. Military wives are using technology and starting home pages on the Internet where they can ask questions about military issues and have them answered by other wives, professionals, and paraprofessionals. Women who are due to be assigned to a foreign country can gain insights about the locations through Relocation Points of Contact. One of the main complaints of the women I interviewed was the division between the wives of officers and enlisted personnel. The Internet enables all military wives, regardless of husband rank, to connect in a way that heretofore was not possible.

Today, the women have a variety of venues for their frustrations and concerns. The NMFA, Family Support Centers, the Marine Corps' Key Volunteers (earlier Key Wives) program, and the Navy's Ombudsman Program have given the wives an outlet for their grievances.

Since the mid-1980s, the military has instituted a burgeoning bureaucracy to take care of family matters. The programs appear to confirm that the military does indeed "take care of its own." Yet this bureaucracy itself provides the military with more extensive control over military wives as programs become institutionalized and subsume the interest of the family to the interest of the service.

Recommendations

Cynthia Enloe points out in *The Morning After*, "In each country someone will be making calculations about how masculinity and femininity can best serve the national interest."[46] Although the military has embraced cutting-edge defense technology, it has been slow to respond to social change. The military requires that personal and family issues come behind military members' commitment to service, duty, and country. The requirement that family members be managed and taken care of has been in the interest of the military mission, not in the interest of the individual.

The "us-and-them" attitude of the military toward the general public has been a deliberate attempt by the military to maintain a strong sense of identity and tradition. Many civilians, uncomfortable with the purpose of the military, encourage this separation, which lessens the need to contemplate the consequences of military action, and allows the military to behave according to its own tenets.

The British military is closing base housing because service families increasingly choose not to live on military bases. Conversely, the U.S. military continues to build and repair base housing, at a time when domestic violence, child abuse, and other negative happenings are escalating. It may be to the military's advantage to keep families under its control, but we should question whether a military base is a healthy environment for women and children.

The U.S. military could follow the lead of many of the world's military services that deploy their forces and leave a family in one location for most of the military members' lives. If the U.S. military adopted such a policy, the military wife would no longer come under the authority of the military commander. She could establish a career, make lasting friendships, and raise a family in a stable environment. The money saved by the government in housing and moving costs could be used to help military members purchase their own homes, making them less vulnerable at the end of their careers when many are financially unable to enter the housing market.

Contemporary military wives are not *dependents* but women able to "jump outside" the military system and speak in unique and authentic voices about the military requirements that control their lives. The government, the media, feminist groups and scholars, working together with military wives could provide a forum for their voices to be heard. When military wives create their own "frame," they, not the military hierarchy, will decide how they can best serve their own and the national interest.

NOTES

1. Edward M. Coffman, *The Old Army: A Portrait of the American Army in Peacetime, 1784–1898* (New York: Oxford University Press, 1986), 113.

2. Linda Grant De Pauw, *Founding Mothers: Women of the Revolutionary Era* (Boston: Houghton Mifflin, 1975), 179.

3. Mary Ormsbee Whitton, *These Were the Women, 1776–1860* (New York: Random House, 1954), 6.

4. Sally Smith Booth, *The Women of '76* (New York: Hastings House, 1973), 181.

5. Grant De Pauw, *Founding Mothers*, 184.

6. Shauna Whitworth, *"The Happy Contagion" or Story of the First Military Wives Club* (Fairfax, Va.: Shauna Whitworth, 1990), 6.

7. Grant De Pauw, *Founding Mothers*, 188–90.

8. Coffman, *The Old Army*, 136.

9. Louise Hall Tharp, *The Baroness and the General* (Boston: Little, Brown, 1962).

10. Grant De Pauw, *Founding Mothers*, 183; Booth, *Women of '76*, 181–82.

11. Coffman, *The Old Army*, 24–25.

12. Ibid., 113

13. *Army Times, Navy Times, and Air Force Times* supplement, *1997 Handbook for Military Families*, 7 April 1997, 12.

14. General Colin Powell with Joseph E. Persico, *My American Journey* (New York: Random House, 1995), 62.

15. Roger W. Little, *The Military Family: Handbook of Military Institutions* (Beverley Hills: Sage, 1971).

16. Nancy Loring Goldman, "Trends in Family Patterns of the U.S. Military Personnel

during the 20th Century," in *The Social Psychology of Military Service*, ed. Nancy Loring Goldman and David Segal, vol. 6 (Beverley Hills: Sage, 1976).

17. U.S. Army, *Historical Antecedents and Philosophical Foundations of Army Family Policy* (Springfield, Va.: Military Family Resource Center Research Department, 1984), 12.

18. "Washington Update," *Fort Worth Star-Telegram*, 17 April 1995, 2.

19. U.S. Department of Defense, "Total Child and Spouse Abuse Reports," in *Family Advocacy Program: Personnel Support Families and Education* (Washington, D.C., 1995).

20. Morris Janowitz, *The Professional Soldier* (New York: Free Press, 1977), 192.

21. Patrick Pexton and Rick Maze, "A Gap in Military Pay," *Air Force Times*, 29 May 1995, 14.

22. Department of the Air Force, AF Regulation 30–51, "Air Force Members' Marital Status and Activities of Their Spouses," (Department of the Air Force, 6 June 1988).

23. E. Van Vranken, Ron Buryk, Elwood Hamlin, eds., *Report on Family Issues: The Army Family Analysis and Appraisal* (proceedings of First Army Family Symposium, 1980).

24. Carmen Noble, "Program Helps People Cope with Military Life," *Air Force Times*, 10 February 1997, 23.

25. Cynthia Enloe, *The Morning After: Sexual Politics at the End of the Cold War* (Berkeley: University of California Press, 1993), 195–96.

26. Mark Thompson, "The Living Room War," *Time*, 23 May 1994, 48.

27. 1993 interview at the Pentagon with Colonel Nelson.

28. Thompson, *Living Room War*, 48.

29. DOD, *Family Advocacy Program*.

30. Thompson, *Living Room War*, 50.

31. Ibid.

32. David Peterson del Mar, *What Trouble I Have Seen* (Cambridge: Harvard University Press, 1996).

33. Lenore E. Walker, *The Battered Woman* (New York: Harper & Row, 1977).

34. Carolyn F. Swift, "Women and Violence: Breaking the Connection," no. 27 (Wellesley, Mass.: Wellesley Center for Women, 1987).

35. "$1.5 Million Bazaar," *Air Force Times*, 2 November 1987, 31.

36. Patricia Y. Stallard, *Glittering Misery* (Norman: University of Oklahoma Press, 1977); Beth Bailey and David Farber, *The First Strange Place: Race and Sex in World War II Hawaii* (Baltimore: Johns Hopkins University Press, 1992).

37. Saundra Sturdevant and Brenda Stoltzfus, *Let the Good Times Roll: Prostitution and the U.S. Military in Asia* (New York: New Press, 1992), 45.

38. Elizabeth B. Custer, *Boots and Saddles, or Life in Dakota with General Custer* (1885; reprint, Williamstown, Mass.: Corner House, 1977), 129.

39. Martha Summerhayes, *Vanished Arizona* (Lincoln: University of Nebraska Press, 1979), 12.

40. See Custer, *Boots and Saddles*; Summerhayes, *Vanished Arizona*; Kathleen Tupper Marshall, *Together* (New York: Tupper and Love, 1946).

41. See Nancy Shea, *The Army Wife* (New York: Harper & Row, 1966); Nancy Shea, *The Air Force Wife* (New York: Harper & Brothers, 1966); Ester Weir and Dorothy Coffin Hickey, *The Answer Book on Naval Social Customs*, 2d ed. (Harrisburg, Pa.: Military Service, 1957).

42. Jim and Sybil Stockdale, *Love and War* (New York: Bantam, 1985).

43. June 1997 interview with Sydney Hickey.

44. Gloria Lauer Grace and Mary B. Steiner, "Wives' Attitudes and the Retention of

Naval Enlisted Personnel," in *Military Families*, ed. Edna J. Hunter and D. Stephen Nice (New York: Praeger, 1978).

45. See Laurie Weinstein and Christie White, eds., *Wives and Warriors: Women and the Military in the United States and Canada* (Westport, Conn.: Bergin and Garvey, 1997).

46. Enloe, *Morning After*, 261.

Autobiography

Perspectives on Being an Insider/Outsider in the Armed Forces

Joan I. Biddle

Editors' note: This article is abridged. The complete version may be viewed at http://www.erols.com/jandjb/insider.htm. For the full theoretical analysis about the socialization of military wives and insider/outsider concepts, see Joan I. Biddle, "Do You Speak Military? The Socialization of Army Officers' Wives to Institutional Expectations" (Ph.D. diss., Boston University, 1992).

As a sociologist, I look at the context within which events occur. So, when I think about the concepts of *inside/outside*, and apply those concepts to military life, I understand that my own perspective depends very much on "who" I am when I claim my point of view.

Who I am depends upon my public or social role—the role that I am judged to occupy by others in my setting—and my own interpretation of my immediate role and my understanding of the circumstances surrounding my interactions from those points of view. Similarly, what I understand about the roles of those who are judging my role and my interpretation of *their* roles have an impact upon how I judge their interpretations of me.

My perspective about military things reflects the variety of separate roles that I have occupied, some of which have overlapped to occur simultaneously.

For example, I was commissioned in the army as an officer, therefore I am an officer. I was an active-duty officer; I am now a reserve officer. I married, therefore, I became, and was viewed as, someone's wife and a married officer. When I resigned from active duty, I was a married reservist and an officer's wife. Later, I became a mother, therefore a married reserve officer and mother, and still an officer's wife. As I began to acquire educational and professional credentials, I came to be identified by those as well. When my husband resigned from active duty, he became a reservist; we became a dual-reservist family, I continued to be a wife, a mother, a sociologist, a reserve officer, and a reserve officer's wife. Sometimes I occupied several roles simultaneously; I recall times during which I was conscious of being in one role while being viewed as in something else by someone else.

When I first went on active duty, I was single. After I married, I was a married officer and a wife. As part of my Army job, I arranged and attended numerous official social functions. My husband, also an officer, often went with me. Usually, officers more senior than either of us addressed him by his rank and me by my first name, even though both of us wore the blue uniform to the function. Very few people ever introduced me by my rank, even though they introduced my husband by his. This practice was especially true when the nonmilitary wives of these officers were a part of the conversation or when the wives were being introduced to me.

My perception about this type of social behavior was that those who called me by my first name felt unsure about how to treat me—as an officer, or as a wife. Addressing me by first name, even though I was wearing a military uniform, too, was a way to place me into a role that made sense to them or to their wives, and to indicate my junior status. I felt that they didn't really regard me in the same way as they regarded my husband, who, as a male, a Vietnam veteran, and an artillery officer, was one of *them*. I occupied a discrepant role because I am a woman, and was viewed as being more like the wives than an officer. These other military people and their wives were unable to reconcile my rank and status to that of a military person.

When I went with my husband to social functions for his unit, I was usually introduced and addressed by my first name. Since I didn't work in his organization, my only connection to these people was through my husband. The officers, all of whom were men, seemed to regard me, a woman officer, as something of an oddity.

The wives seemed to regard me with a mixture of curiosity and suspicion. I remember walking into a room and the room's suddenly becoming silent; all looked at me, then all looked away and resumed talking in their very tightly closed circles that were separate from the men. There usually wasn't room for me in those circles, so I remained with my husband, on the fringes of his groups, where I felt more at ease.

As for the wives of the men in my husband's unit, the rumors that I heard indicated that the wives didn't think that I fit in with them, either, because I was "doing a man's job." This attitude led to suspicion and a quietly stated fear that one of their husbands might become interested in the few military women at the post or, less quietly stated, that military women might become interested in their husbands.

From those perspectives, I, who viewed myself as an *insider* officer, was regarded by some other *insiders*, military men, as an *outsider* because I was a wife and a woman. The wives, viewed me, a wife, as an *outsider* to their groups because I was an officer, therefore not an *insider* to their groups.

So, for both groups, I was both an *insider* and an *outsider*.

On another occasion when I was still on active duty, I was invited to a social function for the wives of the men in my husband's organization. This function was sponsored by the brigade, so the "senior lady" officiating at it was the wife of the colonel who was the brigade commander. My husband was a captain and a company commander in one of the battalions in the brigade. I was a captain and a company commander in another Battalion and Brigade. My "place" in this hierarchy of my husband's unit was simply that of another wife. My own rank and job were irrelevant for this particular organization of women from whom I had received the invitation, and I usually did not go to the wives functions.

The function was held at the Officers Club, and the wives of other brigade, battalion, and company officers were there, some of whom I knew, others whom I did not know. I had been introduced to the Brigade Commander's wife on a previous occasion, and as a matter of courtesy, when I arrived, just like everyone else, I greeted her. I then joined the other women and socialized with them, again, just as everyone else did.

When the social part of the evening moved to the part in which the "senior lady" speaks to the group, one of the first things that she said was "Even though Joan's a WAC, she's welcome here." I remember being very stunned, having had no idea that she would make such a remark, and then not understanding why such a remark had even been necessary.

With hindsight, I can say that the remark was a way to distinguish me from them. I still don't know what motivated her that time, yet I do understand that this "senior lady" deemed it necessary to let the group know that it was "okay" for me to be included in its activities. The remark was a form of "permission" that identified me as an *outsider* to the wives group and then allowed me to enter the group to become an *insider*.

So, I was at first, an *outsider*. Among themselves, the wives were *insiders*. From the viewpoint of the Brigade Commander's wife, I, too, was a wife; *however*, I was also a commissioned officer. As a commissioned officer, I was not expected to be an *insider* among the wives, yet, because I was married to an officer who was a member of that organization, I met the qualifications for entry into the wives group. So, because I was an officer, even though I also met the membership criteria for a wife, I was identified as an officer first, an *outsider*. It was therefore necessary to recognize me as an exception, as one who also qualified as an *insider*. The Brigade Commander's wife identified me as an *outsider*, and then she gave "permission" for me to be included as an *insider*.

Another example shows a distinction that was made by a military *insider*. In 1978, my husband and I lived in Wiesbaden, West Germany, where he was stationed. I was temporarily on active duty in Mainz for my annual Reserve tour. At the end of a workday, I dropped in at a battalion building to wait for my husband, who was then an artillery battery commander. I was still wearing my fatigue uniform. As I walked past the desk of the relatively new S-3/operations officer, the officer, also a captain, as I was at the time, noticed my name tag, stood up, put out his hand for me to shake, and introduced himself to me. He looked puzzled, then explained that he hadn't realized that I was "military too," referring to me as connected to my husband and assuming that we were both active duty. When I told him that I was doing my Reserve tour, he said, "Oh," looked embarrassed, sat down, and lost interest in me.

I remember thinking that it was strange that as many times as I had been in that building no one had ever stood up to greet me or introduce himself to me before in such a manner. I had been wearing civilian clothes on those earlier occasions, and as my husband's wife, seem to have been invisible to the military people who worked there. Another thing about this happening was that the Captain spoke to me in a tone of voice different from that I was accustomed to hearing—a tone reserved for those of equal standing, not the tone reserved for wives and children.

Among military personnel, as a person in uniform, I was a military *insider*, someone worthy of notice, a possible colleague; as someone's wife, I was an *outsider*. Even though I was wearing the same uniform as he was, the other officer viewed me as a wife, and there was no common ground for further discussion or camaraderie.

Meanwhile, at my duty location in Mainz, no one regarded me as someone's wife, I was simply a Reserve officer assigned to work at that location for several weeks. As a uniformed officer, I was treated as an *insider*, and spoken to in the language and jargon of the military. In turn, I was expected to be an *insider*, to act like an *insider*. I was expected to know the rules of the setting, the organization, and the military culture. I was expected to fit in—as an officer.

How does one become an *insider*?

My first awareness about the military as something special occurred when I was a very small child growing up in post–World War II New Jersey. I remember sitting on the boardwalk in Lavalette with my father, a veteran of the World War II Navy, and listening to him identify the navy aircraft that flew along the coast from the nearby naval station at Lakehurst. He'd joined the navy "for the duration" of "The War." I knew that The War had been something *big*, that The War had changed the lives of the people who had fought in it, and that life, for many, was reckoned as being before, during, or after The War.

World War II and the events of that war were, and are still, *the* major events in the lives of the people who lived through it. The military service of those who had "joined" forged their identities. As veterans, they were no longer "active," yet, as veterans, they continued to regard themselves as *insiders* because their experiences gave them that right. They were "special" members of an "elite" group. Those who evaded the call for military service, those who somehow had not served or who had not fulfilled their patriotic duty, were outsiders to this elite group of citizens who had served honorably in the armed forces.

These impressions were my first inklings about a perception by military persons, about *exclusive inclusion* in a unique segment of American society and culture. Those who could claim inclusion into this social group qualified solely by their military service. All others would never qualify, remaining forever *outsiders* to it.

So, why are these perceptions about inclusion/exclusion important? Consider that one's perspective about inclusion/exclusion in a group has a lot to do with one's identity in relationship to that group and to the larger society in which one lives. That image of oneself has much to do with how one defines the world and relates to it.

In the case of perceptions about identification with the armed forces, some very basic concepts apply. One's identification as a member of the armed forces begins as one swears to "support and defend the Constitution of the United States against all enemies, foreign and domestic . . . [and] bear true faith and allegiance to the same."

By swearing the oath, a person voluntarily becomes an official member the armed forces and is subject to military authority. By swearing the oath, a person formally and publicly declares that she/he is a member of a specific branch of service and accepts the obligation to perform whatever duties she/he is given. Furthermore, the oath represents the ideology of the military organization, and by swearing to it, a person gives legitimacy to the military belief system and assumes an obligation to support it. The *oath* is the symbolic gateway through which all *insiders* must pass.[1]

One major distinction, then, between *insiders* and *outsiders* is that *insiders* have taken an *oath* that makes them *members, exclusive insiders,* of the military, of the armed forces, and that *outsiders* have not. The *oath* places upon *insiders* obligations and responsibilities as members of the military and as citizens that outsiders have not sworn to uphold.

The nonmilitary spouse directly associates with the military by way of an oath too; however, the oath is not to the armed forces. It is usually the marriage vow. Obligations are not to the military institution but, rather, to the military husband/wife. Nonmilitary spouses are indirect members of the military institution through the membership of the persons to whom they are married. Because the spouses are not sworn members of the armed forces, they are *not* subject to its authority; instead, they are indirectly subject to its influence, and there is no direct obligation or responsibility attached to them for their participation in military life and culture. Spouses and family members are unofficial/official insiders whose presence is accounted for in numerous official regulations and policies that take into account their needs for housing, medical care, and so on.[2]

Each sworn member of the armed forces receives a Geneva Convention Identification Card, a critical document for every service member and family member. The card contains a picture of the military person and a brief description of personal characteristics. Possession of the card immediately identifies its holder as an exclusive insider, an insider who is entitled to the full range of benefits of the military occupation, a fully responsible member of the armed forces, the military community, who is entitled to access to military installations and the services and opportunities therein.

The spouses of military *insiders* have an ID card, too. The identification and privilege card identifies the spouse and each child ten years and older and enables specific, limited access within the military institution. Moreover, it exists only through the sponsorship of the military person to whom the spouse is married and who is also the parent of the child or children.

Each military person is entitled to wear the uniform of her/his branch of the armed forces. The uniform publicly identifies its wearer as a member of a particular branch. The uniform is an external symbol of commitment to fulfill the oath.

Each military person initially undergoes training in how to be a military person. The point of training for both officers and enlisted members is the same: to learn the basic skills and the specific skills necessary for performing their piece of the military mission.

Along with intense training in military skills, every level of introductory, continuing, or advanced training includes indoctrination into military ideology. The goal is to produce a person whose behavior and attitudes conform to the norms of the institution, someone who will be a dependable part of the military "team." Everything that happens to all trainees and students, officers and enlisted, has a reason. The individual branches of the armed forces—the Army, Navy, Marine Corps, Air Force, Coast Guard—are intentional institutions that exist for specific purposes, and all institutional efforts are directed toward achieving institutional goals.[3]

The result of this intense training is that those who undergo it internalize the ideology of the armed forces as their own. Military training resocializes one to identify with all things military and to think "military" in all aspects of life and living. One learns to define the world in "military" terms—time is reckoned on a twenty-four-hour clock; "duty, honor, country" become a primary directive for daily life; the "needs of the service" come first. Subsequently, military people respond to the world around them according to their new military, ways of thinking and understanding.[4]

Wives' socialization to their roles and culture occurs primarily in social settings. Through their interactions with one another, they learn the rules for their participation in the military institution. They pass this knowledge on to other spouses who are newcomers to the military setting.

How, then, should the spouses of military service members or veterans be regarded? Where do they fit into the picture? First, veterans are our historical predecessors who provide tangible connections between their past experiences and our own experiences, just as we who are future veterans will provide those links to our own successors.

In my opinion, after having lived and observed military life and after having observed the lives and activities of women married to military men for nearly thirty years, I regard the spouses of service members as critical institutional actors. The spouses especially the wives, contribute to the quality of life of the military communities in ways that can't always be measured. The presence of the wives is pervasive and, for the most part, very invisible. Their presence is so well integrated into the military institution as to be totally taken for granted by everyone. Yet, even as the wives are regarded as a natural part of any setting, some persons still view them as superfluous, as institutional outsiders.[5]

A number of years ago when I was a major on active duty during one of my Reserve tours, I overheard a senior colonel talking to another officer about the move that a major organization was about to make to another installation. Part of the discussion involved the issue of housing and how to accommodate the families of the active-duty military personnel who would be required to move to the new post. There was not enough on-post housing to meet the needs of everyone, and off-post housing was not available. What could be done to get the military persons to their destination on time and, simultaneously, to accommodate their families? "Send them home." was the response that I heard the Colonel give.

My first mental reaction to that statement was that the families *were* at home. To what "home" did he propose to send them?

The Colonel was clearly stating his point: the wives and families of the service members making the move were *outsiders*. When one sends people "home," one believes that they belong elsewhere, not where they already are. The Colonel failed to understand that the wives and family members were already at *home*, that they, too, were *insiders*.

To view wives as *outsiders* indicates a failure to comprehend the importance of the roles and responsibilities that the wives (and sometimes husbands) of military persons frequently assume in their communities. Although nonmilitary spouses view themselves as *insiders*, their military spouses, often regard them as *outsiders*, assuming that only persons wearing the uniform and carrying the Geneva Convention Identification Card qualify as *insiders*.

Still, the wives view themselves as institutional *insiders*. Many wives become involved in all kinds of philanthropy for the good of their communities and are important as unofficial, informal conveyors of influence for the commands with which they are affiliated. Wives clubs, such as the Officers' Wives Club (OWC) and the Non-Commissioned Officers' Wives Club (NCOWC) exist at many military installations. Many sponsor events to raise money that is given back to their communities in the form of grants and scholarships.

In terms of influence in their communities, many wives network among themselves in groups that are often structured along the organizational lines of their husbands' duty organizations/chain of command. Among themselves, they meet formally (coffees, teas), informally, and socially to discuss events that affect them as members of their communities. In peacetime, these groups tend to serve primarily symbolic and social functions accompanied by some limited functional responsibilities. In times of crisis, such as during deployments or mobilization or war, the groups assume numerous functional responsibilities for the command, including becoming the bases for family support groups and networks that pass information to family members.

So, what *is* the answer? Who *is* the *insider*? Who *is* the *outsider*?

Personally, I regard myself as an *insider*, in both military and family settings, although there are those who might regard me differently. Certainly, according to the criteria that I've just outlined, I would likely regard those who don't have the experience of military service or of a military spouse as *outsiders*. Being a part of the *inside* of the military is a commitment to its values, its mission. We represent the United States of America, we represent its interests. We serve proudly to support and defend our country.

NOTES

1. Joan I. Biddle, "Do You Speak Military? The Socialization of Army Officers' Wives to Institutional Expectations" (Ph.D. diss., Boston University, 1992), 68.

2. Ibid., passim.

3. Ibid., 99.

4. Ibid., 100.

5. Ibid., passim.

Seven

Civilian Employees in the Department of Defense

Diane M. Disney

Throughout U.S. history, American women have challenged gender boundaries to aid our country's defense. Some have become nurses; others, soldiers; many, however, have made less visible but not less valuable contributions in support roles as cooks, laundresses, and clerks, sometimes in official, paid positions but often as volunteers during times of war. Today, thousands of civilian women work at the Pentagon and at hundreds of military installations throughout the United States and around the globe. Over time, their jobs within the Department of Defense (DOD) have become more diverse and their opportunities for advancement have become more equitable.

During this country's Revolutionary War, some women masqueraded as men to serve as soldiers; some stood beside their husbands and replaced them when they fell in battle; many more served as sutlers, cooks, and nurses. During the Civil War, women's nursing assistance greatly reduced casualties, as Connie Reeves discusses in chapter 1. Other women raised funds, made clothes, developed libraries, produced concerts, wrote letters, and worked as couriers, scouts, and spies.

Opportunities for more formalized service to country arose in the twentieth century, with the creation of the Army Nurse Corps (1901) and the Navy Nurse Corps (1908), as well as the authorization to enroll women temporarily in military positions other than nursing in the Navy (1917) and later the Marine Corps.[1] Most served in clerical positions, as Georgia Clark Sadler details in chapter 2.

World War II brought a great expansion in the number of women serving what was then called the War Department as bookkeepers, secretaries, analysts, and switchboard operators. The Pentagon building, in fact, could not be occupied until telephone service became available. "The system installed in 1942 required 32,000 square feet of space and had more than 200 employees and 125 switchboard positions."[2] The positions were filled by young women. One operator, Marian Bailey, is depicted by a mannequin at a switchboard in a Pentagon exhibit commemorating the building's fiftieth anniversary. Ms. Bailey still works for the DOD, sharing her wealth of experience by providing guided tours for visitors.

In the quarter century following World War II, little happened to change the roles or numbers of women working as civilians for the Department of Defense.

On the military side, the Defense Advisory Committee on Women in the Services (DACOWITS) was founded in 1951 to strengthen the role of women in the armed forces, as detailed in chapter 8. In 1967, Public Law 90–130 repealed the 1948 law that had placed a 2 percent ceiling on the number of women in the armed forces; it also allowed women to become flag and general officers. With the 1970s came the disestablishment of the women's services (WAC, WAVES, and WAF), signifying a growing integration of women into military service, as discussed in chapter 2.

Women on the civilian side, however, faced somewhat different challenges because of their status as civil servants and nonappropriated fund employees, that is, people paid not from tax dollars but from revenues generated by such activities as recreation centers, commissaries, and exchanges. Active-duty military, Reserves, and National Guard members constitute three-quarters of the Department of Defense staff. Their treatment is governed by Title 10 of the U.S. Code. Civilian employees constitute the other quarter, but they are covered by Title 5, which concerns government organization and employees. Civilian workers, then, must cope with the benefits and constraints of the civil service while functioning in a military environment. This combination has at times seemed to limit the number of women working for the DOD. Although women constitute about half of the staff of the U.S. Departments of Labor, Commerce, Treasury, Education, Housing and Urban Development, and Health and Human Services, they have never exceeded 38 percent of the DOD's civil service employees.[3]

At the end of Fiscal Year 1997, the DOD employed roughly 774,000 civil servants and 150,000 civilians working in nonappropriated-fund activities. Although the latter do provide much-needed support, their jobs tend to have higher turnover than civil service positions. More than a third are occupied by military family members, generally wives, and 6 percent by off-duty military; therefore, incumbents change when tours of duty expire. Nearly 60 percent of the nonappropriated-fund jobs are held by women, many of whom work flexible schedules. In a previous chapter, Doreen Drewry Lehr addresses the challenges faced by wives of military members in seeking and retaining employment. The balance of this chapter will focus on civil servants.

Over the past two decades, the DOD's civilian workforce has changed dramatically. From a base of somewhat more than 982,000 in FY 1977, it rose during the 1980s to more than 1.1 million. The fall of the Berlin Wall then brought restructuring and downsizing. Overall numbers are now some 774,000, including foreign nationals, with a considerable shift in the occupational mix.

The Department's insistence on managing the downsizing humanely as well as efficiently has prevented undue dislocation despite the drop. Normally, reductions in force would eliminate jobs of the least-senior people, who were most likely to be women and minorities. However, use of separation incentives and the Priority Placement Program (which finds new jobs in the DOD for employees facing dislocation through no fault of their own) has enabled the Department to retain the diversity it had when the civilian drawdown began at the end of FY 1989.

The DOD's gender profile has changed over the past two decades, with the relative proportion of women increasing from 29.7 percent in 1977 to 37.3 percent in 1997 (table 7.1). The latter figure is noteworthy because it demonstrates that sound transition programs can help preserve and even improve a workforce profile despite downsizing pressures.

The following sections describe drawdown-driven changes and the current reality for civil servants in the DOD in terms of age, grade level, and occupation.

Age

As of the end of FY 1997, the typical DOD civilian employee was 44.4 years old. This represented an increase in the average age of 2.8 years since the drawdown began eight years earlier. If recommendations made in the recent Quadrennial Defense Review are fully implemented, the average age will rise another 1.7 years, to peak at 46.1 in FY 2003.

A comparison of ages of men and women in five-year intervals shows the impact of the baby boom, retirement plans, and changing hiring practices (see figure 7.1). Government agencies and private employers alike are facing problems with an aging workforce caused by the sheer size of the cohort born after World War II.

In the DOD, the military features an inverted pyramid with few flag officers compared to many enlisted men and women. The very large number of military members in their teens and twenties, combined with the "up-or-out" promotion rules, keeps the age profile fairly constant. The civil service, though, does not consciously recruit and train thousands of young people each year, does not have an "up-or-out" program of career development, and (theoretically at least) can permit an outsider to enter at any level in the system. It is not uncommon for a service member to retire or otherwise leave the military and then join the civilian workforce at a comparable rank. Because entry is possible at any level on the civilian side, the civilian and military workforces have different profiles. The civilian workforce features a bell curve with concentration in the forties (see figure 7.1).

TABLE 7.1
Gender Profile of DOD Civilian Employees,
FY 1977–FY 1997

Fiscal Year	Total	% Male	% Female
1977	964,016	70.3	29.7
1982	964,590	66.7	33.3
1987	1,051,447	63.7	36.3
1992	956,668	63.1	36.9
1997	736,663	62.7	37.3

NOTE: Table includes only U.S. citizens paid from appropriated funds.
    SOURCE: U.S. Department of Defense, Defense Manpower Data Center files.

FIGURE 7.1

Age and Sex Profile of DOD Civilian Employees, FY 1997

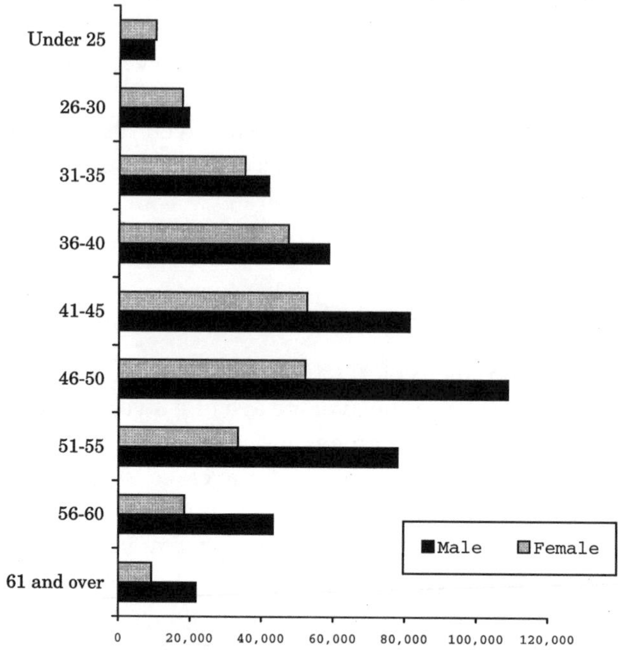

SOURCE: U.S. Department of Defense, Defense Manpower Data Center files.
NOTE: Figure reflects only U.S. citizens paid with appropriated funds.

The noticeably high numbers in the forties and early fifties also reflect the "golden handcuffs" of the Civil Service Retirement System (CSRS). This defined-benefit plan provides a guaranteed annuity for those who reach the prescribed combination of age and service (generally fifty-five years of age with thirty years of service). Because people covered by the CSRS are not also covered by Social Security, and there is no indexing to accommodate years outside the system, workers reaching middle age often feel tied to the civil service for retirement security. The Federal Employees Retirement System (FERS), for workers hired since the mid-1980s, incorporates Social Security with a thrift savings program and a small defined benefit. Younger workers, then, should regard their benefits as more portable, making them less likely to feel compelled to try to stay in the civil service until reaching the minimum retirement age of fifty-five to fifty-seven. The current mix of retirement plans is expected to lead to an exodus beginning in 2001 when the oldest baby boomers turn fifty-five.

There are more than twice as many men as women in the categories older than forty-five, but also greater parity in successively younger age brackets: a 22 percent gap between women and men in their thirties; less than 5 percent for those in their twenties (see figure 7.1). If this trend continues, the Department could have a very well-balanced workforce in the next two decades.

As of the end of FY 1997, the DOD's typical male employee was three years older than the typical female employee (45.9 years versus 42.9 years). The

DOD's microsimulation model projects that the age differential will fall to 2.4 years (47.2 versus 44.8) in FY 2003 if planned and recommended reductions are made.

The drawdown since FY 1989 has not affected all age categories equally (see table 7.2). Before the drawdown began, the DOD typically hired about 65,000 civilians for permanent jobs each year; the yearly total is now down to 20,000. The combination of fewer accessions and seniority rules for retention has significantly altered the age profile.

Table 7.2 indicates that over the past eight years, there has been a decline in every five-year age category except for that of people aged forty-six to fifty. Much of this is the result of workers in a large baby boom group retaining their positions as they near pension eligibility. (CSRS-covered employees who are involuntarily separated are eligible for an immediate annuity if they have twenty-five years of service at any age or if they have twenty years of service and have reached age fifty.) During the drawdown, the DOD has been able to limit official reductions in force (RIFs) to less than a tenth of the overall reductions. When RIF do occur, those with the longest tenure are almost always the ones who retain their jobs, adding to the tendency of CSRS-covered employees to try to stay. Before anyone receives an official RIF notice, the employing DOD unit offers voluntary-separation incentive payments (or "buyouts") to individuals whose departure could free a position for those who might otherwise become unemployed. Individuals who are at or near retirement age frequently base retirement decisions upon the availability of such payments. Thus, the existence of buyouts also affects behavior of people in the forty-six to fifty-five age categories.

Table 7.2 also shows that the largest single drop during the drawdown has been among women aged twenty-five or younger. Much of the drop is attributable to the overall drop in accessions, and part to the sharp decline in clerical positions, which will be described later.

As mentioned earlier, the average age of female civil servants within the DOD has increased over the past eight years. Table 7.3 indicates how the proportional representation has changed by age category. Women twenty-five and

TABLE 7.2
Changes in Age Profile of DOD Civilian Employees, FY 1989–FY 1997

Age	Male N	Male %	Female N	Female %	Total N	Total %
≤25	−19,524	−67.6	−29,553	−74.8	−49,077	−71.8
26–30	−36,991	−65.8	−36,879	−67.9	−73,870	−66.8
31–35	−36,201	−46.5	−26,582	−43.1	−62,783	−45.0
36–40	−46,918	−44.4	−14,664	−23.9	−61,582	−36.8
41–45	−37,567	−36.6	−5,219	−9.0	−42,786	−24.2
46–50	10,634	+10.9	10,305	+24.7	20,939	+15.0
51–55	−7,055	−8.3	884	+2.6	−6,211	−5.3
56–60	−10,795	−20.0	−3,403	−15.7	−14,198	−18.7
61+	−4,966	−18.6	−3,932	−29.9	−8,898	−22.4
Total	−189,383	−29.1	−109,083	−28.4	−298,466	−28.8

NOTE: Table includes only U.S. citizens paid from appropriated funds.
SOURCE: U.S. Department of Defense, Defense Manpower Data Center files.

TABLE 7.3
Age Profile of DOD Female Civilian Employees, FY 1989 and FY 1997

Age	FY 1989 Number	%	FY 1997 Number	%
≤25	39,499	10.3	9,946	3.6
26–30	54,282	14.1	17,403	6.3
31–35	61,616	16.0	35,034	12.7
36–40	61,921	16.0	47,257	17.2
41–45	57,712	15.0	52,493	19.1
46–50	41,774	10.9	52,079	18.9
51–55	32,497	8.5	33,341	12.1
56–60	21,732	5.7	18,329	6.7
61+	13,138	3.4	9,206	3.3
Total	384,171		275,088	

NOTE: Table includes only U.S. citizens paid from appropriated funds.
SOURCE: U.S. Department of Defense, Defense Manpower Data Center files.

younger now represent only 3.6 percent of the female workforce, as opposed to more than 10 percent in FY 1989. A similar drop is evident for all those under thirty-one.

On the other hand, there has been a decided increase in the share of women aged forty-six to fifty: before the drawdown, they constituted just less than 11 percent of the female workforce; they now account for nearly 19 percent. Until accessions increase and the bulk of the baby boomers reach retirement age, the share of women in the older categories is likely to continue to increase.

Grade Distribution

Women working for the DOD are far more likely to be in white-collar jobs than blue-collar ones, as table 7.4 shows. Even before the drawdown eliminated 40 percent of the blue-collar jobs, women held less than 10 percent of them. Beyond this distinction, however, much has changed over the past two decades. The percentage of women in entry-level jobs (General Schedule levels 1–4) has steadily fallen, from 38.9 percent in FY 1977 to 13.1 percent now. Part of this drop is attributable to the general reduction in hiring, part to the decline in clerical positions, and part to promotions and other circumstances enabling women to reach higher levels than before.

Particularly noteworthy is the increasing representation of women in GS-9 through GS-12 positions because these are journey levels and supervisory positions. Fully a third of the female employees now hold positions at these levels. There has also been an increase in the share of women at managerial levels (GS-13–GS-15). Less than 1 percent of the women two decades ago, these managers now constitute more than 6 percent.

Although the number of female members of the Senior Executive Service (SES) remains too small to show on table 7.4, that number also has risen, from 13 at the GS-16 level in 1977, before the SES was created, to 167 now. In addition, over

TABLE 7.4
Grade Distribution of DOD Female Civilian Employees, FY 1977–1997

Category/Grade	FY 77, %	FY 82, %	FY 87, %	FY 92, %	FY 97, %
N	(286, 65)	(321, 25)	(381, 44)	(353, 359)	(275, 08)
			White-collar		
GS 1–4	38.9	31.3	25.3	16.1	13.1
5–8	36.8	39.5	38.9	40.2	38.4
9–12	10.4	15.7	21.0	28.5	32.5
13–15	0.7	1.0	2.0	4.1	6.1
SES	0.0	0.0	0.0	0.0	0.0
Other	3.6	3.3	4.3	4.1	4.5
Total	90.5	90.8	91.5	93.0	94.8
			Blue-collar		
WG 1–4	2.9	2.7	2.3	1.5	1.3
5–8	2.6	3.3	3.0	2.9	2.3
9–12	0.7	1.0	1.3	1.4	1.4
13+	0.0	0.0	0.0	0.0	0.0
Other	3.3	2.2	1.9	1.1	0.2
Total	9.5	9.2	8.5	7.0	5.2

NOTE: Table includes only U.S. citizens paid from appropriated funds.
SOURCE: U.S. Department of Defense, Defense Manpower Data Center files.

the past five years, women have been named for the first time to such positions as Secretary of the Air Force, General Counsel, and Director of Defense Research and Engineering.

Occupations

As indicated in the preceding section, men dominate the blue-collar occupations within the Department of Defense. Table 7.5 shows that twelve times as many men as women hold blue-collar positions. Further, more than a third of the men hold blue-collar jobs, as opposed to just one-twentieth (5.2 percent) of the women. On the other hand, there are five times as many women as men in clerical positions.

Within the white-collar area, men's positions are most likely to be administrative (22.8 percent) or professional (21.2 percent). Jobs held by women are fairly evenly distributed across clerical (26.3 percent), administrative (26 percent), and technical areas (25.8 percent). Over the past two decades, the occupational distribution of women working for the DOD has changed substantially. Clearly, the most significant change has occurred in the clerical area. Where nearly two-thirds of the women working for the DOD held clerical positions in 1977, only one-quarter do now (see table 7.6). Advanced levels of education and experience have enabled more women to enter administrative, technical, and professional areas. This increasing occupational diversity, in turn, acts to make women more central to the operations of the DOD than at any time in the past.

TABLE 7.5
Occupational Profile of DOD Civilian Employees, FY 1997

Category, Percentage	Male		Female		Total
	N	%	N	%	N
(N)	(461,575)		(275,088)		(736,663)
Professional	98,009	21.2	44,664	16.2	142,673
19.4					
Administrative	105,152	22.8	71,533	26.0	176,685
24.0					
Technical	59,411	12.9	70,900	25.8	130,311
17.7					
Clerical	14,655	3.2	72,476	26.3	87,131
11.8					
Other white-collar	15,013	3.3	1,318	0.5	16,331
2.2					
Total white-collar	292,240	63.3	260,891	94.8	553,131
75.1					
Blue-collar	169,335	36.7	14,197	5.2	183,532
24.9					

NOTE: Table includes only U.S. citizens paid from appropriated funds.
SOURCE: U.S. Department of Defense, Defense Manpower Data Center files.

Conclusion

Life in the Department of Defense has always been substantially different from that in other federal departments. The mixture of active-duty military, National Guard and Reserve members, and civilians has by itself posed challenges beyond those faced in domestic agencies. In addition, the DOD civilians constitute nearly half of the federal civil service, making every change that happens in the DOD seem as potentially significant for the rest of government.

Rather than becoming less complicated after the dissolution of the Soviet Union, the day-to-day life of a DOD civilian has become more complex. With 30 percent of the civilian positions already eliminated and another 14 percent possibly slated for elimination over the next five years, the workers who remain must be more broadly educated and more capable of shouldering extra responsibility than were their predecessors.

Data presented in this chapter indicate that the Department has taken major steps toward more fully employing the resources of its civilian women. Women

TABLE 7.6
Occupational Profile of DOD Female Civilian Employees, FY 1977–FY 1997

Category	FY 77, %	FY 82, %	FY 87, %	FY 92, %	FY 97, %
(N)	(286,658)	(321,252)	(381,440)	(353,359)	(275,088)
Professional	3.3	6.8	8.7	10.3	16.2
Administrative	10.1	15.0	20.0	25.0	26.0
Technical	12.7	14.9	14.6	16.7	25.8
Clerical	61.1	53.3	47.7	38.7	26.3
Other white collar	0.2	1.7	1.6	0.9	0.5
Total white collar	87.2	91.7	92.5	91.6	94.8
Blue collar	12.8	8.3	7.5	8.4	5.2

NOTE: Table includes only U.S. citizens paid from appropriated funds.
SOURCE: U.S. Department of Defense, Defense Manpower Data Center files.

continue to perform the duties that were characteristically theirs when the Pentagon was built in World War II. But more and more, they have come to hold other positions as well. From a situation in which nearly two-thirds of all women were in one occupational category, the DOD has moved to one where no more than 26 percent of women fall into any single occupational area.

Women have also reached and succeeded in key leadership positions in law, acquisition, science and engineering, personnel management, finance, intelligence, environmental security, and other areas. They have done so in all of the military departments as well as the defense agencies, field activities, and the Office of the Secretary of Defense. Just as important, the growing numbers of women acquiring experience in midlevel positions have increased the pool of candidates from which additional promotions will be made.

Taken together, the data on civilians in the Department of Defense suggest a steady change toward greater equality between men and women in type, level, and responsibility of positions. One senior official captured this change by noting that she looked forward to the day when she could tell her parents that her daughter had just become a secretary—the Secretary of Defense.

NOTES

1. Department of Defense, Research Division, "A Review of Data on Women in the United States," 21 February 1986.

2. Alfred Goldberg, *The Pentagon: The First Fifty Years* (Washington, D.C.: Office of the Secretary of Defense, 1992).

3. U.S. Department of Labor, *1983 Handbook on Women Workers: Trends and Issues* (Washington, D.C.: Government Printing Office, 1994), 21.

Autobiography

Bridging Gaps: Reflections of Two Civilian Professors at the U.S. Naval Academy

Helen E. Purkitt and Gale A. Mattox

Although differing to varying degrees in personal experiences, scholarly training, and research interests, we share the experience of being members of the first generation of women civilian professors at a federal service academy. We were the first two female civilian instructors hired by the Political Science Department at the United States Naval Academy (USNA) in 1979 and 1981, respectively. Our autobiographical sketches chronicle remarkable similarities in early socialization and later academic and personal experiences. We leave it to the more theoretically inclined to judge how important the common factors were in our subsequent careers. Throughout this essay we detail anecdotes of our experiences in "bridging gaps" in the classroom and with male civilian and military colleagues at USNA, the wider Department of Defense (DOD) community, and in international contacts. In recounting the experiences, we highlight how certain expectations and norms of behavior changed over time as increased numbers of women demonstrated that they could succeed professionally as military officers, civilian academicians, and midshipmen at the USNA.

Female midshipmen are now widely accepted members of the Brigade of Midshipmen, but we believe that problems persist because women remain a highly visible and distinct minority in the Brigade, the faculty, and the administration. While we do not propose specific policy prescriptions, our conclusions reflect our experiences about how to change conventional wisdom, stereotypes, and discriminatory policies.

Autobiographical Sketches

We shared two elements that provided a personal bond as well as a solid grounding from which to integrate and to succeed in the military culture at the U.S. Naval Academy. We both had family backgrounds in the military and roots in the Vietnam generation.

On the first point, our upbringings exhibited some striking similarities. We both were "Army brats" who had moved around the world often, including postings to Germany. For the uninitiated, this means that our fathers were Army officers. We grew up in a culture that included specific expectations, discipline, and men in positions of authority. Although we shared many of the values of those in uniform, we were also a product of the Vietnam War generation who refused to acknowledge that being female presumed exclusion from graduate school and professional careers. We shared a determination to make our way in what we had experienced as a predominantly male world.

Helen was born in a British ambulance in the Soviet Zone of a divided Germany the same year Gale moved to Germany. Gale's later professional focus on German issues and interest in national security issues was probably rooted in these early years. Helen's German experiences, however, left a more indirect impression. Her first memories of military officers stem from the age of five when her father headed the ROTC program at Princeton University. She remembers the well-mannered junior officers who frequently visited the home and let her slide down the banister from the second story and, occasionally, the third! In both cases, international travel and military backgrounds provided a similar basis for later educational and career choices.

For Helen, studying in Mexico and pursuing course work at the University of California at Los Angeles (UCLA) and the University of Southern California (USC) were formative in developing interests in the politics of developing countries and political psychology. Gale lived a total of six years in Germany and a year in Japan, which certainly played a role in her interest in international relations in college and graduate school.

We both faced a number of hurdles during graduate school that we managed to work around by making the best of what was available and pushing the envelope of opportunities available to women in the 1970s. In Helen's case, the USC School of International Relations offered a fully funded fellowship to obtain a master's degree. Accepted into the Ph.D. program because of a strong academic record, she was told she would not receive a fellowship; several of the more senior professors thought she "was not Ph.D. material." This assessment was similar to the ones received by other women in this Ph.D. program.

The mind-set of many male faculty in the United States throughout the 1970s and into the 1980s was that it was a waste of resources to award graduate fellowships to women because they would get married and never practice their profession. This mind-set prevailed at the University of Virginia (UVA), where Gale enrolled in the M.A. program on the urging of a supportive male professor at Mary Washington College. She then worked for the Congressional Research Service for two years to avoid working in a congressional office where all the women, including professional women with advanced degrees, started as receptionists. Gale returned to UVA to accept a formal offer to pursue a Ph.D. degree only to hear on the first day that "we thought you would be married and pregnant by now."

Meanwhile, Helen had decided to pursue a Ph.D. in international relations despite the lack of funding. She worked on several research projects simultaneously and also taught part-time in a local community college while most of the male graduate students received fellowships. The research and teaching experiences obtained from part-time jobs provided Helen with methodological skills and new research interests that proved invaluable in later years in such diverse fields as African politics and political decision making. Gale was also able to benefit from practical work experiences with research on arms control and its impact on Europe, an area she had determined was being overlooked during her time with Congress. Both benefited from male mentors who encouraged their progress and, in Gale's case, steered her to vital funding from the Institute for the Study of World Politics. Neither graduate program had a female faculty member of any rank in international relations and male mentors were critical to their success under sometimes veiled but tenuous circumstances.

After completing the course requirements for a Ph.D., Helen accepted a tenure-track position in political science at Texas Tech and was one of two women faculty in the department: the first women to be hired in several decades. Gale taught part-time at two women's colleges (one of which hired its first full-time female faculty member only in the 1980s) while completing her degree. She pursued the research on her dissertation as a Fulbright scholar in Germany at an institute where the presence of women in the field was even more striking than in the United States. She was usually one of the few females at professional conferences in Germany, as well as elsewhere in Europe.

Although both of us are daughters of career Army officers, we applied and accepted the offers of tenure positions from the Political Science Department at the USNA for reasons not consciously affected by our early socialization. We both felt that the Washington, D.C., area offered greater professional opportunities. The lure of sailboats and offices overlooking Chesapeake Bay were additional incentives. An even more important factor was our reaction to observing a political science class at the Academy. We both concluded during our job interviews that midshipmen would be an interesting group of students to teach.

We also liked the fact that the USNA encourages its faculty to pursue research. In addition to her African interests, Helen wanted to investigate how people make political decisions. Although experimental studies of politics were not yet widely accepted in most political science departments, the Defense Department was a major funding source for studies on political decision making, and units of DOD-designed procedures were used to train foreign area experts. Therefore, she felt that the Academy would be one of the few universities where her unique combination of research interests would be well received. Gale liked the opportunity to pursue research in nearby Washington and later remained at USNA because of the flexibility to take leave to work on a range of European and nonproliferation policy issues at the State Department.

For these reasons, we accepted our positions when they were offered. We were both told during interviews that the ability to teach a broad range of classes was the principal reason we were selected. Timing also appeared to play a role, for most of the political science faculty had decided it was time to hire women.

After becoming accepted members of the department, our civilian colleagues admitted that prior familiarity with the military and therefore the ability to "blend in" were important factors in our selection from a large pool of qualified applicants. In Gale's case she knew the USNA also as the granddaughter of a 1917 USNA graduate.

As the first woman in the department, Helen joined the faculty for the 1979/80 academic year—the year the USNA graduated its first cohort of women. Although the administration and Brigade of Midshipmen were officially supportive of integrating women, the issue of whether the public should pay for women to attend the service academies, given their exclusion from combat billets and the larger question of whether women should fight in wars, was a hotly debated issue. Women constituted approximately 10 percent of the entering class and were a highly visible minority group in the Brigade.

Although several female military officers had served as faculty instructors since 1973, Helen was the third civilian woman to join the permanent faculty of the USNA. In her late twenties, she was only a few years older than the students. The first day she walked into class, the midshipmen assumed that she was a secretary. When she started to review the course requirements, some mids seemed rather stunned. However, the novelty of having a female instructor quickly wore off as she announced due dates for homework and research assignments. Midshipmen tend to judge their instructors rather quickly in terms of competency and temperament. She was gratified to hear the same types of questions and groans as she explained course research requirements that she had encountered in civilian universities.

One novelty in those early years that disappeared with the passage of time was that a few midshipmen felt compelled to comment on our apparel on student evaluations. Those more positively inclined would make comments such as "She dresses well"; those who felt less positive tended to criticize certain outfits. These types of comments and many other aspects of male-midshipmen attitudes toward women professors changed dramatically over time as new generations of entering midshipmen, raised by working mothers, entered the Academy.

Bridging the Gap

In addition to the hiring of female faculty at the USNA, a number of changes affecting attitudes toward women occurred after the admittance of female midshipmen in 1976. One of the most encouraging trends has been the steady progress that female midshipmen have made as they competed successfully with their peers and became accepted members of each graduating class.

From the outset, women as a group outperformed male classmates academically. Over the years, female-midshipmen varsity sports teams increased in popularity and status, and a number of teams gained national prominence. In 1983, Kristine Holdereid became the first midshipman to rank number one in her class, a designation derived from both academic and military rankings. In 1990, Aimee

Hodges was the first female to direct the Naval Academy Foreign Affairs Conference, which was chaired by Gale, the first female faculty member to chair the conference. With the appointment of Juliane Gallina in 1992 as Brigade Commander, female midshipmen occupied all levels of leadership at the Academy.

As civilian instructors, we also noted some significant albeit subtle changes in the behavior of female midshipmen in the classroom. In the early years, many female midshipmen walked to class in pairs, remained quiet but attentive during class discussions, and tended to study and socialize with friends from same-sex sports teams—good examples of the maxim that the more in a minority (11 percent) a group is, the more reluctant are its members to stand out. These behaviors changed significantly over twenty years. Many decisions taken by the USNA administration were instrumental in encouraging integration—dispersing women into all the companies while also rooming them together within the company. Additionally, the administration developed closely matched physical requirements and other measures to put the males and females on an equal footing.

Most encouraging from our perspective is the fact that the behavior of female midshipmen in class now varies more with the level of preparedness and personality of the individual than with gender. Two factors that seem to play a key role in explaining the behavioral changes are the socialization patterns of women throughout society and the disappearance of the early opposition to women at the Academy by many male midshipmen, some company officers, and even a few men in senior administrative or faculty positions. Some female mids in the classroom still exhibit the reluctant characteristics observed generally throughout society in educational settings, but many are now often among the first midshipmen to volunteer comments and differing views during class discussions.

By the end of the 1980s, as women in the workplace became the norm rather than the exception, new generations of midshipmen entered the Academy, and female midshipmen became an increasingly accepted and expected aspect of life at the USNA. The officers and faculty had more positive and supportive attitudes—some of the officers had served in the Gulf with women who had more than proved their mettle as dependable colleagues.

Although most Americans until recently have supported the fact that women were being excluded from combat billets on physical grounds, we have never understood the justification until 1973 for not hiring female faculty. To our knowledge neither military service nor any minimum level of physical fitness was ever required of male civilian faculty. In any case, as the number of female faculty rose, the gender status of the students' professors became a largely irrelevant attribute for most midshipmen.

In the early 1990s, the Political Science Department hired its fifth female professor, making our department one of the most gender-balanced on campus with one of the largest percentages of women among U.S. political science departments. When our new junior colleague walked into class, midshipmen no longer assumed that the young woman at the head of the class was a secretary. Instead, like most uniformed officers and civilian professors, they now accept the presence of women and recognize that success at the USNA and in their future career as Navy or Marine Corps officers requires them to work well with and gain the respect of individuals from both genders and diverse ethnic backgrounds.

Some Americans have the impression that life at the USNA is rife with problems because of a few highly publicized incidents. However, the Academy, much like the rest of the Department of Defense, is at the forefront of American society in implementing rules and incentive structures designed to promote meaningful social integration and equal employment opportunities for individuals, irrespective of ethnicity or gender. Progress has not been without problems, but it has been steady.

Civilian Educators and Naval Policy Toward Women at Sea

There is probably nothing more sacred to a Navy than its combat ships. They are, in essence, the raison d'être of the U.S. Navy. Prior to 1992, women were not allowed to serve on board combat ships. This restriction caused problems as women successfully competed for and entered billets as pilots and officers serving both on land and on noncombatant ships. Although the line between combat and noncombat billets became increasingly difficult to define, the official policy regarding prohibitions against uniformed women officers and enlisted personnel serving on combat ships did not waiver for a number of years. We experienced the contradictions of this policy firsthand when we signed up in the early 1980s for the Educator at Sea Program designed to acquaint USNA civilian faculty with life at sea for naval personnel and our former students.

We were eager to take this opportunity to understand better the needs of our students for their future careers. However, the Navy's best-laid plans quickly experienced problems—our suspicion is that it had not anticipated women's responding to the offer. Prior to our departure, we were informed that we would be unable to ride naval vessels to and from Guantanamo, Cuba, because there were no ships available with accommodations for women. Arrangements were made for us to fly on military transport planes to Cuba, and the three male faculty traveled on an aircraft carrier.

Our differential and disappointing itinerary put us in Cuba several days early and turned out to be a mixed blessing when we encountered a base commander who was very supportive of women in the Navy and arranged for us to visit a number of ships prior to the arrival of our male colleagues. More important from our perspective was the Admiral's promise that we would be able to ride any ship in port at Guantanamo. This sponsorship was critical to our goal of experiencing as many different naval vessels as possible.

We toured a number of ships during our visit where we were warmly received by captains, naval officers, and enlisted personnel. The differences in terms of sophisticated equipment, operational mission, captain's command style, and crew morale were fascinating to observe. We learned a great deal about deployments at sea and the importance of summer cruises to midshipman training.

The range of reactions of naval officers to our visit, however, was the most remarkable aspect of this experience. One frigate captain, who was preparing to leave the next day for a tour in the Persian Gulf and Africa, invited us to join the cruise. Unimpressed by traditional lore about the bad luck associated with women on ships, he assured us that it would be easy to make room for us on board and that it would be an excellent experience for both us and the crew.

We tactfully declined this informal, unauthorized offer, but his hospitable reaction was in sharp contrast to the reaction of another captain of a significantly larger guided-missile cruiser when we pulled alongside. Because the sea was becoming rough, we were looking forward to getting on board quickly. The Captain was opposed to having female visitors and showed his displeasure by physically blocking Gale from stepping onto the deck from a long rope ladder. As the two of them had a face-to-face conversation at the edge of the ship, Helen remained swinging on the rope ladder below.

Gale insisted that the captain contact the base commander to verify that our visit was authorized and approved by the U.S. Navy. Initially, the captain refused to give ground, declaring that as captain he had the final say on who would board his ship. Fortunately, after conversing with the base commander by radio, this recalcitrant changed his mind and permitted us to board. He apologized and provided us with a professional and instructive tour.

These visits left us with a much better appreciation of both the range of attitudes and behaviors that our female uniformed colleagues were encountering on a daily basis, as well as the complexity of implementing change throughout the Navy, even for a seemingly benign educational program. Much like our female colleagues in uniform, we learned that the most efficient way to change stereotypic thinking is to challenge the underlying attitudes head-on.

The most important lesson learned from the varied reactions to our ship visits, however, concerned the critical role of command leadership in implementing policy changes at the fleet level. A seemingly inconsequential program intended to familiarize civilian educators with the needs of the Navy forced the military leadership to reexamine its policy. Although the Navy subsequently canceled the Educator at Sea Program for lack of funding, we nonetheless believe this vignette illustrates the importance of individuals' firmly asserting their rights, when necessary, by standing one's ground, or, as in this case, not retreating down a very long rope ladder hanging from a swaying ship at sea.

Traveling and Working Abroad

The importance of equal opportunity for all U.S. citizens in our modern armed services is communicated abroad in a myriad of ways. Most of these are unseen and rarely appreciated by the American public. The following vignettes describe Gale's experiences working with the German Defense Ministry and Helen's experiences as one of the first, if not the first, American, female employee of the Department of Defense to visit the South African Military Academy at the end of the apartheid era. These illustrate how the commitment of the U.S. military to

1. A group of cadet nurses from Keuka College report at Geneva General Hospital, c. 1944–45. Courtesy of the Geneva Historical Society, Geneva, New York. P. B. Oakley Collection.

2. Wrapping surgical dressings at Red Cross work rooms in Geneva Masonic Temple Building, c. 1944–45. Courtesy of the Geneva Historical Society, Geneva, New York. P. B. Oakley Collection.

3. Two WAFs at Sampson Air Force Base sitting on several of the 1,000 and 2,000 lb bombs stored at the base, early 1950s. Courtesy of the Geneva Historical Society, Geneva, New York. P. B. Oakley Collection.

4. A WAVE and companion land a trout from Seneca Lake waters at Geneva, New York. Courtesy of the Geneva Historical Society, Geneva, New York. P. B. Oakley Collection.

5. Blanche Van Deusen is sworn into the Women's Army Corps (WACs) on January 1, 1945 at State Armory. Courtesy of the Geneva Historical Society, Geneva, New York. P. B. Oakley Collection.

6. Mrs. Evelyn Marie Vance and Mrs. Flora MacLean take jobs as guards at Seneca Ordnance Depot during World War II. Courtesy of the Geneva Historical Society, Geneva, New York. P. B. Oakley Collection.

7. WAVES Mary E. Meyering from Rochester, New York, Helen C. Lupinski, from River-
dale, New York, and Mary Kester, from Akron, Ohio, share apples with Professor Richard
Wellington of the New York State Agricultural Experiment Station. Courtesy of the Geneva Historical Society, Geneva, New York. P. B. Oakley Collection.

8. Karen Johnson (USAF-Lt. Col.), retired from the U.S. Air Force Nurse Corps in 1992. During her twenty-year term of service, she completed her M.S. at Yale University. She is currently Vice President for Membership of the National Organization for Women (NOW). Courtesy of Karen Johnson.

9. Vietnam Women's Memorial, Washington, D.C. Courtesy of Francine D'Amico.

10. African American USO dance during World War II. Courtesy of the Geneva Historical Society, Geneva, New York. P. B. Oakley Collection.

11. U.S. Army Sgt. Harold Miner, stationed in Puerto Rico during the early days of the war and his Puerto Rican bride, c. 1944. Courtesy of the Geneva Historical Society, Geneva, New York. P. B. Oakley Collection.

12. Mrs. Irma S. Spike and son read a telegram from her husband, Lt. Clarence Spike, from somewhere in Europe, c. 1944–45. The officer was wounded on two different occasions and was awarded the Purple Heart, shown at left in photo.

13. Learning to become riveters, Arlene Forbes and Anna Illacqua are students at Geneva's War Training School, c. 1944–45. Later, many students who trained here were employed by the Andes Range Company to make airplane parts for the government. Courtesy of the Geneva Historical Society, Geneva, New York. P. B. Oakley Collection.

14. Mrs. Michael (Lee) Calabrese sews a sixth star on her service flag denoting six sons in the service. After the photo was taken, another son went into the Army.

15. Margaret (Maggie) Gee, a Chinese American WASP, in her silver wings and Santiago blue uniform. Courtesy of the Maggie Gee Collection.

16. A group of junior hostesses at Geneva's USO to entertain servicemen. Courtesy of the Geneva Historical Society, Geneva, New York. P. B. Oakley Collection.

gender equality often forces other countries to deal with issues related to professional women in their militaries.

In any discussion of the German military from an American perspective, it is necessary to highlight three factors: first, the much higher degree of public suspicion of the military based on Germany's history during the two world wars; second, the slower advancement of women in Germany in certain professions and particularly in academia; and third, the lack of career shifts between academic and policy positions. The American model of professors who go "in and out" of government and former policy makers who accept academic positions after leaving government is virtually unheard of in Germany.

For this reason, Gale's request to work at the Ministry of Defense (MOD) during her year (1984/85)—sponsored by the Robert Bosch Foundation in Germany for fifteen young American "leaders" on the issues on which she had written fairly extensively—met initially with rejection. A foreign professor within the walls of the Defense Ministry, even one from a military academy? Impossible! The position was saved only by the defense minister himself, whom Gale coincidentally had interviewed at a much more junior level. But when she showed up at the assigned office miles away from the ministry, there was open-jawed amazement that the professor was a female. In the end, whatever opposition there had been was not in the least evident as the relationship proved mutually beneficial to the research efforts of Gale and the MOD office.

In fact, Germany's history has also produced another interesting twist. Unlike the United States, where women's groups largely initiated and supported the introduction of women into the military, German women generally have been opposed. Those on the left argue that the military is a necessary evil and that female participation would be a step back for the country. The more conservative women argue that women should stay at home (*Küche, Kirche, und Kinder*). Only the small liberal free-market party has supported women in the military. Despite the lack of political, particularly female, support, in the early 1980s military interest in allowing volunteer women to serve arose for a quite pragmatic reason: predictions of a precipitous decline in the availability of sufficient numbers of men to serve. Among other projects during her four months at the ministry, Gale was given access to considerable data on the issue of women in the military, as well as other issues, and she found her time there fascinating.

Helen's visit to the South Africa Military Academy at Saldanha Bay in 1992 occurred at a time when U.S.–South African diplomatic relations were increasingly contentious. Helen had been advised that there was a chance that her visa application for a research trip might not be approved by South Africa. Thus, she was somewhat surprised when the naval attaché in Washington called and invited her to tour the South Africa Military Academy during her stay in Cape Town.

Helen accepted this invitation and visited during an exceptionally tense time in the political negotiations in South Africa. The African National Congress had walked out of the negotiations for a transitional government and was sponsoring protests and strikes against intransigence and backsliding by the government negotiators. Although most believed the negotiations would eventually resume, many South Africans were voicing long-held concerns about whether time would run out for a negotiated settlement.

During the car ride to Saldanha Bay with a South African Defense Force (SADF) colonel, the conversation turned to the similarities between the South African and U.S. militaries in Angola and Vietnam, respectively. The colonel suggested that in both conflicts the minority of soldiers who actually saw combat had paid a heavy personal price while having to live in a society where a majority of citizens no longer supported the war effort. He noted repeatedly that he had found this to be an important, common bond in his interactions with career U.S. military personnel in Angola.

Unlike the U.S. Naval Academy, where both civilian and officer faculty are expected to make contributions to the mission of the Academy and their local communities, the military officers working at Saldanha Bay led a rather solitary life during the apartheid era. Civilian instructors, including a few women professors who taught at Saldanha Bay, commuted from Stellenbosch University a few times a week to teach specific courses and were not involved in academy life beyond the classroom. The military instructors and officers at Saldanha Bay during the sanctions era knew little about recent changes in the American military and society. Helen's South African colleagues were especially interested in hearing about the U.S. experience integrating women and minorities at the service academies and throughout various DOD commands. They were also surprised to learn about the large number of civilian instructors, particularly women, who taught at the USNA.

During a formal luncheon ceremony held in honor of Helen's visit, the commandant, who was not very fluent in English, seemed to relax after making a formal speech by calling for a toast to mark the first visit to Saldanha Bay by a female employee of the U.S. military. With the formalities over, Helen listened to some good-natured kidding about the sorry state of the modern military in which wives and daughters were invading even the most sacred male bastions. This seemingly inconsequential visit appears to have entered the local lore among career officers in the former SADF who remained in the military after the 1994 election. On subsequent visits to South Africa, Helen continued to run into military officers whom she had met during the visit or who had heard about her visit.

Addressing the Issues

Although they were in positions to evaluate the issues confronting women at the U.S. Naval Academy and in the national and even international community at large, both Helen and Gale found it difficult to address problems at the Academy whether based on tradition, legislation, or lack of access to decision- and policy-making processes. In the first few years, we eagerly participated and helped form the female Faculty, Officers, and Midshipmen Group with the objective of providing support to the female mids. Unfortunately, the female mids had enough problems with being singled out by the press and others; they never showed up for the meetings. They wanted—even needed—to integrate to succeed, and the attention of such a meeting contradicted that objective. The group dissolved quickly.

Helen and Gale had also anticipated female mids would confide in them when confronting difficulties. This turned out not the case. To the contrary, the USNA authorities and role models initially presented to the female mids were male warriors, and it was clear that not only did civilians not fit those models, female civilians definitely did not. We certainly understood the impulse not to confide.

Helen became involved in other efforts to input some of the concerns many faculty had with regard to women and minority integration. She chaired one of the committees on academic affairs for the first internal study designed to determine the reasons for higher rates of attrition among African American midshipmen, worked on the Mid-Atlantic Self-Study for accreditation, and served on the Admissions Board. Gale became involved in the midshipmen study trip to Germany, making sure that women were included, and she also tried to encourage women to participate in the Naval Academy Foreign Affairs Conference.

As the novelty of female midshipmen subsided and as more senior female officers came to the Academy to serve in officer and faculty billets, female and male officers increasingly served as credible role models for midshipmen. The current prevailing norm communicated to midshipmen by our uniformed colleagues is that a successful naval career officer and effective military leader is an individual able to earn the respect of men and women from diverse backgrounds in her or his command. In recent years, the Academy has also benefited from the participation of naval officers who have had classmates of both genders during their period at the Academy. Finally, there have been a number of internal studies that have sought to diagnose and address the problems of female and minority midshipmen.

Gale also worked outside the Academy as the first vice president and later president (1996–) of Women in International Security (WIIS; pronounced "wise"), an organization dedicated to encouraging more women to enter national security–related professions and enhancing career opportunities for women in international security jobs worldwide. Gale founded and then chaired the first seven years of the WIIS Summer Symposium for Graduate Students, which has tried to encourage female graduate students in the United States and other countries to enter occupations related to international security. With almost one thousand women and men members and the names of more than five thousand women in a data bank from which conference organizers and employers draw, WIIS has become an important vehicle for showcasing and promoting women in international relations. Helen and Gale have brought a number of naval officers and DOD civilians into the organization and introduced midshipmen as well to WIIS.

WIIS represents the collective beliefs held by most successful female professionals currently working in international security–related careers that young women still need access to information, mentors and role models, alternative networks, and opportunities in order to prove that they can and should be judged on performance and aptitude rather than gender.

There is no doubt that there has been progress at the Academy. The appointment of the first female secretary of state and the first female three-star Marine Corps general are proof that women are starting to gain recognition in the military, national security, and foreign affairs. However, the number of women who have managed to break through the glass ceiling and who are now working at the upper levels of public and private organizations involved in international security affairs remains modest. A recent high-level international conference of national security experts with more than 15 percent female attendees had only one female speaker out of thirty-four speakers. This gender imbalance was yet another reminder that women professionals in and out of uniform have not yet achieved the goal of equal access to high-status activities or recognition for their achievements.

Conclusion

Our parallel autobiographical sketches suggest some remarkable similarities in our early socialization as daughters of career U.S. Army officers stationed in Germany after World War II. Our early familiarity with the norms of the military profession and family life abroad meant that the transition from a civilian to a military college environment was a relatively easy one for both of us. However, these life histories also reveal substantial variation in terms of personal and professional careers.

Our sometimes humorous combined experiences in "bridging gaps" in the classroom, with colleagues at USNA and with foreign military officers, document some of the remarkable changes in perceptions of women, opportunities for women, and gender interactions that have occurred. We believe our parallel experiences in the United States and abroad over almost twenty years support the idea that gender integration in the U.S. military is important for challenging outmoded practices and norms of behavior worldwide. We also believe that our experiences at the USNA and elsewhere support conventional wisdom about the critical role of leadership in promoting change in hierarchical organizations. We have witnessed firsthand that for social change to be effective, full commitment and support of leaders both at the top and in field positions are required. Conversely, most of the gender-related problems and "scandals" at the Academy in recent years can ultimately be traced to command management failures at varying levels in the formal chain of authority.

Notwithstanding some of the remarkable changes that have taken place in recent years as women have become accepted in the brigade and as respected members of the faculty, it is clear that the Academy, like the wider U.S. Navy and American military, has not yet achieved total gender integration. Problems continue that may not be remediable, given the fact that female midshipmen remain a distinct and highly visible minority within the Brigade. A hiring freeze on new civilian faculty limits the number of civilian women and men who can be hired in coming years. More informal societal norms continue also to limit the number of military and civilian women working in top administrative positions. Undoubtedly, some constraints will change as societal norms change in the direction of promoting greater gender equality. However, efforts by the U.S. military to implement standards that promote equal opportunity for men and women of diverse backgrounds in the United States and abroad will be a gradual, cumulative process involving thousands of Americans, including civilian, female professionals.

Eight

Volunteer Services and Advocacy Groups

Francine D'Amico

Countless women have volunteered in civilian organizations that provide the military with vital support services, and many others participate in advocacy groups for women in the services, women veterans, and military wives. This chapter describes some of the organizations, and advocacy groups, and programs related to military service and highlights two: Judith Youngman writes on the history of the Defense Advisory Committee on Women in the Services (DACOW-ITS), and Judith Lawrence Bellafaire describes the activities of Women in Military Service to America (WIMSA). A brief list of related groups and organizations appears in the appendix.

Organized support for the U.S. military from women on the home front and at or near the battlefield has a long history. Since the Civil War, many women have volunteered with the American Red Cross, founded by Clara Barton (see chapter 1). For the doughboys of World War I, there were "doughnut dollies" at train stations and other points of embarkation, serving coffee and doughnuts and distributing care packages. These civilian women and those who rolled bandages, knitted, baked, wrote letters, cared for wounded soldiers, performed civil defense drills, and organized scrap drives also served.[1] During World War II, women staffed Red Cross clubs and clubmobiles, volunteered in stateside hospitals and recreation centers, shipped food to American and Allied POWs, and packed bandages and comfort items for troops and war refugees.[2] Besides its well-known nursing service, the Red Cross also provided a blood donor service and communication services linking soldiers and their families.[3]

Women also participated in civilian organizations under the umbrella of the United Service Organizations (USO), which formed in 1941 to coordinate the efforts of the Young Men's Christian Association (YMCA), the Young Women's Christian Association (YWCA), the National Catholic Community Service, the National Jewish Welfare Board, the Travelers Aid Association, and the Salvation Army. More than three thousand USO clubs operated during World War II to provide a "home away from home" for service personnel on leave in the United States and overseas, and USO road shows traveled around the world to provide entertainment respites from the war.[4] The USO continues to provide these services today.

Other civilian organizations in which women served during World War II include the Public Health Service (PHS) and the Cadet Nurse Corps (CNC). PHS nurses served with the Coast Guard, in civilian hospitals, and at Japanese-American "relocation" camps. The PHS administered the CDC program, which paid for tuition, fees, uniforms, and a monthly stipend to nursing students in exchange for service in military or veterans hospitals or other federal facilities. More than 124,000 nurses, including 3,000 African Americans, graduated from the CDC program between 1943 and 1948.[5]

Besides nurses, other health care specialists, including dietitians and physical therapists, served in the Army Medical Department "as civil service employees even before the United States entered World War I" and were not given temporary military rank until 1943; they, along with occupational therapists, finally received permanent military status in 1944.[6] The many ways women attempt to heal the wounds of war require further investigation and documentation.

The skills of women pilots were first put to use during World War II. Nancy Harkness Love directed the Women's Auxiliary Ferrying Squadron (WAFS) of the Army Air Transport Command, a program in which experienced pilots ferried new aircraft, weapons, supplies, and personnel to military installations. Jacqueline Cochran designed the women's flight-training program, in which pilots learned to tow targets for antiaircraft gunner trainees and pilots in pursuit aircraft or became instructor pilots themselves. The two programs were merged on 5 August 1943, to form the Women's Airforce Service Pilots (WASP). More than one thousand WASP members flew before the organization was disbanded on 20 December 1944; thirty-eight died in air fatalities. Although the WASP performed services for the military, it was officially a civil, not a military, service. However, in 1949, many of its former members were offered commissions in the U.S. Army and Air Force Reserves; some of these reservists were called to active duty during the Korean conflict. In November 1977, Congress conferred veteran status on all other former members of the WASP.[7]

NOTES

1. See Dorothy Schneider and Carl J. Schneider, *Into the Breach: American Women Overseas in World War I* (New York: Viking, 1991), and Lettie Gavin, *American Women in World War I: They Also Served* (Niwot: University of Colorado Press, 1997).

2. Judith Lawrence Bellafaire, "We Also Served," in *In Defense of a Nation: Servicewomen in World War II*, ed. Jeanne M. Holm (Washington, D.C.: Military Women's Press, 1998), 135–37.

3. Ibid., 138.

4. Ibid., 138–40.

5. Ibid., 140–43.

6. Ann M. Ritchie Hartwick, "Army Dietitians, Physical Therapists, and Occupational Therapists," in Holm, *In Defense of a Nation,* 123–32.

7. Yvonne C. Pateman, "Women Airforce Service Pilots: WASP," in Holm, *In Defense of a Nation,* 111–21.

Defense Advisory Committee on Women in the Services (DACOWITS)

Judith Youngman

It was 1951. The United States was embroiled in the Korean War. Once again, the need was great for additional sources of military personnel. Retired General George C. Marshall, the Secretary of Defense, personally invited fifty civilian women to meet with him in Washington. Assistant Secretary of Defense for Manpower, Personnel, and Reserves Anna Rosenberg served as chair for this group of women representing business, education, civic organizations, and a variety of geographical locations. Their mission? To advise the Secretary of Defense on how to recruit more women for the armed forces, increase their retention rates, and better utilize their capabilities. The group organized that November was the Defense Advisory Committee on Women in the Services (DACOWITS). Five DACOWITS working groups were established: Training and Education; Housing and Welfare; Utilization and Career Planning; Health and Nutrition; and Recruiting and Public Information.

During its first year, DACOWITS made fifteen official recommendations to the Secretary. A unified recruiting program initiated nationwide succeeded in attracting many women into the service of their country (see chapter 2). DACOWITS field trips to military installations were initiated in this first year.

In its forty-sixth year, 1997, DACOWITS was made up of thirty-five women and men from diverse geographical locations representing the professions of medicine, education, law, business, the military, and community service. The committee was divided into three subcommittees: Equality Management; Forces Development and Utilization; and Quality of Life. It worked directly with the Assistant Secretary of Defense for Force Management Policy. During the year, DACOWITS issued six official recommendations to the Secretary and visited fifty-nine installations in the United States and eighteen installations overseas during the Executive Committee's trip to WESTPAC. At the request of Secretary of Defense William J. Perry, DACOWITS also initiated visits to training installations.

By 1997, DACOWITS envisioned an America where our daughters would have the same opportunities to serve the nation as our sons and where full partnership between our women and men would strengthen the power of America's military to guarantee our nation's freedom.

Between 1951 and 1997, the DACOWITS had become more targeted in policy focus, more public in activities and decisionmaking, and more representative in membership. But some things had not changed. DACOWITS continued to serve as another set of eyes and ears in the field and the fleet for the Secretary of Defense, and to represent the perceptions and priorities of military women to the senior civilian and uniformed leadership of the armed forces. Most of all, DACOWITS never wavered from its original mandate from Secretary of Defense Marshall: to strengthen the national defense and to pursue optimal mission readiness through better recruitment, retention, and utilization of military women.

DACOWITS Process

DACOWITS remains a highly visible advisory committee within the Office of the Secretary of Defense. Chartered biannually by Congress under the Federal Advisory Committee Act (FACA), its processes are transparent and its deliberations are open to the public. The DACOWITS primary mandate is to listen without agenda to the troops in the field and the fleet and to report back directly to the Secretary of Defense on any issues that concern service members. DACOWITS also provides feedback from the field and the fleet on how departmental policies and actions affect military women, the gender-integrated military, and military readiness, and, when appropriate, recommends policy objectives for the Secretary's or services' consideration. Both DACOWITS functions are founded upon the same process: DACOWITS installation visits, first initiated in 1951.

Every year, members of DACOWITS conduct visits to military installations to meet in small groups with service members of all ranks. In 1997, for example, DACOWITS members met with more than 6,600 service members at seventy-seven installations and vessels in the continental United States (CONUS) and overseas. Although the travel costs of the overseas trips are funded by the Department of Defense, DACOWITS members bear the cost of all CONUS installation visits themselves. Visits are conducted with active-duty troops of all five services and their reserve components, as well as at ROTC units and service schools and training bases.

A single protocol is followed for installation visits. Installation selection is a collaborative process between the DACOWITS member, the DACOWITS office in the Office of the Secretary of Defense, and the services. Visits typically last one day and include inbriefs and outbriefs with installation commanding officers, and focus groups with both women and men, as well as enlisted and officer personnel. Usually, focus groups are segregated by gender and rank, such that separate groups are held with E1–E3, E4–E6, E7–E9, O1–O3, and O4–O6 personnel. DACOWITS requests that service members either volunteer or be randomly selected for the focus groups. A video about DACOWITS with a message from the Secretary of Defense discussing the DACOWITS visit is shown to service personnel before the DACOWITS member arrives.

During a focus group, the DACOWITS member asks open-ended questions to generate discussion, such as, "If you had five minutes with the Secretary of Defense, what would you want to tell him?" The DACOWITS member promises confidentiality and nonretribution for participation in group discussions. Only the DACOWITS member and focus group members are allowed in the room. The DACOWITS member records what is discussed simply by taking notes. Following a focus group, the installation commanding officer is fully briefed by the DACOWITS member on the general issues raised.

After an installation visit, the DACOWITS member forwards written notes to the DACOWITS office for transmittal to the service hosting the visit. The DACOWITS chair and the coordinator of installation visits also review the DACOWITS member's notes in order to track and monitor the policy issues raised during the visit. Four times a year, information received from installations is summarized and shared with all DACOWITS members and the public. The coordinator orally briefs attendees of the DACOWITS spring and fall meetings on the major issues raised in installation visits during the previous six months. A written Overseas Installation Visit Report and an Annual CONUS Installation Visit Report are submitted to the Secretary of Defense in September and January, respectively.

The DACOWITS Executive Committee is the first to review the annual CONUS Installation Visits Report; this is done in February during the first of two annual meetings. The issues raised by service members in the field and the fleet help DACOWITS define its vision and goals for the year. During the fall Executive Committee meeting, members also review issues raised during the summer overseas trip. Occasionally, the Secretary of Defense may ask DACOWITS to make a certain type of issue a priority in its goals and deliberations, for example, quality of life.

Issues raised by service members in the field and the fleet are discussed with the services, reviewed, and assessed during subcommittee meetings at the spring and fall meetings. The subcommittees may recommend that DACOWITS make an official recommendation on an issue; they may request more information from the services or the Department of Defense; or they may recommend no action. All deliberations are open to the public. All recommendations or requests for information must be approved by DACOWITS in a public general voting session. Recommendations may be made to the services, as well as other departments throughout the Department of Defense.

DACOWITS Organization

Every Secretary of Defense has the option to modify the DACOWITS organizational structure and placement within the Office of the Secretary of Defense during the biannual congressional renewal of the DACOWITS charter. The organizational structure of DACOWITS, however, has remained relatively stable over its forty-seven year history.

DACOWITS's mission is to provide the Secretary of Defense, through the Assistant Secretary of Defense for Force Management Policy, advice and recommendations on matters and policies relating to women in the armed forces. To accomplish this mission, DACOWITS remains organizationally within the Office of the Secretary of Defense. It is headed by a chair selected annually by the Secretary from third-year DACOWITS members. Each year, the Secretary selects ten to fourteen new DACOWITS members from nominations forwarded by the White House, members of Congress, the services, the Chairman and Vice Chairman of the Joint Chiefs, and third-year DACOWITS members. Selections of members annually are made to ensure demographic diversity of the membership. DACOWITS also includes four ex officio members: the Assistant Secretary of Defense for Reserve Affairs; the Deputy Assistant Secretary of Defense for Military Personnel Policy; the Deputy Assistant Secretary of Defense for Equal Opportunity; and the Deputy Assistant Secretary of Defense for Personnel Support, Families, and Education.

Each of the service branches and reserve components also designates commissioned and noncommissioned officer Military Representatives and Military Liaisons to the committee. Their roles are to provide advice and counsel to committee members during the members' assessments of issues and decisionmaking on requests for additional information and recommendations. The military representatives and liaisons do not vote on DACOWITS decisions, but their technical expertise is critical to the committee's success.

The DACOWITS chair annually recommends persons for membership on the Executive Committee to the secretary for consideration. The Executive Committee in 1998 comprises a vice chair, coordinator of installation visits, and chairs and vice chairs of the three DACOWITS subcommittees. The eight-person Executive Committee is drawn from second- and third-year DACOWITS members and is also demographically diverse. Its functions are to develop annual goals, to set meeting agendas, and to chair subcommittee meetings. Executive Committee members also undertake an annual two-week visit to overseas military installations. The DACOWITS Executive Committee typically meets quarterly in Washington, D.C.

Administrative, technical, and advisory support to DACOWITS is provided by a military staff in the Office of the Secretary of Defense that also serves as the women's policy staff for the OSD. This staff of officer and enlisted women and men includes a representative from each of the services and is headed by the Military Director, DACOWITS and Military Women Matters.

DACOWITS Recommendations and Influence

During its forty-seven-year history, DACOWITS has remained an unfailing advocate for military women and the critical roles that they play in the nation's defense. The issues DACOWITS has addressed and its recommendations have echoed the same themes for nearly fifty years:

- The nation's defense is strongest when military women have opportunities to serve as full partners with military men.
- Full partnership depends upon women having opportunities to serve that are commensurate with their abilities, not based upon preconceived or popularly held notions of "women's roles."
- Full partnership also requires the availability of support systems essential to individual readiness, such as adequate women's health care.
- Full partnership depends upon respect for women in uniform and for their service as soldiers, sailors, and aviators in the nation's defense because respect within the ranks underlies unit cohesion, morale, and good order and discipline.

Consistent with these themes, DACOWITS recommendations over the years have included opening new jobs to women by lifting the 2 percent limitation on representation of women in the armed forces, lifting promotion ceilings, and opening to women the service academies and ROTC programs as well as operational positions in aviation, combat aviation, combat support fields, combat ships, engineering, intelligence, and many other career fields. The expansion of career opportunities for military women since 1948 reflects a dynamic between military women's success in the field and the fleet, the need for recruits with women's abilities and capabilities, and constant pressure and attention from DACOWITS and other supporters of an expanded role for military women. Most recently, DACOWITS has recommended the design of all new vessels to house gender-integrated crews, including submarines, and the opening of new field artillery weapons systems to women as well.

DACOWITS also has been continuously concerned that women receive not only promotions in rank but career opportunities and development necessary to position them for leadership in all branches and career specialties open to women. DACOWITS has been vigilant in identifying leadership-selection criteria unrelated to critical job needs that exclude women from leadership roles in the armed forces, such as qualifications to command military hospitals and the nomination and selection processes for command sergeant majors in the Army.

Working in an environment that enables every service member to contribute to the best of his or her abilities is critical to a strong national defense. Eliminating harassment, discrimination, and retaliation in the military have topped issues raised by military women, and the DACOWITS issue agenda, for years because harassment, discrimination, and retaliation undermine the unit cohesion and good order and discipline essential for mission readiness. Sexual-harassment-prevention programs, informal dispute-resolution procedures, and core values and leadership training are all initiatives recommended by DACOWITS to ensure that military climates and cultures are based upon respect for all service members.

Since its inception, DACOWITS has continuously recommended improved support services for military women. As new positions have opened to women in new branches and career fields, and as the percentage of service members who are women has increased from 2 to nearly 15 percent, DACOWITS has responded to the concerns of service women on quality of life by pressing for adequate housing for women and their dependents, access to specialized women's health care, victim-assistance programs, child-care availability, recreational activities available to women, and just plain combat boots and uniforms that fit. Many of the DACOWITS quality-of-life initiatives have equally benefited all service members, such as recommendations on child care, dental care, housing, and compensation. Finally, when needed, DACOWITS also takes to the road to help the armed forces recruit more women during national security crises, as originally for the Korean conflict as well as for Vietnam.

But throughout its history, DACOWITS has performed two roles that no other advisory committee in the Department of Defense has performed. DACOWITS has ensured that the senior civilian and uniformed leadership of the armed forces, as well as members of Congress, have heard the voices of military women, no matter how few or junior they might be. DACOWITS has also worked to ensure that military women have the respect, the opportunities, and the support services that they need to work to the utmost of their abilities in the nation's defense. As another set of eyes and ears for the Secretary of Defense in the field and the fleet, DACOWITS has consistently ensured that even the most junior service members are heard by the Secretary.

DACOWITS: Prospects

With many more positions in the armed forces now open to women, critics of military women and the gender-integrated military are declaring that DACOWITS has outlived its usefulness. But exactly the opposite may be true.

Women are still excluded from key jobs in all of the services and have yet to rise to senior leadership positions in either the commissioned or noncommissioned officer corps. Even the representation of women among the senior civilian leadership of the Department of Defense is sporadic at best. The recruitment of larger percentages of women in recent years challenges the armed forces to respond with sufficient career opportunities and support services to retain the best military women. Most military women work daily in units in which they are a small minority, and where more-senior service members are hesitant to mentor them for fear of perceptions.

In this environment, DACOWITS remains the only organization or group within the Department of Defense or U.S. government that constantly listens to women service members and transmits what it hears to the Secretary of Defense. Its meetings, where issues are openly debated and discussed, are open to all military personnel and the public, and serve as a unique forum for information and experience sharing by the services as well as military women.

But most important, DACOWITS serves as an unfailing advocate for military women consistent with the needs of mission readiness and a strong national defense, without regard for the popularity or unpopularity of its recommendations. The message that DACOWITS advocates has changed little in nearly fifty years. The gender-integrated military is the result of a century of steady progress in a single direction for our armed forces. Every citizen willing to serve the nation as an active patriot in uniform is necessary to maintain a strong national defense. Women in uniform have proven their dedication and ability to meet national defense challenges during war and in peacetime. They have done so by working side by side with men in uniform for nearly one hundred years. Throughout the twentieth century, the increasing gender integration of the armed forces and expanded roles for women have contributed to the ability of the armed forces to maintain well-trained forces capable of meeting the challenges of downsizing, war, new missions, heightened operational tempos, and career uncertainty without flinching.

In recent years, the armed forces have met drawdown and budgetary challenges without sacrificing the readiness of our forces and military capabilities. America's armed forces remain the best in the world. The gender-integrated military—and military women—are part of that success story.

Women in Military Service for America Memorial Foundation, Inc. (WIMSA)

Judith Lawrence Bellafaire

The Women in Military Service for America Memorial Foundation, Inc. (WIMSA) is a nonprofit foundation dedicated to honoring women who served with and in the American military from the founding of the nation through to the present. WIMSA's goal is to make the historic contributions of servicewomen a visible part of our national heritage and to inspire others to emulate, follow, and surpass them. To do this, the Foundation collects, preserves, and displays at the Memorial materials relating to military women. In addition, the Foundation disseminates information about women's military contributions through the publication of a variety of historical materials.

The Memorial is located at the main entrance to Arlington National Cemetery. It includes an exhibit gallery, an interactive computer register, the Hall of Honor, a gift shop, and a theater for special events. The Foundation also maintains an off-site research center and archives that are open to researchers by appointment.

The Memorial, opened in October 1997, is the result of almost ten years of planning and work by Foundation President Brigadier General Wilma L. Vaught (USAF, retired), the Board of Directors, and the Foundation staff.

The Creation of the Women's Memorial

In the fall of 1982 the American Veterans Committee (AVC), a national organization of veterans of the United States armed forces who served in World War I, World War II, the Korean War, and the Vietnam War, approved an initiative to launch a national project to establish a memorial in the nation's capital to honor women who have served in defense of the country. The AVC National Board set up the Women Veterans Memorial Committee, key members of which included June Willenz, the Executive Director of the AVC and author of *Women Veterans: America's Forgotten Heroines*, and Ralph Spencer, Vice Chairman of the AVC.[1]

In a separate initiative in May 1985, Congresswoman Mary Rose Oakar, Chairperson of the House Subcommittee on Libraries and Memorials, introduced legislation for a memorial to recognize the contributions of women in military service. Oakar held a series of hearings on the issue and spoke on behalf of the proposed legislation before a Senate committee that had initially voted against the proposal. The Secretary of the Interior expressed some reservations about the proposed memorial, as did the National Park Service. They believed that other monuments being planned—the Vietnam Women Veterans Memorial and the Navy Memorial, both to include women—would make another women's memorial duplicative. After further, persuasive testimony by AVC officials, distinguished women veterans, and active-duty officers, the National Capital Memorial Commission unanimously voted in favor of the proposal. The Secretary of the Interior then withdrew his opposition to the project.[2]

AVC monitored the legislation's circuitous route through Congress and actively lobbied on its behalf. AVC also provided a clearinghouse of information and advice about the progress of the legislation to women veterans, interested organizations, and the media. In 1985, AVC's attorney drew up articles of incorporation for the Women in Military Service for America Memorial Foundation, Inc., and filed them in the District of Columbia.[3]

In late fall 1986, the House and Senate both unanimously passed the bill, which was signed into law by President Ronald Reagan on 6 November (Public Law 99–610). The Women in Military Service for America Memorial Foundation was authorized to establish the memorial on federal lands in Washington, D.C., or its environs to honor women who have served with and in the U.S. armed forces.[4]

On 17 December 1986, AVC convened an organizational meeting and invited a group of distinguished military and civilian women to participate on the Foundation's Board of Directors. Brigadier General Wilma L. Vaught (USAF, retired); Lieutenant Colonel Yvonne C. Pateman (USAF, retired); Colonel Bettie Morden (USA, retired); Mrs. Ilse Whittemore; and Ms. June Willenz agreed to serve. Vaught was elected Foundation President in March 1987.[5]

The National Park Service assisted the Foundation in identifying potential sites for the Memorial within the national capital area, many in isolated areas far from other monuments. At the conclusion of a guided tour of the sites, the Park Service official drove by the old ceremonial gateway to Arlington National Cemetery, whose 270–foot neoclassical hemicycle is on an axis with the Lincoln Memorial. Vaught asked the purpose of the structure and commented that it seemed to be neglected and incomplete. The official gave her a brief history of the structure.[6]

The hemicycle, dedicated in 1931, was built as the ceremonial entrance to Arlington National Cemetery. In 1938, the National Commission on Fine Arts decided that it interfered with the view from Arlington House to Memorial Bridge. The commissioners attempted to lessen its impact with ivy, and the hemicycle slowly fell into disrepair.[7] The Foundation believed that the main-gate structure could be preserved and restored, and would find new meaning as a part of a new memorial. Initially, Park Service personnel warned of the substantial cost of restoration, but Foundation directors believed that restoration would bring back a piece of the country's lost history. And what better place could there be to acquaint the public with the "lost history" of women's military contributions? The Park Service decided to support the Foundation's request for the site.[8]

Within six weeks, the Foundation secured approval of its site choice from the National Capital Memorial Commission, the Commission on Fine Arts, and the National Capital Planning Commission. Final approval came on 28 July 1988.[9]

In December 1988, the criteria for the selection of a winning design for the Memorial were approved by the National Capital Memorial Commission. It was deemed imperative that the "view lines" be maintained from Memorial Bridge to Arlington National Cemetery and from Arlington House to the Kennedy grave site. The new memorial would have to blend harmoniously with the memorials already in place nearby. The Foundation also wanted to give the Memorial gateway the civic presence originally intended and to create an image to which servicewomen could relate.[10]

The design competition was open to all American citizens. A panel of nine judges, consisting of women veterans and distinguished architects and designers, was selected to oversee its first phase. More than 130 registrants sent in designs, and in June 1989 the submissions were reviewed. Four top contenders were selected and invited to participate in phase two of the competition.

The three finalists were the architectural firms of Weiss/Manfredi of New York City; Norton, Harp and Associates of Tybee Island, Georgia, and New York City; and Galford and Antonis of Philadelphia. A fourth design, by the firm of Seigel and Derwent of Chicago, received an honorable mention, and its creators were invited to continue in the competition.[11]

The reviewers gave each of the final four designs a nickname. "The Candles" included glass spires attached to the hemicycle wall. "The Grove" consisted of sculptured bronze trees on top of a glass floor. The central feature of "the Spiral" was a shallow outdoor bowl in a unique spiral form. The "Beaux Arts" placed the education center behind the hemicycle wall, unifying the entire site with a classical, symmetrical plan.[12]

In September, the National Endowment for the Arts announced a $50,000 grant to the Foundation to support the second stage of the design competition, in which the four finalists refined their designs. That stage was judged by six distinguished reviewers, several of whom had participated in the first stage. In November, the Foundation announced the winner of the competition: "The Candles," designed by Marion Gail Weiss and Michael Manfredi. It featured ten tall glass spires whose inner lights would glow softly at night. During the day, the spires would serve as skylights above the rooms of the education center, to be built immediately behind the restored hemicycle wall. Four sets of stairs would ascend through the blank niches of the hemicycle to the upper level of the structure, symbolizing the passage of servicewomen through the barriers that have existed for them in the military.[13]

The National Capital Memorial Commission had reservations about two critical elements of the Weiss/Manfredi design. It deemed the glass spires incompatible with the other structures already within the Memorial corridor; light from the spires would diminish the visibility of the Kennedy flame. And, the commission questioned the necessity of breaking into the wall of the historic hemicycle to build the four stair ways. During the redesign, Weiss and Manfredi replaced the spires with a skylight to be made of clear glass tablets. The tablets would be inscribed with quotations by or about military women throughout the centuries that would be reflected onto the inner marble wall of the Memorial as the sun passed overhead.[14]

The revised design was approved by the following reviewing bodies and agencies: the National Park Service, the National Capital Memorial Commission, the National Capital Planning Commission, the Advisory Council for Historical Preservation, the District of Columbia Historic Preservation Office, the Virginia State Historical Preservation Office, and the Commission on Fine Arts.[15]

The Foundation now launched an enormous fund-raising campaign. It received early, generous contributions from AT&T, General Motors, Continental Airlines, and others.[16] Sales of commemorative coins produced by the U.S. Mint netted more than $3 million.[17] Thirty state legislatures, responding to a foundation initiative, by mid-1997 voted to contribute.[18] In November 1993, Congress enacted legislation that included a federal grant of $9,538,000 to be used solely for the repair, restoration, and preservation of the main gate structures, center plaza, and hemicycle wall (more than 40 percent of the cost of construction for the entire project).[19]

In 1995, the Foundation obtained a $2.3 million line of credit to meet the total needed to start construction. The groundbreaking ceremony was held 22 June 1995.[20]

In January 1996, Clark Construction Group of Bethesda, Maryland, was selected as the general contractor. Contractors restored the hemicycle wall, excavated behind it, and built the Memorial's education center. The Memorial was opened on 18 October 1997, during a four-day gala dedication celebration packed with special events and attended by approximately thirty thousand people.

Current Activities of the Women Veterans Memorial Foundation

Visitors to the Women Veterans Memorial see a series of thematic exhibits that tell the story of women's contributions to the American military over time. They may also use the computerized register to access the individual stories of thousands of the 1.8 million women who have served or are serving in defense of our nation. Each entry in the register contains an individual woman's name, her record of service, a photograph of her in uniform, and a short story relating her most memorable military experiences, if provided.

The public may also visit the Hall of Honor, which lists the names of women who died in the line of duty. Until the advent of the Women Veterans Memorial, no single central depository compiled records of female casualties, and many records have been scattered and lost over time. For this reason, the rolls of names are constantly being revised as research slowly uncovers more information about these women. The process of registering military women is ongoing. If you or someone you know would like to register with the Memorial, contact the WIMSA office (see appendix).

To increase the American public's knowledge and awareness of the contributions of women to the country's military history, the Foundation has established the Military Women's Press, which publishes scholarly manuscripts pertaining to the history of women in the military. The Foundation supplies researchers with topical bibliographies upon request and continues to expand its archive collections of official documents, photographs, memoirs, scrapbooks, and letters written by military women, and books and articles written about military women. The Foundation also collects and preserves uniforms and military-issue items worn and used by military women. To visit the archives or to donate items to the Memorial, call (703) 533–1155.

NOTES

1. Statement by the American Veterans Committee before the National Capital Memorial Advisory Committee on a proposal to set aside public lands in the District of Columbia for a memorial to honor the women who served in the Armed Forces, November 14, 1985, History of the Memorial File, WIMSA Archives; Statement of the American Veterans Committee before the Subcommittee on Public Lands of the Senate Committee on Energy and Natural Resources on S.J. Resolution 156 to establish a memorial in the District of Columbia to honor women who served in the Armed Forces, October 29, 1985, History of the Memorial File, WIMSA Archives; see June A. Willenz, *Women Veterans: America's Forgotten Heroines* (New York: Continuum, 1983).

2. *Register,* quarterly newsletter of the Women in Military Service for America Memorial Foundation, fall 1988, 5; Memorandum from Director, National Park Service to Legislative Counsel dated December 20, 1985, Subject: S.J. Res. 156—Women in the Armed Forces Memorial, History of the Memorial File, WIMSA Archives.

3. Statement by the AVC, November 14, 1985, and Summary of AVC Activities on Behalf of the Women in Military Service for America Memorial, 1982–1986, History of the Memorial File, WIMSA Archives.

4. Public Law 99–610 Joint Resolution, *Congressional Record,* 4, 6 November 1986, vol. 131; and 16, 17 October 1986, vol. 132.

5. Minutes of the introductory meeting of the Women in Military Service for America Memorial Foundation, Inc., December 17, 1987, in Michael Beasley's office, Washington, D.C., History of the Memorial File, WIMSA Archives.

6. *Register,* fall 1988, 1; Marion Weiss, "Underestimated Sites" (paper presented at the Inherited Ideologies Conference), History of the Memorial File, WIMSA Archives.

7. Perry G. Fisher, "Historical and Design Issues: Memorial Avenue and the Great Entrance to Arlington National Cemetery," and Richard A. Etlin, "The Proposed Women in Military Service for America Memorial In Historical Context," reports prepared for the Women in Military Service for America Memorial Foundation, Inc., May 21, 1991, History of the Memorial File, WIMSA Archives; "Prisms Selected for Memorial Honoring Military Women," CAUS News, spring 1990, 4, History of the Memorial File, WIMSA Archives.

8. Author's conversation with Brigadier General Wilma L. Vaught, president, Women in Military Service for America Memorial Foundation, 27 June 1997, foundation offices.

9. *Register*, fall 1988, 1.

10. Weiss, ''Underestimated Sites.''

11. Oehrlein and Associates, ''Final Report: Site Investigation Report of the Memorial Gate, Arlington National Cemetery, For the Women in Military Service for America Memorial Foundation, Inc., January 19, 1989,'' 4, History of the Memorial File, WIMSA Archives; ''Competition X 3,'' exhibit script, National Building Museum, March 1990, History of the Memorial File, WIMSA Archives; *Register*, spring 1989, supplement, 1.

12. Benjamin Forgey, ''Women's Memorial Winner,'' *Washington Post*, 9 November 1989.

13. Fisher, ''Historical and Design Issues''; Etlin, ''The Proposed . . Memorial''; ''Prisms Selected,'' 4; *Register*, spring 1990, 1.

14. Weiss, ''Underestimated Sites.''

15. *Register*, fall 1992, 1.

16. *Register*, spring 1995, 1.

17. *Register*, summer 1994, 1.

18. *Register*, spring 1997, 1.

19. *Register*, spring 1994, 1.

20. *Register*, fall 1995, 1.

Part III

Outsiders
Women *and* the Military

Nine

No War without Women
Defense Industries

Joan E. Denman and Leslie Baham Inniss

Throughout history, women have been needed to provide supplies to the military in times of war. This relationship existed before the American Revolution but was especially true beginning with the Civil War. The two world wars saw the need for women's help in maintaining defense industry production. Although World War II in particular increased job opportunities for women in traditionally male-segregated positions, those advantages have not been maintained in spite of the increase of working women to more than 45 percent of the workforce by 1990.

One of the main reasons is gender discrimination. In a process that Reskin and Padavic call "construction of gendered work," women are generally segregated from men and concentrated in lower-prestige occupations.[1] The consequences of this segregation are that women have less chance for advancement and earn less income relative to men. This is especially true for women of color.

In this chapter, we briefly examine the role of women in the defense industry from the 1700s to the present. The defense industry is dependent on the activities and goals of the military and vice versa. President Dwight D. Eisenhower warned of the spread of the "military-industrial complex," and we will examine the extensiveness of this relationship and show how it depends on women's participation. As Cynthia Enloe states, "Virtually any job *can* be militarized, that is, made dependent on the military force and its goals."[2]

A Brief Background: 1700s to 1940

The American Revolution saw colonial women providing food, clothing, hats, and other items from their homes to family members who went off to fight. By the time of the Civil War, some white women were working in factories, mostly in textile mills and shoe factories. The majority of African American women, however, worked as slaves on Southern plantations, raising food and producing clothing and other items for soldiers. Contemporary accounts estimated that 300,000 more women worked for wages than would have sought jobs without the war. This increase in women workers presented its own set of problems.

For one thing, although women were now earning wages, their entrance into the labor market also brought the de-skilling of their work. Highly skilled jobs that they once may have performed at home were now broken into parts and controlled by management. For example, women who had learned sewing at home were not defined as having a skill and thus were paid less than men for the same type of job. This, the beginning of skills being gender-bound, has continued to the present day.

The nineteenth century also saw the development of the "cult of domesticity." This ideology stated that a woman's proper place was in the home, not in the paid labor force. By the beginning of the twentieth century, 40 percent of single women and girls over ten years of age were working outside the home, whereas only 6 percent of married women were employed. Beginning in 1874, states passed laws limiting the number of hours women could work and the weight amounts women could lift. By 1900, these "special protections" were widely common and limited women's ability to obtain jobs with better hours or higher wages. In addition, marriage "bars" limiting married women's employment were enacted in certain occupations.

Within ten years, women were working in the electrical and chemical industries, paper production, food processing, and metalworking. World War I brought additional opportunities to white women in an array of other occupations, where they produced bombs, grenades, firearms, and ammunition. In the glass factories, they produced optical equipment; in the leather industry, they made holsters, covers, tents, belts, and other items. In airplane plants, some were able to assemble motors and others did semiskilled work. Nearly twelve thousand African American women also found jobs, often in the same factories where white women worked, but only as cleaners and janitors. As railroad workers, African American women repaired tracks, cleaned cars, and did various yard duties.[3] With the conclusion of World War I, however, many of the job gains were lost as women, both black and white, were replaced with returning soldiers.

The years 1920–1940 saw a small increase in the labor-force participation rates of women, from 21 to 25.4 percent. World War II is usually seen as the catalyst of change in that it ended the depression and heralded the entry of great numbers of women into the workplace. In 1940, women's participation rate was more than 27 percent; nearly 12 million women were working. This increased to 37 percent or almost 19 million women working, by 1945; women constituted 36.1 percent of the civilian workforce.[4] Another change brought on by World War II was the variety of jobs women held, many of which had been traditionally "male" occupations.

World War II

World War II as a campaign of production brought extensive changes in the sexual and racial makeup of employees. The attack on Pearl Harbor cost not only many American lives but also great material losses in ships and planes. The

United States had to catch up, and women became essential to this goal as factories were converted to manufacture war materials.

By mid-1942, war industries were facing labor shortages because of men's being drafted and the expansion of the workload at the plants and shipyards. In addition, shipyards, aircraft and munitions plants, and other factories were springing up all over the country, and labor demands were not being met because of such rapid expansion.

In mid-1942, the Office of War Information (OWI) was established and, along with the War Manpower Commission and the War Advertising Council, its job was to "sell the war." Major advertising campaigns using magazine and newspaper articles, radio spots, special short films, posters, and billboards were created to encourage more men and especially women to work.

Higher wages were one of the main appeals of defense-industry jobs. Although some women applied out of patriotism, many, if not most, did so out of economic necessity. Prior to the war women and many men had been unemployed or held low-paying jobs. Jobs in defense industries might double or triple what a woman made previously. Women of color seldom attained the highest-paying jobs, but even as laborers or janitors they made considerably more than they had made in laundries and service jobs, or as domestics.

Women became associated in some way with every type of defense work. By November 1942, they made up 10 to 88 percent of the workers at many war plants. Around the nation women operated lathes and grinders, shoveled coal, ran hydraulic presses, tested bombers, mined ore, worked as guards, and produced tanks and trucks. They worked in railroad yards, lumber mills, rubber plants, glass works, and aluminum plants. Women operated heavy cranes, and performed tests on machine guns, antiaircraft guns, and other weaponry. Martin and Boeing were two of the aircraft plants that hired a few female engineers. Also, although the numbers were small, there were some women employed as chemists and others as draftsmen at shipyards.

Even as women were entering the workforce, the December 1942 census estimated there were 17 million women homemakers without children under ten, still at home and potentially available. Hence, the first major advertising effort directed at women emphasized that war work not only paid good wages but was as pleasurable and simple as operating a home sewing machine. Copy was also aimed at husbands, urging them to encourage their wives to take part, while assuring them not to fear the loss of their wives' femininity.

Maureen Honey's study found that when appeals were made involving patriotism, it was emphasized that women would be doing their part and that if they did not do their part, a soldier would die. These patriotic appeals always related to the women on personal terms, that is, they would not be helping their country but, rather, their husband, boyfriend, son, or other male relative. The whole campaign always had as its premise " 'that the woman's primary role in life was as wife and mother.' "[5]

Women did respond to the efforts of the OWI. Those who had been married and homemakers prior to Pearl Harbor now were about 25 percent of wartime-

employed women. Women who had been students accounted for about 20 percent. One-third of the homemakers found jobs in primarily war manufacturing
industries. Homemakers made up nearly 60 percent of the new workers in
agriculture.[6]

During the military buildup women almost doubled their participation rate.
In durable-manufacturing industries—ships, aircraft, steel, machinery, and cars—
1.7 million women were employed in 1944; overall, nearly 2.7 million women
worked in unskilled or semiskilled factory jobs.

By September 1943, so many women had left their poor-paying jobs as store
clerks, teachers, waitresses, and laundry and nursery workers that the government now needed to convince them that these "essential civilian" jobs, as they
were officially called, were just as vital to the nation. It is important to note that
the majority of working women did fill these "essential civilian" jobs.

Women entering the workforce held thousands of jobs that had previously
been done only by men. These occupational changes included work in shipyards,
aircraft plants, auto and electrical manufacturing, as well as in the munitions
industry, to name a few. Yet, industries had to change in order to accommodate
this influx of workers.

Shipbuilding and other heavy-industry jobs were considered as highly skilled,
and men performed these craft jobs after serving apprenticeships of three to four
years. This tradition was strongly enforced by unions, and because many West
Coast yards were closed shops, the unions objected to the hiring of women.
However, the labor shortage was so severe by November 1942 that women were
finally allowed to join the unions and be hired.

Federal funds were used to establish training programs for women and men
wishing to learn welding, riveting, drafting, sheet-metal work, and other skills.
To accommodate the vast numbers of new male and female workers, jobs were
broken into smaller tasks. Mass-production techniques were introduced, which
allowed for training in a few days or weeks for some of the simpler skills. New
workers would then be given very specific tasks, saving the more complicated or
varied tasks for the few "skilled" journeymen, all of whom were male. Thus, a
ship or airplane could be produced quickly with great numbers of people all
doing a task or two each. In addition to this training, the suspension of state
"protective" labor laws allowed women to obtain jobs on all three shifts and
carry some of the heavier equipment and materials. Occupations with marriage
"bars" suspended them for the war emergency.

The numbers of women entering shipyard work was dramatic. Only thirty-six
women were employed in the yards nationally in 1939, yet by 1943, women
made up 4 percent of the workers, and by 1945 nearly 10 percent, with some
shipyards reporting up to 27 percent women.[7]

In shipyards, women held an array of jobs, such as pipefitters, riggers, sheet-
metal workers, painters, machinists, boilermakers, shipfitters, laborers, welders,
burners, and electricians. The largest numbers of women were working as clerical
workers or "general helpers." Women were relegated to mostly semiskilled jobs,
in what Ruth Milkman; in her study of the automobile and electrical manufactur-

ing industries identifies as the "idiom of sex typing." Women were associated with " 'light, repetitive work, demanding manual dexterity.' "[8] It should be added that women were often associated with domestic work and relegated to cleaning jobs. Even in the few instances when women did obtain supervisory positions, they did not receive the appropriate wage or status.

By mid-1943, women were 65 percent of the new workers in the shipyards. The percentage of women of color was considerably less and reflected the areas of the country. In the South, a smaller number of African American women were employed, working only as janitors and laborers.

Employment figures for women of color in particular war industries are difficult to obtain due to lack of or incomplete company records. Japanese Americans were relocated from the West Coast to internment camps inland. More than 27 percent of the Chinese American population was in the San Francisco Bay area in 1940. This region had several shipyards and other defense industries, where an estimated five hundred to six hundred Chinese American women worked.[9] Figures and information regarding other racial groups either were not kept or were deemed insignificant.

Examining other minority groups, we also find limited data. The prejudices of the times account for the secrecy and invisibility of lesbians. There were some reports of lesbians working in the West Coast aircraft plants. However, because quite a few "single" women were part of the workforce we can assume lesbians were employed in many of the defense jobs. Physically challenged women were employed in some plants where their finger dexterity could be used. The gauging of machine parts became the specialty of some blind women. Age restrictions were gradually eliminated, and women over thirty-five were hired in many industries.

Women who responded to the government's call were not always welcomed, however. When women would first enter a previously all-male company, they often met hostility and noncooperation from the men. Women were often hampered on their jobs when male coworkers or supervisors would not instruct or assist them as they would men. Certain jobs or activities were considered strictly male.

In many of the war industries women were required to wear slacks and sturdy shoes or boots, and to cover their hair, not only for safety on their jobs but to avoid distracting men. Women were to remain feminine but not too attractive.

The aircraft industry, being relatively new, was the most receptive to women; workforces in some plants were 45 to 50 percent female. By 1944 475,000 women were employed in the industry. On production lines women were found to be more accepting of tedious assembly-line work. Women also became noted for their ability to work in the small, cramped space of a plane's nose or tail. Work on gauges and other electrical and communication mechanisms that needed precision and dexterity came to be considered "natural" for women.

Each plant or industry, however, varied in jobs given to women. In New Jersey, only women would drive the trucks in one plant; in another, only men. Women would be working in X rays at one company; at another, only men were allowed to do so. Such inconsistencies were evident in the auto and electrical manufacturing plants as well. Women constituted only 5 percent of autoworkers in 1940, but as the plants were converted to producing tanks, military vehicles, and aircraft, the percentage rose by 1944 to slightly more than 24 percent. Though job classification specifics are limited, women appear to have held jobs similar to those they held before the war. A July 1944 United Auto Workers (UAW) report showed that women's chief job classifications were assembly, inspection, drill press, punch press, sewing machines, filing, and packing.[10]

Between 1940 and July 1944, women increased their participation rate from 32 to nearly 49 percent of electrical manufacturing production workers. This industry had a tradition of hiring women and so was less resistant to the increase, especially because the majority of new women continued to occupy positions normally handled by females. However, African American women were especially discriminated against; in 1942, for example, one thousand who had completed vocational training courses could get jobs only as cleaners and inspectors.[11]

Race was a barrier to African American women regardless of geographic location. They received the lowest-paying and usually the dirtiest, heaviest, hardest jobs with the worst hours. In the South, if they were able to get jobs in war industries, they were segregated from the white workers, as they often were at other plants around the country. The aircraft companies in southern California seem to be the only industries where they had some opportunities to work beside white women.

Prejudice was stronger in the San Francisco Bay area where the African American population tripled because of Southern migrants. There, African American women found jobs in a variety of industries such as shipyards, military supply depots, canneries, hospitals, and service occupations. Railroads were vital for moving materials and military personnel, and African American women worked as laborers in the yards. As one worker explained years afterward, " 'Discrimination was hard, but we've been doing it for years and years. At least we got paid for putting up with it out here.' "[12]

The munitions industry was another sector in which African American women made some inroads. Before Pearl Harbor, there were about thirty thousand women already working in the munitions industry in jobs that were particularly dangerous. The jobs required great caution, as well as extraordinary precision and patience to turn out error-free products safely. Located in rural or isolated areas to guard against inflicting widespread damage in the event of accidental explosions, the industry hired from a labor pool different from those of most other makers of war material, whose plants were in more populous locales. That fact often meant a higher percentage of African American women employees, but usually only after the supply of white women had been exhausted. At Alabama's Huntsville Arsenal, where colored-smoke munitions, gel-type incendiaries, and mustard and other gases were produced, African American women were 11 percent of the workforce in September 1944.[13] All women were paid less than the minimum rate paid to men.

Often overlooked, agriculture was another area where hundreds of thousands of women were vital. By mid-1942, as more and more men were leaving the land for military service or more lucrative industry jobs, the labor hostage was becoming acute. In April 1943, the federal government set up the Women's Land Army (WLA) under the U.S. Extension Service. Although some areas were already offering programs in gardening, poultry raising, and dairy management, the WLA placed more systemic attention on recruitment and coordinated the placement of women on farms.

Approximately three million women, mostly white, worked on farms during the years 1943–1945. The number of African American women is unclear because they were prohibited from working in some of the WLA programs in the South.

Ads and posters called upon women to participate in food and fiber production, to set " 'their vacation plans against a calendar of crop seasons.' "[14] Women drove tractors, operated pickup balers, transported grains, hoed, raked, picked, pruned, milked cows, cared for chickens—in short, whatever needed to be done—and their efforts were essential to the Allied prosecution of the war.

Whether it was higher wages or patriotism that drew women to war jobs, they came, they worked, and they succeeded. The chairman of the War Production Board put it this way: By 1942, " 'the output of our war factories equaled that of the three Axis nations combined. In 1943 our war production was one and one half times, and in 1944, more than double Axis war production.' "[15]

Although the OWI had waged a campaign to recruit women workers, the intent was always that women's paid employment was a remedy "for the duration." By the spring of 1944, ads showing the unhappiness of children with working mothers began to appear, as did ads featuring women as postwar consumers rather than producers. By 1945, ads with recruitment themes had disappeared. The new advertising focus was the role of women as homemakers. Although women of color made up about 10 percent of war-industry workers, they were not featured in the new propaganda effort and once more were rendered invisible.

There may not be extensive records on women of color, yet there have been some studies of the experiences of African American women and Chinese American women. The biggest benefit from the war for African American women was the opportunity to move out of the poverty-stricken rural South to greater job opportunities in urban centers around the country. The opportunities did not always lead to permanent gains. African American women's " 'postwar jobs fell into two categories: irregular, part-time or seasonal work in garment factories, canneries, and domestic service; and full-time, long-term employment, usually in the governmental sector.' "[16]

The war effort did produce advances for Chinese American women. Xiaojian Zhao's study of Chinese American women in the San Francisco Bay area reports some of these gains. In the days following Pearl Harbor, the general American print media published articles on how to distinguish the "friendly" Chinese from the Japanese (China and the United States were allies). This was a start toward removing the negative stereotypes that had persisted for years. The war industries needed the Chinese American workers and advertised for these in local Chinese-language newspapers.

Most Chinese American women workers were second-generation daughters, and high school, if not college, graduates. This enabled them to get shipyard jobs as office staffers, draftswomen, welders, burners, and other semiskilled workers rather than as manual laborers. Because they were not segregated from the white women, there were opportunities to meet and socialize with people of other ethnic groups. Their experiences gave many a feeling of acceptance by white American society. Race relations improved for them after the war years, and the majority of them found jobs outside their isolated communities.

Post–World War II

In 1944–1945, the Women's Bureau of the U.S. Department of Labor conducted a study of women workers' postwar plans. It found that 75 percent of the women planned to continue to work after the war. Many had themselves or families to support; others enjoyed the money and challenges of their jobs. However, most employers viewed them as temporary workers hired only for the duration of the war and thus they were usually the first to be fired.

By the end of 1944, female shipyard workers were being laid off, and those with some skills could not even find jobs in ship repair, which was in need of workers. Their few skills were not sufficient for repair work, which required journeymen.

In June of 1945, women factory workers were starting to be laid off; by September, one-fourth had lost their jobs. As a case in point, at Boeing, women had constituted about half of the total wartime workforce. The Seattle plant's employees dropped from 35,000 to 6,000; the Wichita, Kansas, plant's from 16,000 to 1,500 immediately after Japan surrendered.[17]

Industries no longer producing war materials had to reconvert to consumer goods. In the auto industry, for example, during the initial reconversion process people were laid off. When the plants began to rehire workers, they usually did so on the basis of seniority. Even with union contracts, women were not seen in the same light as the men. For one thing, returning veterans who had previously worked at a plant had seniority rights over women who had worked there during the war. Most women agreed with this aspect of plant policy. However, when young men with no job experience were hired and women were not, many women took issue. Taking issue was not always successful, however. For example, in Detroit if women protested when they were passed over, they might be placated by being given "women's jobs." If they continued to protest, the auto plants would often give them the worst or heaviest of "men's jobs." The women then faced a dilemma. If they protested about job conditions, it was seen as unwillingness to meet job requirements. If they went along, they often had to quit or were fired for not being able to perform as well as men.

After reconverting, some industries, such as electrical manufacturing, hired many of the women back, but once again they were segregated into women's jobs, and many received as much as a 17 percent pay cut. Women who worked after the war, then, usually did so at lower-wage jobs, mostly in clerical, sales, and service.

Another factor that prevented many women from working after the war was the reestablishment of the marriage bars in many states and industries. Protective laws were again enforced because management asserted it could not hire women for certain jobs or give them overtime. Whatever the reason, the biggest deterrent to women's working was the management forces within each industry.

Women's labor force participation dropped sharply as women continued to be laid off and others returned to their homes. The proportion of women in the national workforce had fallen from the high of 36 percent to 29 percent by August 1946. Some women chose to resume or take on the homemaker/mother roles when a husband or boyfriend returned from service or war work. However, married women did not stay at home for long; by 1948, their labor force participation rate was higher than the wartime peak in 1944 (23 percent) and the participation rate of all women slowly rose to nearly 30 percent by 1950. In some industries women began to regain some of their losses, yet mainly in sex-segregated jobs.

In 1944, the auto industry employed 185,000 women, 24.8 percent of its workforce; in 1950, 70,700, or 10 percent; in 1983, nearly 96,000, or 14 percent. The same pattern held in the electrical manufacturing field. In 1944, women held 380,000 jobs, or 48.9 percent of the workforce; in 1984, 960,000, or 43 percent of the total workforce.[18] However, not all of the workforce in these industries deal with military products. In other words, women have never regained in overall percentages their wartime rates of labor force participation even during postwar military buildups.

The start of the Cold War in 1948 brought increases in manufacturing and other industries. With the Korean War and the desire of the United States to stay ahead of the Soviet Union, defense expenditures again grew rapidly. However, the defense industry has changed greatly since World War II. For example, with higher personnel costs along with technological advances in airplane design, fewer planes are now being manufactured. In the years 1940–1945, more than 300,000 planes were produced. During the 1950s, 3,000 tactical aircraft were built; in the 1960s 1,000 a year; and in the 1970s, 300 a year.[19]

The 1950s and 1960s saw more women, especially married women, entering the workforce. Some had worked during World War II and now, with their children grown, they wanted or needed employment. Others simply needed a second income. Whatever the reason, they could not be viewed as temporary workers, as they had been in World War II. The majority of these new hires went into clerical, sales, and service jobs, which were expanding and welcoming of women.

Women increased their participation in the manufacturing trades yet were still concentrated in sex-segregated industries such as textiles, apparel, and electrical manufacturing. Regardless of the industry, women in all manufacturing faced obstacles. Though they received some support from unions, when industries expanded, the new jobs went to men and women were once again denied new or better-paying jobs or overtime. Management again rationalized that restrictive labor laws hindered its hiring of women or giving them overtime. It was not until 1967 that the executive board of the UAW started to support strongly the elimination of state labor laws that served to limit women.

Increasing union support along with the establishment and enforcement of affirmative action laws opened more opportunities to women. However, with downsizing and changes in the defense industry their participation remains low.

In recent years, the most military-dependent industries have been aircraft and missile engines, radio and communication equipment, private ordnance, and shipbuilding. Together, these industries supply almost half of all defense purchases. In 1970, 77 percent of their employees were male, and 23 percent were in "professional, technical, and kindred" jobs—in this category, women constituted approximately 6 percent.[20] Since World War II, the defense industry has become increasingly more white and male because of the high concentration of engineers and other technical positions. The importance of the technical positions can be seen in the increase in research and development: in 1945, 5 percent of the positions were for research and development; since the late 1950s, between 30 and 50 percent.[21]

In the durable defense industries, it is only in shipbuilding that the production workforce, rather than the managerial or clerical workforce, still is the majority. Shipbuilding remains a very labor-intensive and highly skilled industry. The 1990 census showed 587 women boilermakers, 2 percent of all boilermakers, including those in commerce and defense.

Another industry in decline is munitions, which inevitably stagnates during peacetime. Large stockpiles are not cost-effective with advances in armor technology.

During the defense buildup of the Reagan years, added jobs were mostly in managerial, administrative support, professional, and technical and service occupations. Clerical work has steadily increased over the years. In 1985, in the Los Angeles area, it was estimated that women were employed in 80–90 percent of all clerical defense jobs, 4 percent of professional jobs, and 7 percent of managerial jobs.[22]

Studies have found that in 1990 the aerospace industry employed the majority of private defense workers; two-thirds, 1.7 million, were working in aircraft and parts, missiles and space, or electronics and communications.[23] Census data showed that women held 9 percent, or slightly fewer than twelve thousand aerospace engineering jobs. This can be attributed to the growing percentage of females among engineering majors, 13 percent by the late 1980s.[24]

In spite of the shrinkage of the shipbuilding and munitions industries, other types of defense-related industries have expanded and changed over the years. Besides the most obvious, such as the building of missiles and planes, there are thousands more. Corporations like Coca-Cola, Beatrice Foods, Borden, General Foods, and Ralston Purina were in the top hundred defense contractors in 1970.[25]

Since then oil companies have replaced the food companies as some of the prime recipients of defense money. Other changes have seen universities receiving more and more research dollars. In 1990, half of $976 million budgeted by the Department of Defense for research went to institutions of higher education.[26]

The government has estimates of the number of defense jobs, direct and indirect, created per dollar amounts spent on purchases. The indirect jobs are in supplier industries, that is, subcontractors and lower tiers, which can often number in the thousands. For example, when Boeing was making the Minuteman missile, approximately 40,000 suppliers were involved.[27]

In terms of numbers of jobs created, in 1965 it was estimated that for every $1 billion in purchases, 80,000 jobs were created, or about 2.1 million total. Because of inflation, $1 billion bought fewer jobs over the years. In 1983, with the defense buildup of the Reagan years, it was estimated that there were 2.9 million jobs; in 1985, 3.2 million.[28] These figures, however, do not include induced jobs, those that are estimated by means of the "multipler effect." "Multipler-effect" figures are estimates of jobs created when defense or military employees buy goods and services. The "multipler effect" was easier to see during World War II, when millions of jobs were induced because male employees were being drafted and women were needed to fill their shoes.

Along with the exclusion of induced jobs, another problem with the DOD figures is that they do not include NASA jobs, which are under the Department of Energy. Although not all aspects of the space program are military-related, a substantial number are, especially the "Star Wars" program. Additionally, the figures do not include U.S. military sales to foreign countries. Allowing for these drawbacks, we have difficulty estimating the participation rates for women. Suppliers to the military are widely based. Census figures are for broadly based occupations and cannot be allocated to individual industries.

All types of fabricated textile products such as tents, equipment covers, parachutes, lanterns, and the like are defense industry products. The construction and mining industries, along with those that manufacture chemicals, drugs, and ammunition, employ defense-related workers. Manufacturing paper and paper products, paints, furniture, and apparel can also be classified as defense-related occupations. Radio, television, and other communication products, aircraft and parts, various transportation vehicles and parts, all sorts of machine products, various glass products, metal containers, parts and supplies, metalworking equipment, gasoline and petroleum products, and computers are all produced under defense contracts. Business and clerical services, hotels, entertainment and amusement industries, and research facilities and personnel at universities and colleges can also fall under the classification of defense-related occupations.[29]

Borrowing from Cynthia Enloe's statement that any job can be militarized, we suggest that even today the case of indirect suppliers and induced jobs is yet another example of this omnipresent militarization of the employment sector. Thus, we can see that although manufacturing jobs in the main defense industries have decreased over the years, there has been a proliferation of defense-related jobs. It is hard to say how many women are actually employed in defense industries, but we can say that their numbers have decreased in durable defense manufacturing since World War II but increased in other manufacturing and in service firms. Women are at least indirectly working for the military in working for the thousands of subcontractors supplying services, materials, and goods. Women hold a substantial proportion of these jobs; in 1990, they were more than 45 percent of that sector's workforce. They just are not as visibly working for military defense as they were in World War II.

NOTES

1. Barbara Reskin and Irene Padavic, *Women and Men at Work* (Thousand Oaks, Calif: Pine Forge Press, 1994), 8–12.

2. Cynthia Enloe, *Does Khaki Become You? The Militarization of Women's Lives* (London: Pandora Press, 1988), 175.

3. Jacqueline Jones, *Labor of Love, Labor of Sorrow: Black Women, Work, and the Family from Slavery to the Present* (New York: Basic Books, 1985), 166; Maurine W. Greenwald, *Women, War and Work: The Impact of World War I on Women Workers in the United States* (Westport, Conn.: Greenwood Press, 1986), 21–25.

4. Susan Hartmann, *The Home Front and Beyond: American Women in the 1940s* (Boston: Twayne, 1982), 21.

5. Maureen Honey, "Remembering Rosie: Advertising Images of Women in World War II," in *The Homefront War: World War II and American Society*, ed. Kenneth O'Brien and Lynn Parsons (Westport, Conn.: Greenwood Press, 1995) 93.

6. D'Ann Campbell, *Women at War with America: Private Lives in a Patriotic Era* (Cambridge: Harvard University Press, 1984), 72–73.

7. Mary Martha Thomas, *Riveting and Rationing in Dixie: Alabama Women and the Second World War* (Tuscaloosa: University of Alabama Press, 1987), 7; Amy Kesselman, *Fleeting Opportunities: Women Shipyard Workers in Portland and Vancouver during World War II and Reconversion* (Albany: State University of New York Press, 1990), 6.

8. Kesselman, *Fleeting Opportunities*, 34.

9. Xiaojian Zhao, "Women and Defense Industries in World War II" (Ph.D. diss., University of California, Berkeley, 1993), 11; Xioajian Zhao, "Chinese American Women Defense Workers in World War II," *California History*, summer 1996, 141.

10. Ruth Milkman, *Gender at Work: The Dynamics of Job Segregation by Sex during World War II* (Urbana: University of Illinois Press, 1987), 50, 54.

11. Ibid., 50, 55.

12. Gretchen Lemke-Santangelo, *Abiding Courage: African American Migrant Women in the East Bay Community* (Chapel Hill: University of North Carolina Press, 1996), 122.

13. Kaylene Hughes, "Women at War: Redstone's World War II Female 'Production Soldiers'" (paper presented at U.S. Army Historians Conference, June 1994), 2.

14. Judy Barrett Litoff and David C. Smith, "To the Rescue of the Crops: The Women's Land Army during World War II," *Prologue* 25, no. 4 (1993): 353.

15. Doris Weatherford, *American Women and World War II* (New York: Facts on File, 1990), 124.

16. Lemke-Santangelo, *Abiding Courage*, 125.

17. Eugene Rogers, *Flying High: The Story of Boeing and the Rise of the Jetliner Industry* (New York: Atlantic Monthly Press, 1996), 80.

18. Milkman, *Gender at Work,* 155–56.

19. Jacques S. Gansler, *The Defense Industry* (Cambridge: MIT Press, 1981), 21.

20. Rebecca Blank and Emma Rothschild, "The Effect of U.S. Defense Spending on Employment and Output," *International Labour Review* 124, no. 6 (November–December 1985): 693.

21. Gansler, *Defense Industry,* 101–2.

22. Ann R. Martusen, *Dismantling the Cold War Economy* (New York: Basic Books, 1992), 163.

23. James N. Dertouzos and Michael Dardia, *Defense Spending, Aerospace and the California Economy* (Santa Monica, Calif.: Rand, 1993), 4.

24. Claudia D. Goldin, *Understanding the Gender Gap: An Economic History of American Women* (New York: Oxford University Press, 1990), 215.

25. Carroll W. Pursell, Jr., *The Military-Industrial Complex* (New York: Harper & Row, 1972), 316.

26. Nancy J. Perry, "More Spinoffs from Defense," *Fortune,* spring-summer 1991, 63.

27. Gansler, *Defense Industry,* 43.

28. Richard P. Oliver, "Increase in Defense-Related Employment during Vietnam Buildup," *Monthly Labor Review* 93, no.2 (February 1970): 3; David Henry and Richard Oliver, "The Defense Buildup, 1977–1985: Effects on Production and Employment," *Monthly Labor Review* 110, no. 8 (August 1987): 8.

29. Oliver, "Increase in Defense-Related Employment," 4–5.

Oral History
My Silver Wings

Margaret "Maggie" Gee, Compiled by Xiaojian Zhao

Editor's note: During World War II, Margaret "Maggie" Gee worked as a welder at a Richmond shipyard and then as a draftsman at the Mare Island Naval Shipyard. In 1944, she joined the Women's Airforce Service Pilots (WASP). After the war, she went for graduate training in physics and worked as a physicist at the Lawrence Livermore National Laboratory.

I was born in 1923 in Berkeley. There were about twenty Chinese families in Berkeley at that time, most of them came from San Francisco after the earthquake of 1906. We were the only Chinese in the neighborhood. On Sundays we would go to the church to play with other Chinese children in town.

My father was a merchant from Hong Kong. My mother was born in the United States. Her parents—my grandparents—came from China in the 1870s. They settled in a fishing community in Monterey Bay, California. My parents had an arranged marriage. Although my mother was an American citizen by birth, her citizenship was taken away when she married my father. *[Editor's note: The Cable Act of September 22, 1922, states that "any woman citizen of the United States who marries an alien ineligible to citizenship shall cease to be a citizen of the United States."]* They lived in San Francisco for a few years. Later on my father built a house in Berkeley and the family moved to the east bay. My father had a warehouse in San Francisco's Chinatown. He imported rice and other food prod-ucts from China and exported things like soap and toothpaste. I was a only seven-year-old when my father passed away. My uncle told me that my father invested heavily in the stock market. When the market crashed during the Great Depression, he lost all the money and had a heart attack.

My parents had six children, and I am the third from the top. I have one older brother, one older sister, two younger sisters, and one younger brother. We were well off up to the time of my father's death. We had a car, and my mother learned to drive very early. When my father died, my mother was thirty-four. To support her six children, she took in sewing. Sometimes I woke up two o'clock in the morning and could still hear her sewing.

I began to work while I was in high school. I delivered newspapers and did domestic work for other families. I helped take care of the babies and cooked a little bit. I was not very good at doing housework or cooking. At home my mother did everything herself. I learned a lot from working at these families, such as the proper way to set the table in Western style. At that time I didn't like chopsticks at all; I do now, of course. I just didn't want to be that way as a kid. I would say, "Let's eat with forks, do the way the other people would do." We ate Chinese food at home. My mother was an excellent cook. I liked my mother, but I really didn't appreciate her that much until I was older. I think that's true with every generation. When you're young, you think you are smarter then your mother. During the summer when there was no school, I worked in a cannery. I also worked in a dime store for a while. I did pretty much what other children of my age would do at the time. A lot of us high school kids had jobs.

Berkeley High was an integrated school and I associated with both white and black kids. I remember that as a Chinese, I could not go swimming in community pools and could not join clubs organized by white students. But I didn't care—I am not a sensitive person and I was not good at swimming anyway. Although I joined the Chinese student club, I was too busy to spend time there. After school I had to work and to go to Chinese language school.

When I was in fourth grade, my uncle was going to take my sister and me to China to study. We had a going-away party. Then came the news that the Japanese had invaded Manchuria in China. So my mother decided that we had to cancel the trip. I felt terrible because we had to go back to school after having said goodbye to our friends. My mother was very involved in the war effort in China, especially after 1937. She took us to many fund-raising activities and rallies in San Francisco. I felt so bad when I heard about the "Rape of Nanjing." I mentioned it to my American friends, but they didn't seem to know what had happened. My mother was very unhappy when one of my sisters dated a Japanese boy. We wouldn't buy anything Japanese. If there was something made in Japan in the house, my mother would be sure to break it. I also didn't like the Japanese because of the war, but I had Japanese friends, they were different.

After high school, I attended college at the University of California, Berkeley. Going to college was not a big financial burden for our family since we lived in a college town. To my mother, it was just putting a bowl of rice on the table a little longer. The fee was only twenty-eight dollars each quarter, which I could earn myself. My brother was thinking about going to medical school. That's different and he couldn't make it financially. So he chose to be an accountant. I had no idea what I would do with a college degree. I went to college because in a college town, everyone went to college after high school. On Sunday, 7 December 1941, I went to Doe Library on campus to study. I was surprised to see that people were talking and no one was studying. That's how I heard about Pearl Harbor. This incident really changed everything. Suddenly everyone wanted to be involved and everyone wanted to do something. My mother was one of the first women to join defense industrial work. She got a job at one of the Richmond shipyards. She loved that job and she enjoyed meeting people. This was the first time she worked outside the home (her sewing job was mostly done at home).

My older brother joined the Army. I was eager to do something too, and my mother must have suggested I find a job in the shipyard. I took a graveyard-shift job welding in a Richmond shipyard while still a student at Berkeley. Working at night was boring because you had no one to talk to. You worked outdoors in the dark by yourself, and you were sleepy because you were taking classes during the day and didn't get much sleep. Sometimes when the job was slow I would fall asleep, but it was so cold out there at night you couldn't sleep for very long. Welding was not very difficult. You basically repeat the same job again and again—just like my mother sewing the sleeves in those years.

A few months later, I found a new job as a draftsman at Mare Island Naval Shipyard. It was a daytime job, and we had about thirty people working in the department. There I met two friends of my age. Jean is white, and Mary is a Filipino girl. We worked in the same room. The three of us used to meet every day at ten o'clock at the ladies' room. The ladies' room had this nice little sitting area, and we would sit there and have a cup of coffee. Here, we were in a war industry, but we all wanted to do more. We used to say, ''We can't stay here and do this; we must get involved directly in the war effort.'' Mary had been flying since she was fifteen, and she said that we could all become pilots. I was so excited about the idea because that was the most glamorous thing to do. Everyone liked to fly. My father used to drive us to Oakland Airport to watch airplanes taking off. I also read about women flying from the magazines, but I didn't dream to fly myself. We learned that there was this aviation school in Nevada and that all you needed was $800 to enroll, including room and board. I had saved a little bit of money while working in the Richmond shipyard. As a draftsman, my salary was $1,444 a year, a little over $100 a month. And I saved every penny I could. That day when we finally cashed all of our war bonds, $800 apiece, the three of us tossed the money in the air and laughed and laughed— we were overjoyed.

We took a temporary leave from our jobs and boarded a bus to Nevada in 1943. There were about fifteen students in the flying class, including quite a few women. It didn't make any difference if you were a man or a woman in training. I was the only Asian woman learning to fly. A lot of people in town thought I was an American Indian. We graduated in about two months. Before we went home, someone from the WASP—Women's Airforce Service Pilots—interviewed us. The men were interviewed separately by the Army recruiting people. While our files were under review, we all went back to our old jobs at Mare Island. I was ready to go to the war, but it was also nice to go back to work. I used up all of my savings and I needed the money. A lot of our coworkers came to ask us about what we had done in Nevada. They asked many questions about flying. Some people I guess were envious of us. We were able to do something different from building and repairing the ships.

Shortly after, I received a call from the WASP. Mary did not make it because of her eye problems. Jean joined but washed out. I couldn't believe that I made it! Everyone in my family was happy for me. The whole family, except for my older brother who was already in the Army, went to the train station in Berkeley to see me off. My mother was a little concerned about my safety, but she said, "If I were young I would like to fly too." She was very proud of me.

In February 1944, I boarded a train to west Texas. The train was so crowded that I had to sit on my suitcase near a restroom most of the way. I didn't even have a seat. I don't know how I did it. I was only twenty at the time. I arrived at Sweetwater, Texas, and reported to the Blue Bonnet Hotel in town. Next morning, they came to pick up us. There were 107 women in my class. All of us were very young and were very excited. We lived in the barracks, six women to each bay. We each had a cot and a locker. I didn't bring much stuff. One suitcase was all that I had, so that was fine. Located between the bays were two big shower heads, two toilets, and two washbasins to be shared by twelve of us. We had to shower together. Some of us were very shy because we had never been in gym before.

Our class was divided into two flights and the trainees spent half of each day on ground training and another half on cockpit. We would get up early in the morning, get dressed, make the beds, line up, and march to the mess hall for breakfast. We marched to the mess hall, we marched to the gym, we marched to classes. You had to line up and march everywhere you went. We used to sing when we marched, just like in the movies. We had very little free time; every minute was taken. We took a lot of classes: physics, math, aerodynamics, and PE. We also had night flying. On Sundays I would go to town with friends. Pretty girls got dates. I and some friends used to hang around with a bunch of guys. We established good friendships. Each time after you passed a test, you would wait and hope your friends pass too. We really cared about each other. So many people were washed out. We cried with them and they were sent home. And you always wondered: "Am I going to be the next?"

The WASP was under the Army. We flew army airplanes and we had to follow all the rules and regulations. If you broke the rules, you would be sent home. We had our passes, and we were all considered officers. But there was this big debate on whether women pilots should be given military status, and not until 1979 did we receive our veteran status. Our uniforms were Santiago blue, which was distinct. Avenger Field was an all-women aviation training ground, but our instructors were mostly men. If you put it in the context of today, the male instructors really resented us. They would say, "You ought to go home to have babies. What are you doing here flying?" I just had to ignore them. It was [that way] at that time; things are very different today.

I was the only Chinese American woman in my class. Hazel Ah Ying Lee and I are the only two Chinese American WASPs. She was in one of the earlier classes; I never met her. She was later killed in action. All of my classmates were white. The fact that I was a Chinese didn't make a difference; we were all very nice to each other. The WASP accepted two Chinese American women but not a single black. I heard that eight black women pilots applied for the job, but none of them were accepted. There was a lot of resistance to women flying. Jacqueline Cochran did not want to take in black women pilots because she had enough problems to deal with. This was before the civil rights movement. The South was segregated and our training field was in Texas. We flew over a lot of southern states.

While in training, I got to fly different types of military airplanes and did cross-country flying. Once I got in very late. When I came in I said, "I am going to show these people how good I am." I made a nice landing, but then I lost my concentration. So the airplane ground looped. It did not go straight, as it should, but drifted into a circle. That was a small accident; no one was hurt. I was so ashamed of myself and would not get out. Because of that, I got checked out. The civilians checked you out, and the Army checked you out. But I did complete all the training and pass all the tests. The day when I finally graduated and got my silver wings, I was so excited! All together the WASP accepted about 2,000 women, but only 1,074 graduated. I had seen so many people washed out, and some lost their lives. I guess I was very lucky indeed.

Before graduation, we were asked where we would like to work and whom we would like to work with. We had a few choices. My baymate and best friend Elaine Harman, who was from Baltimore, and I decided to come to the West Coast. We both began our active duty at the Las Vegas Army Air Force Base in September 1944. There were about thirty WASPs working on the base. I was an instrument instructor, giving flying instructions to male pilots. I also did some copiloting. I flew mostly single-engine airplanes. Then one day in October 1944, we were notified that the WASP would be disbanded. By then, there were many men around and women pilots were no longer needed. On 20 December 1944, WASP was officially deactivated and our WASP squadron at the Las Vegas Army Air Force Base was shut down. We were all sent home. I felt terrible because the war was not over yet.

My experience at the WASP definitely had a great impact on my life. It was a very short time in my life but I got to spend time together with the people I worked with. We had such a small, closely knit group. We did something unique and we all liked what we were doing. Since we lived, trained, and worked together, we developed a good friendship. I feel I know these people well regardless of their social background. Many of them were from well-to-do families. People like me, Mary, and Jean had to earn money to learn how to fly. It would have been impossible if I didn't have the chance to work in defense industries. Most of the women in the WASP were older than I was, and many of them are now in their eighties. Some had commercial licenses already when they joined the program. They had been flying before the war, and some of them did that for their own pleasure. But that didn't matter, the war brought us together to the military service.

I have attended many of our reunions. A lot of us were there for the big reunion of 1979, when we finally got veteran status. I still see other WASPs. I talk to Elaine Harman often. I feel I can drive across the country with the little book that has our names and addresses in it and when I come to any town, I can call up a WASP and go to her house, even if I have never met her. After all, I am one of them. Some of them have come to see me in Berkeley. I feel very comfortable with them. Having worked and lived with these women, I had no problem moving into any social circle later on. People of my generation from my background would not find it easy, but my experience as a WASP did make a difference. It gave me a lot of confidence. I felt comfortable and confident about myself.

When I returned home, I felt that there were a lot of things that I could do. After the war I returned to Berkeley to study physics. In those days, Chinese parents taught their children to be quiet and gentle, especially the girls; you were supposed to develop your potential. My mother was not a strict person. Two of my sisters were active in junior high school. They were leaders of Chinese student clubs at that stage. But I was never that way; I was shy. I got to do one more thing to make the change, to take one more step. It was my service at the WASP during the war that made the difference. Returning to Berkeley campus after the war, I saw many young Chinese students, a lot of them came back from the Army. I said, "I want to be the president of the Chinese Students Association." So I did that.

When I was in graduate school, my sister and I looked for an apartment. That's how I found out what it was like to be a Chinese. We talked to a landlady on the phone and she told us she had an apartment available for rent. So we went to see the apartment. When she realized that we were Chinese, she said the place was taken. My sister said, "We should just say that we are Chinese on the telephone then. Don't bother." It took us a little while before we finally got a place. When I talk to people, I often say that I had an advantage of being a Chinese who grew up in Berkeley. But not in this case, though.

I worked at Berkeley Radiation Laboratory while attending graduate school. Later, I worked in Washington, D.C., at the Bureau of Standards and then lived in Europe for three years. In late 1950s, I came back to California and began working at the Lawrence Livermore Laboratory as a physicist. I was the only woman in my department for many years.

Ten

Military Prostitutes and the Hypersexualization of Militarized Women

Katharine H. S. Moon

To God, Country, and the Ladies. Three toasts before dinner. This was a familiar routine for all the men in uniform in the banquet room. It was a military banquet held in Seoul, Korea, in the spring of 1991 by members of the U.S. Eighth Army. Men led each toast although both sexes present in the room were expected to salute God and Country; when the toast to the Ladies came, only the men in uniform uttered the words, raising their glasses and offering a reverential nod to the wives, girlfriends, and dates. I was used to saluting God in church and the flag in school, but I had never been in a place where God, Country, and Ladies were saluted together as part of a ritual litany.

In *Women and War*,[1] Jean Bethke Elshtain reminds us that Ladies, not simply women, are necessary for the maintenance of the social construction, myth, and identity of men as warriors. They need the "Beautiful Souls" who represent civilization, culture, home, family, morality—and peace—for whom they fight (defend) and sacrifice their lives. In this masculinist gender regime, all the varied categories of women, including whore and soldier, cannot be included. A prostitute is by definition antithetical to a Lady, and a woman who can defend herself and others does not need a man to defend her. A Lady, then, is neither whore nor soldier. Presumably, she is a good wife and mother.

But how separate and distinct are these categories of women for the U.S. military? Have they remained constant through history? Are there identities, roles, or symbolisms that they have in common? How do the women in the different categories of soldier, wife, prostitute negotiate the different identities and perceptions? How do these categories inform women's relationships to national security? This chapter argues that despite the rhetorical and normative need for Ladies and Beautiful Souls to justify militarized masculinity, the U.S. military has conflated the different categories of woman to suit its organizational and normative designs. Sexualization of militarized women serves as the common denominator. The particular aim here is to highlight the prostitute as the prototype of militarized women, rather than the most marginalized.

Who is/was the military prostitute? As there is no one type of woman, there is no one type of prostitute or sex worker. The causes, conditions, and consequences of sex work vary for different women. Some were runaways, some were kidnapped by flesh traffickers, others were physically and sexually abused as children, and still others followed their sexual curiosity about men in uniform. Historical conditions of war and military occupation have helped foster socioeconomic conditions that have forced women and girls, as refugees, widows, and orphans, into sexual labor for the military. In general, they have been grouped together as *camp followers*, women who have made their sexual and other forms of feminized labor, such as cooking and washing, available to troops either voluntarily or involuntarily. Some women have been paid in cash for their sexual services; others have been provided with food and shelter.

Soldier-men have treated such camp followers with as much variety as there are women and men. Some have loved them, married them, provided for their children. Others have helped the women flee oppressive pimps and bar owners. Others have toyed with the women, promised them the world, beaten them, impregnated them, and abandoned them and their children. In the worst of cases, the men have brutally murdered them, as Private Kenneth Markle did to Yun Kumi in Tongduchon, Korea, in the fall of 1992.

The degree to which military prostitutes' lives have been controlled or regulated by the armed forces has depended on the availability of medical knowledge and services regarding sexually transmitted diseases, wartime or peacetime status of military engagement, and the prevailing social and moral norms of the day. For example, post–World War II developments in medical technology have allowed for more accurate testing and treatment of venereal diseases. These have helped justify the regulation of prostitution, whereby local police and health clinic officials regularly examine, certify, and, if necessary, treat (through medication and/or quarantine) infected women. Military and local governmental authorities usually require women to carry certificates of health indicating whether they are free of infection or not. Such has been the mandate in the camp towns near the U.S. bases in Okinawa, South Korea, and until 1992, the Philippines. Most sex workers around the overseas bases in Asia have by now become accustomed to getting their VD and HIV checks every week and every six months, respectively. But they also have experienced more heavy-handed regulation procedures enforced by authorities from the U.S. military and the host government. Forced injection of penicillin, even without proof of infection, and "roundups," in which women have been herded into trucks or vans and taken to the local health clinic to undergo gynecological and blood examinations, are but two examples.[2] The modern "military and medical mind,"[3] which emphasized bureaucratic and scientific efficiency, has institutionalized and systematized prostitution into daily military practice.

Negotiating the conditions of the system of prostitution available to troops has consumed a great deal of time and effort at both the local and top levels of the U.S. military and the host governments/authorities involved. In World War I, General "Black Jack" Pershing, head of the American Expeditionary Forces in Europe, Premier Clemenceau of France, U.S. Secretary of War Newton Baker, and their staffs passed numerous verbal and memo exchanges regarding military prostitution, morale and welfare, and VD conditions affecting American and European forces. During and after World War II, Congress, health and law enforcement officials at both the top and local levels of government, medical associations, women's organizations, and social welfare groups mobilized the general public to fight against regulated prostitution near military camps and war factories and sexual habits that could invite or exacerbate venereal diseases among the populace.[4] In the 1970s, controlling and regulating prostitution and venereal disease served as a major item of foreign policy negotiation and joint governmental action in the bilateral relationship between the U.S. and South Korean governments.[5]

In all three of these cases, the exigency of war or warlike conditions has served to justify heavy-handed methods of regulating people's sexual activities by governments and military authorities. Such conditions have justified the compromise of rights that are normally available in peacetime. For example, the Chicago Bar Association stated emphatically in its 1942 report, "Brief Re: Control Program— Prostitution—Venereal Disease in a War Period," that war "transforms and transplants the individual and his rights and responsibilities," "compels new or changed appraisal of existing rights and duties," and "demands the setting up and creating of new and different values."[6] And therefore, the "national government has the right and duty to insist that officials of state and local governments do their full share" to suppress any activity that is linked to VD.[7] The American Bar Association, in a 1943 report, echoed verbatim these rationales for governmental intervention in the sexual activities of the public.[8]

Although military institutions in many ways stand apart from society—for example, they have their own legal systems—they do reflect the general norms of society at a given time. And the individuals who make up the armed services of course embody the norms and practices they were exposed to before donning the uniform. The U.S. military's attitudes and practices about sex, marriage, and prostitution have therefore varied in time and place. Colonial America witnessed the movement of women, most of whom were not legal wives, alongside the men of both the British and American troops. This was normal military practice in that time. In both of the forces, some of the women were officially on the rations roll.[9] Although the U.S. military today monitors the tens of thousands of women who work as prostitutes around military installations overseas and in the United States, it does not permit—and neither would the larger society— such female camp followers to become its official wards.

And although current feminist scholarship and activism generally criticize and critique a "cult" of military masculinity that requires the sexual domination and abuse of women and the feminine,[10] the U.S. military leadership has at least once promoted a different kind of masculinity that required the very opposite: sexual continence. Progressive Era values and norms regarding sex and morality influenced military practice during the World War I era: "In contrast to World War II policy, there was no mass distribution of condoms, though doctors were aware at the time of their usefulness in disease prevention."[11] Rather, a "Spartan" camp discipline regarding continence was emphasized. The language of Progressivism echoed in exhortations to the troops demanding *"self*-discipline, *self*-denial, *self*-sacrifice, and *self*-control."[12] For General Pershing, who spearheaded this Spartanism among his forces in Europe, sexual continence was intended to reflect the moral superiority and political invincibility of American democracy:

> He [Pershing] wanted the AEF to remain clean, wanted his men to return home in moral and physical strength. It seemed a large hope, but hope ran with the American cause in Europe—if the war might make the world safer for Democracy, Democracy should defend the purity of its knights.[13]

Racist norms and myths prevalent in American society have also helped induce and even justify sexual abuse of women through military men's participation in prostitution. I interviewed a U.S. Army chaplain in the spring of 1994 who stated:

> What the soldiers have read and heard before ever arriving in a foreign country influence prostitution a lot. For example, stories about Korean or Thai women being beautiful, subservient—they're tall tales, glamorized. . . . U.S. men would fall in lust with Korean women. They were property, things, slaves. . . . Racism, sexism—it's all there. The men don't see the women as human beings—they're disgusting, things to be thrown away. . . . They speak of the women in the diminutive.[14]

One Navy man I interviewed in the spring of 1991 commented that some officers would tell their men that prostitution is a part of Asian culture and that Asians like prostitution.

The Sexualization of Militarized Women

Whether wife, prostitute, or soldier, the sexualization of women related to troop life has been built into the history of the U.S. military. The military has treated women's sexuality, and their very physical presence, as suspect—at best disruptive, at worst destructive to military order. The tendency to conflate these categories of women has kept women on the margins of military life. Because any sex act out of wedlock could indict a woman as a prostitute or sex delinquent throughout most of U.S. history, military and governmental authorities have viewed any female presence near military areas as sexually promiscuous. A history of women camp followers of the American and British forces during the Revolutionary War conveys the ambivalent and dualistic attitudes of military men and observers toward women in the camps: they are variously described as dutiful women with the "natural desire . . . to care for their men" and "lewd women" who were "chattering and yelling in sluttish shrills . . . and spitting in the gutters."[15] In this age-old portrait of woman as lady or whore, even wives were deemed "disorderly women" for "suffering any Soldiers coming back to their Barracks at an unseasonable time of night."[16]

For authorities overseeing the sex life of military men, the line between lady and whore has been unclear and, hence, permeable: "[D]uring World War I, *any woman* walking unescorted near a military base ran the risk of being labeled a 'suspected prostitute'" (emphasis added).[17] The Interdepartmental Social Hygiene Board of the War Department included girls and women who had never sold sex for a price in its survey of 15,010 "sex delinquent" girls and women from 1918 to 1920. Part of an effort to control venereal disease among the soldier population, the survey placed 4,884 of the subjects in the category "suspicious conduct, public places." At least 1,620 reported "no sex experience at all," yet they were still subject to government surveillance as women who could threaten national defense by spreading VD.[18]

The study also assumed that the wife and the whore were one and the same in 1,982 cases."Separation from husband" was ranked at the top of the list of reasons for prostitution/sex delinquency, and the study noted that the separation could be a result of the husband's military service, desertion, divorce, or death.[19] The implication was that sex delinquency and wifehood are not mutually exclusive.

In the 1970s, joint efforts at regulating prostitution by the U.S. military in Korea and the Korean government led to frequent cases of Korean wives of American servicemen being stopped by local police. The assumption was that any Korean woman near a U.S. base was a prostitute or a potential prostitute. A police chief in one of the major Air Force camp towns in Korea stated candidly that there is "no way of determining who is an unregistered streetwalker, Korean citizen, or U.S. dependent."[20] African American wives of soldiers near a U.S. base in Florida were also suspected of being prostitutes, according to the base race relations officer: " 'This was embarrassing when it turned out to be a colonel's wife.' "[21]

Numerous accounts and testimonies of women's experiences as members of the armed forces also underscore the military's hypersexualization of their female identity: "In opposing women's presence in the Army, 'the-men-we-have-to-work-with' routinely focus on the supposed hypersexuality of women soldiers, who somehow manage the feat of being prostitutes and lesbians simultaneously."[22] Paula Coughlin, who publicly exposed the sexist practices of the Navy at Tailhook, was recast as "slut" and "bitch" to discredit her story.[23] Military women and prostitutes share the same plight: female identity is reduced to sexual object.

Indeed, the *Tailhook Report* underscores military men's sometimes willing conflation of female soldier with prostitute. Officers interviewed for the report "frequently opined that gauntlet participants could not or *would not* differentiate between the [female] groupies and prostitutes who had been part of Tailhook for many years, and other women [military women] who attended Tailhook '91" (emphasis added).[24] Navy Lieutenant Kara Hultgreen—who later lost her life in 1994 when her F-14 Tomcat crashed into the Pacific Ocean—recalled her Tailhook '91 experience of being called a hooker: "The carrier pilots who attended the convention expected, if they saw a woman at Tailhook, that she either wanted to get laid by an aviator . . . or she was a prostitute or a dancer." A male naval captain who recognized her clarified the situation: "That's no hooker. . . . That's an A-6 pilot."[25]

Civilian women hired as military employees have also encountered this problem of sexualization and conflation of female identities. For example, "fixed post workers" hired by the Interdepartmental Social Hygiene Board during World War I to oversee reformatories and to spread awareness of VD in local communities saw all women who came into contact with soldiers—including women who worked in military camps—as the root of the VD problem.[26]

Even during a period when the notion of "lady" was taken seriously by the American public, women from "good families" were not exempt from the taint of their association with the military. Retired Air Force Major General Jeanne Holm states that despite the military's "prudish concern for protecting military women's virtue, chastity, and reputation—individually and collectively" during World War II, WACs (members of the Women's Army Corps) had to contend with verbal and physical sexual abuse. She relays the words of one corporal: " 'You can't even go into the chow hall without running the gauntlet. . . . You feel naked and you want to hide.' "[27]

Servicewomen of color have especially had to contend with uninvited and unwelcome sexualization of their identities as military women. Black women and Asian women have often been treated by their own in uniform and by local townspeople as sex providers and common whores. Holm notes that in the highly segregated armed forces of the 1940s, white male commanders would "request black WACs for the 'morale' of black troops. Although not usually stated openly in so many words, the ulterior motive was often implicit in the request."[28] Asian American women in the military have been subject to a similar kind of assumption, especially when they have been stationed in Asia.[29]

The military has not only sexualized women's identities but also deemed women's sexuality aberrant. Many feminist writers have noted that the military as an institution promotes its own version of "hegemonic masculinity," eschewing homosexuality in men and women as well as female sexuality. What is not acceptably masculine in the military's eyes is not accepted, and women—because they are not men—deviate from the gender norm. Observers deemed female camp followers of the British troops during the Revolutionary War as immoral, unreliable, dangerous women "who were apt to make trouble, get drunk and shift their partners."[30] With rising awareness of sexually transmitted diseases, women were constructed as transmitters of disease, agents of both physical and moral contamination. Indeed, prostitutes have often been equated with "contagion." Women's sexuality, therefore, became a direct threat to the health and well-being of men, especially those in uniform: "[F]ear of women's sexual natures underlay many of the policies that the War Department initiated" in order "to make military camps morally safe and free of venereal disease."[31] In 1942, the Chicago Bar Association supported the War Department's fight against VD by likening prostitutes to disease-carrying insects, calling prostitution "a swamp which offers a most likely breeding ground for the germ of the disease."[32] In the 1970s, the U.S. military and local Korean authorities referred to Korean prostitutes as the "reservoirs" of VD.[33]

Militarized women have also been at the mercy of governing authorities who have been inclined to view them as mentally, in addition to sexually, aberrant. For example, the Reverend William Lawrence, a military health educator, declared in his lecture at the Harvard Medical School in February 1918, "Venereal Diseases in the Army, Navy, and Community," that 50 percent of prostitutes were intellectually deficient.[34] A comprehensive public awareness report on VD and prostitution authored by the Social Protection Division (of the Office of War Services of the Federal Security Agency) in 1945 lumps prostitute and military wife together as "disintegrating and demoralizing" agents of community health and well-being:

> The girl in a red-light district, the girl who plays the hotels, the adolescent who hangs around street corners after school, the serviceman's wife who distributes her favors in return for a good dinner, are simply more or less acute sufferers from the same dangerous tangle of different kinds of social, economic, psychological and sometimes mental lacks.[35]

The report emphasizes that "[m]any are sick, mentally and physically" and that "[m]any prostitutes are extremely neurotic people, badly in need of psychiatric treatment. . . . Almost every available study stresses this immaturity."[36] The report does not clarify whether "neurotic" and otherwise psychologically and mentally unstable girls and women tend to become sex delinquents or if the life of prostitution and sexual abuse makes them so. Nor does the report question whether the men who use prostitutes are "neurotic." In fact, the report asserts that *any girl or woman* who does not abide by socially sanctioned sexual behavior can become a prostitute; the implication is that all women have the potential to be, or already are, mentally and psychologically abnormal.

Although the military itself did not create the views of women as sexually aberrant and psychologically immature, it has viewed women as a particular burden to its organizational mission. Even in the days when camp followers were considered a useful part of troop life as cooks, cleaners, and sutlers, military men saw women as a financial drain, a threat to troop discipline, and a public relations problem. For example, George Washington was criticized for deciding to give army rations to women above and beyond the portion recommended by the Secretary of War and the Superintendent of Finance. Concerned that his soldiers not impoverish themselves by giving a part of their rations to their women, Washington let the military assume the financial responsibility. Camp followers were also blamed for "annoying and insulting the prudent and decent women of cottages and farms adjacent to their line of march" and robbing civilian homes along the way.[37]

In the 1970s, the U.S. military, together with the South Korean government, viewed Korean camp town prostitutes as bad "PR agents" and tried to reform them into useful ones.[38] They were blamed for the racial tensions and violence in the camp towns adjacent to the bases. This in turn became a contentious issue between the U.S. forces in Korea and U.S. lawmakers in Washington. The military in Korea feared that its mission would not be supported by the Congress. Since the 1960s, Korean wives of U.S. servicemen stationed in Korea, many of whom were former sex workers, have also been blamed for the active trade in blackmarketed U.S. goods in Korea. The *New York Times* reported on 5 July 1997, that the new U.S. military policy to reduce the monthly ration of duty-free beer from thirty cases to eight cases per soldier in Korea might be targeted at military wives. Why any soldier needs to buy thirty cases of beer a month seems not to have been the focus in the decision making.

The argument against women in combat is born of the basic belief that women in general are an organizational burden to the military. Oft-repeated reasons for combat exclusion focus on women's sexuality as obstructing deployment and combat readiness and effectiveness, namely, menstruation and pregnancy.[39] House Speaker Newt Gingrich revealed his uninformed views of women's and men's biologies, in declaring that women should be barred from combat because "females have biological problems staying in a ditch for 30 days," and men are "biologically driven to go out and hunt giraffes."[40] But those who rebut the woman's-body-as-military-liability claims argue that menstruation does not incapacitate or debilitate most women and that "female military nurses have had a long history of functioning in wartime under primitive, unsanitary conditions without questions being raised about menstruation interfering with the performance of their duties."[41] Some argue that pregnancy may be a "legitimate reason to exclude women from actually engaging in some forms of combat" but that "it does not justify the stringency of the current restrictions," especially given that only about 10 percent of women are pregnant at a given time and that pregnancy affects the physical capacity of women differently.[42] Some criticize pregnancy as a deterrent to military effectiveness, but the fact that men have proven more costly to the national treasury and to military preparedness and discipline rarely gets publicized. Holm cites a 1977 DOD study that found that "men lost much more duty time on an average than did women for absence without leave, desertion, alcohol/drug abuse, and confinement."[43] Military men find all sorts of reasons, many unfounded or inaccurate, to keep women out of the military or on the sidelines: "[L]ike witches who cause the cattle to die or the beer to go sour, Army women are responsible for poor morale and unit unreadiness."[44]

Women's exclusion from combat is a clear reflection of the military's belief that women who bear arms and are directly responsible for defense are threatening to national security. But in this line of thinking, women in general represent a threat to national security. For example, the double perception of women as wives (or ladies) and as whores constitutes the contradictory identity and function of militarized women, whose sexuality can both save and threaten troop effectiveness and national defense. Women's presence can be construed to have a humanizing effect on warring men but also a corrupting and debilitating one: "[F]rom first to last during those seven years of imperial struggle, women had helped or encumbered the combatants—helped in the drudgery of camp life, hampered in the long marches and harassed in the throes of wilderness fighting."[45] In writing women into the history of the Revolutionary War, historian

Walter Blumenthal attributes the American victory to the relative lack of female camp followers in the American forces as compared to the British forces. He draws an image of sexual and moral chasteness among the Americans to contrast the lack thereof among the British:

> In the exigencies of camp life and marches the wives [women] with the American troops may have been forced to neglect parlor attire, but there is no trace of dissolute abandon among patriot campfollowers such as commonly characterized overseas armies. Nor was there widespread drunkenness; for (with some falling from grace) the Americans were intoxicated only by the prospect of new-found freedom from a rankling thrall.[46]

George Washington was suspect of the women among his own forces and ordered his officers in Philadelphia to prevent women from meeting soldiers because they approach the men "with an intent to entice the soldier to desert."[47] Blumenthal believes women's presence and self-assertion in military life can mean victory or surrender. He notes a lesson to be learned from the French and Indian War: at an English garrison that was captured by the French in Oswego in August 1756, "[t]he women screamed for an end to hostilities, besought the defenders to run up a white flag, and thus hastened the surrender by their clamor."[48] Preservative love, which Ruddick and other "maternal peace" advocates would promote,[49] would translate into humiliating "clamor" for militarist patriots like Blumenthal.

Of course, women as prostitutes have been viewed as a direct threat to national security since World War I. On anti-VD posters created by the U.S. military and government, the disease was personified as a woman.[50] During World War II, the U.S. military and government worked to prevent girls and women from threatening the war-fighting capacity of American men through debilitating diseases by distributing pamphlets noting the enormous number of man-days lost to VD during the World War I and the fact that more than 60,000 of the first million American men physically examined for the draft were rejected because of VD infection.[51] The American Bar Association, in writing reports to support the War Department's campaign against VD during World War II, equated VD with "sabotage" and called prostitution and VD the "enemy" in the war for democracy.[52] The Federal Security Agency, writing on VD prevention in 1945, reminded readers that "[i]n the first 2 years of World War II, the Japanese killed 36,000 Americans. Syphilis killed 33,000."[53] More recently, U.S. military officials told Korean prostitutes that their racially discriminatory behavior in camp towns can threaten the national security of their country and U.S. interests in Asia because North Koreans could use it to hurt the U.S.-Korean alliance.[54]

Resisting Hypersexualization

Why should we bother analyzing the inconsistencies and contradictions in the seemingly separate categories of lady, whore, and soldier? Because without understanding how these categories are interconnected, we cannot expect long-term positive changes in the military's treatment of female soldiers or hope that access to all combat positions will solve the problem of sexual harassment. Nor can we hope that military wives will not be subsumed by the identity of their husbands. And assessing how ideals of "proper womanhood" are created and sustained by the military can help us challenge the depiction and treatment of prostitutes as "bad women." We need to start out at the most basic level of analysis: the military's assumption that all women are actually or potentially sexually deviant, untrustworthy, and corruptive of military order and national security. We need to acknowledge that the prostitute, rather than lying on the fringes of military society and militarized gender relationships, occupies the core because of her role as the hypersexualized woman. Although militarized women experience sexism contextually, they are in the same boat. As Francine D'Amico notes, "The focus on soldier-mothers leaving children to go off to the Gulf, the military's complicity in prostitution around bases, and continued sexual harassment serve as reminders that women are 'outsiders.' "[55]

Making the connections among the categories of women is also necessary for feminist activism to succeed in improving conditions for militarized women. D'Amico informs us of the hopeful possibilities of collective identity and action among militarized women as "[o]ld antagonisms between military women and anti-war civilian feminists and between spouses and women in uniform are being bridged."[56] But we need to include the identity and interests of military prostitutes if we are to "facilitate resistance to efforts to retrench the gender line"[57] successfully.

So far, military wives and female soldiers have themselves been complicitous in marginalizing the prostitute and thereby serving as an "insider" contingent of what D'Amico calls the "gender police." In particular, women who advocate women's equality and increased participation in the armed services often distinguish themselves from other militarized women, particularly prostitutes, in order to assert their professional identity. I once asked a retired female army general who has been an outspoken advocate of female soldiers' interests if female soldiers who are stationed in Asia have any interaction with the local prostitutes near the bases. My naive hope was that some kind of interaction would point to women's solidarity in a male-dominated military world. But she immediately answered 'no' and stated that servicewomen may feel sorry for the prostitutes but that the two groups had nothing to do with each other.[58] The implication was that the two types of women were categorically different; she was emphasizing the professional identity of female soldiers while shunning the sexual identity of camp town sex workers. Cynthia Enloe also notes that military personnel treat Asian wives of soldiers with suspicion and do not welcome them into the military family because of a "widespread fear that Asian women are likely to be little more than prostitutes latching on to a naive American soldier in order to gain access to an immigration visa and economic security."[59] It is likely that many American military wives share this suspicion and disdain. Asian wives of servicemen are often noted as the most isolated, marginalized, and abused among military wives.

The way male servicemen interact with one category of women affects the way they relate to another. For example, DACOWITS (Defense Advisory Committee on Women in the Services) has verified that the military's use of local sex workers in Asia as "entertainment" and the prevalent practice of buying local women for sex in the Navy and Marine Corps severely affect the welfare and morale of female servicewomen stationed in Asia. The author of this report noted that her team encountered "macho," sexist, and abusive behavior at each of the installations in the western Pacific and Asia it visited in 1987: Headquarters, U.S. Pacific Command; Commander in Chief–Pacific Fleet and Marine Corps Air Stations in Kaneohe Bay, Hawaii; Subic Bay and Cubi Naval Air Station in the Philippines; Okinawa; and Atsugi Naval Air Station and Yokosuka Naval Base, Japan. One of the most egregious abuses the team discovered involved activities on board the USS *Safeguard*:

> [T]he commander's shipboard activities which allegedly included public sex, attempts to "sell" female sailors to the Koreans. . . . From our discussion with Navy women elsewhere during our trip such behavior should not be considered surprising given the Service's support for such on-base activities as "peso-parties" (Subic/Cubi terminology for the liberal and routine public "use" of Philippine females at places such as the enlisted, NCO and Officers' Clubs), noon-time burlesque shows and "dining-ins" that emphasize sexually-oriented entertainment.[60]

The DACOWITS report continued: "[O]n-base activities such as these contribute to creating an environment in which all females are regarded with little or no respect and abusive behavior toward all women is not only passively accepted and condoned but encouraged."[61]

More recently, the *Tailhook Report* found that the harassment of women and the other indecencies at Tailhook '91 were also linked to the way men behave at overseas camp towns, where R&R (alcohol and prostitutes) abound. "Many officers likened Tailhook to an overseas deployment. . . . Dozens of officers cited excessive drinking, indecent exposure, and visits to prostitutes as common activities while on liberty [in foreign ports]."[62] Moreover, blatant sexism against "insider" women at home mirrors that against "outsider" women in foreign countries. The *Tailhook Report* states that some male officers at the 1991 gathering wore T-shirts that read "WOMEN ARE PROPERTY" on the back and "HE MAN WOMEN HATERS' CLUB" on the front.[63] An activist against U.S. militarism in Asia has reported that U.S. servicemen from the Kadena Air Base on Okinawa walk around wearing T-shirts that depict an illustration of a woman along with the letters "LBSM." The letters stand for Little Brown Sex Machine.[64]

And in a twisted logic that attributes the military's sexual and organizational problems on women, mothers and wives have been blamed for servicemen's bad habits of seeking out prostitutes. Mridu Gulati paraphrases from "The Prostitute and the Mother Imago," a paper delivered by Winfred Lay on behalf of military officials seeking to rectify the VD problem during World War I:

> Naturally socialized to expect ready compliance, a son could not but turn to a prostitute who acquiesced to his desires in a way that his wife would not. In fact, some men, Lay claimed, overwhelmed by their desires, were troubled by the thought of sullying respectable girls with their sexual energy. They turned to a prostitute with the "noble" idea that they were not ruining a good girl.[65]

Lay did not include the category of woman-soldier as somehow responsible for men's "turning to" a prostitute—perhaps because she could not imagine women as professional soldiers then, though we now entrust women with B-52 bombers. But whether wives, soldiers, or sex workers, women are still made in the image of the military. And in that image, the prostitute stands front and center.

NOTES

1. Jean Bethke Elshtain, *Women and War* (New York: Basic Books, 1987).

2. Katharine H. S. Moon, *Sex among Allies: Military Prostitution in U.S.-Korea Relations* (New York: Columbia University Press, 1997), 98.

3. Barbara M. Hobson, *Uneasy Virtue: The Politics of Prostitution and the American Reform Tradition* (New York: Basic Books, 1987), 181.

4. U.S. Office of Community War Services, Division of Social Protection, *Challenge to Community Action* (Washington, D.C.: Federal Security Agency, 1945).

5. Moon, *Sex among Allies*.

6. Chicago Bar Association, "Brief Re: Control Program—Prostitution—Venereal Disease in a War Period" (1942), 1.

7. Ibid., 1–2.

8. American Bar Association, Committee on Courts and Wartime Social Protection, *Venereal Disease, Prostitution, and War* (1943).

9. Walter H. Blumenthal, *Women Camp Followers of the American Revolution* (Philadelphia: George S. MacManus, 1952).

10. Wendy Chapkis, "Sexuality and Militarism" in *Women and the Military System*, ed. Eva Isaksson (New York: St. Martin's Press, 1988); Susan Brownmiller, *Against Our Will: Men, Women, and Rape* (New York: Bantam Books, 1975).

11. Hobson, *Uneasy Virtue*, 180.

12. Allan M. Brandt, *No Magic Bullet: A Social History of Venereal Disease in the United States Since 1880* (New York: Oxford University Press, 1985).

13. Frank E. Vandiver, *Black Jack: The Life and Times of John J. Pershing* (College Station: Texas A&M University Press, 1977), 775–76.

14. Interview, Washington, D.C., 19 April 1991.

15. Blumenthal, *Women Camp Follower*, 61, 66.

16. Ibid., 66.

17. Hobson, *Uneasy Virtue*, 167.

18. U.S. Interdepartmental Social Hygiene Board, "General Analysis of the answers given in 15,010 case records of women and girls who came to the attention of field workers of the United States Interdepartmental Hygiene Board, and of its predecessors, the War

Department and the Navy Department commissions on training-camp activities" (Washington, D.C.: Government Printing Office, 1922) 172–73.

19. Ibid., 174.

20. *Pacific Stars and Stripes*, 4 September 1971.

21. Quoted in Cynthia Enloe, *Does Khaki Become You? The Militarisation of Women's Lives* (Boston: South End Press, 1983), 81.

22. Billie Mitchell, "The Creation of Army Officers and the Gender Lie: Betty Grable or Frankenstein?" in *It's Our Military Too! Women and the U.S. Military*, ed. Judith Hicks Stiehm (Philadelphia: Temple University Press, 1996), 39.

23. Ibid., 38.

24. U.S. Department of Defense, Office of the Inspector General, *The Tailhook Report: The Official Inquiry into the Events of Tailhook 91* (New York: St. Martin's Press, 1993), 85.

25. Jean Zimmerman, *Tailspin: Women at War in the Wake of Tailhook* (New York: Doubleday, 1995), 9.

26. Mridu Gulati, "The United States Military's Campaign against Venereal Disease: The Changing Definition of the Prostitute and the Detention Home During World War I" (undergraduate honors thesis, Harvard University Archives, 1993), 27.

27. Quoted in Jeanne Holm, *Women in the Military: An Unfinished Revolution*, rev. ed. (Novato, Calif.: Presidio Press, 1982), 69.

28. Ibid., 70, 78.

29. *The Invisible Force: Women in the Military*, documentary film (1987). Available from the University of Massachusetts, Amherst.

30. Blumenthal, *Women Camp Followers*, 46.

31. Hobson, *Uneasy Virtue*, 175.

32. Chicago Bar Association, "Brief Re:," 1.

33. Moon, *Sex among Allies*, 97.

34. William Lawrence, "Venereal Diseases in the Army, Navy, and Community" (Washington, D.C.: U.S. War Department, 1918).

35. U.S. Office of Community War Services, *Challenge to Community Action*, 2.

36. Ibid., 4.

37. Blumenthal, *Women Camp Followers*, 80–81, 64, 26.

38. Moon, *Sex among Allies*, ch. 4.

39. Jeff Tuten, "Germany and the Two World Wars," in *Female Soldiers: Combatants or Noncombatants? Historical and Contemporary Perspectives*, ed. Nancy Loring Goldman (Westport, Conn.: Greenwood Press, 1982), 47–60.

40. Quoted in Laurie Weinstein, introduction to *Wives and Warriors: Women and the Military in the United States and Canada*, ed. Laurie Weinstein and Christie White (Westport, Conn.: Bergin and Garvey, 1997), xv.

41. Mady Weschler Segal, "The Argument for Female Combatants," in Goldman, *Female Soldiers*, 273-74.

42. Lucinda Peach, "Gender Ideology in the Ethics of Women in Combat," in Stiehm, *It's Our Military Too!*, 170-71.

43. Holm, *Women in the Military*, 303.

44. Mitchell, "Creation of Army Officers," 39.

45. Blumenthal, *Women Camp Followers*, 51.

46. Ibid, 63.

47. Ibid., 66.

48. Ibid., 48.

49. Sara Ruddick, *Maternal Thinking: Toward a Politics of Peace* (Boston: Beacon Press, 1989).

50. Gulati, "United States Military's Campaign," 77; Brandt, *No Magic Bullet*, ch. 4 (see poster illustrations).

51. Philip Broughton, "Prostitution and the War," *Public Affairs Pamphlets* 65 (1942): 2.

52. American Bar Association, *Venereal Disease*, 1–2.

53. U.S. Office of Community War Services, *Challenge to Community Action*, 9.

54. Moon, *Sex among Allies*, 89.

55. Francine D'Amico, "Policing the U.S. Military's Race and Gender Lines," in Weinstein and White, *Wives and Warriors*, 220.

56. Ibid., 223.

57. Ibid., 223.

58. Conversation, Washington, D.C., June 1990.

59. Enloe, *Does Khaki Become You?*, 81.

60. Jacqueline K. Davis, "Memorandum to General Anthony Lukeman, USMC: 1987 WestPac visit of the Defense Advisory Committee on Women in the Service," 26 August 1987. Available from the DACOWITS office, Washington, D.C.

61. Ibid.

62. U.S. Department of Defense, Office of the Inspector General, *Tailhook Report*, 84.

63. Ibid., 85.

64. Aurora Camacho de Schmidt, "Voices of Hope and Anger: Women Resisting Militarization," in *The Sun Never Sets: Confronting the Network of Foreign U.S. Military Bases*, ed. Joseph Gerson and Bruce Birchard (Boston: South End Press, 1991), 110.

65. Gulati, "United States Military's Campaign," 30.

Eleven

Women Oppose U.S. Militarism
Toward a New Definition of Security

Gwyn Kirk

The largest proportion of U.S. federal income-tax dollars, $627 billion (or 52 percent) in 1997-1998, supports current and past military operations.[1] We are told that the country needs a strong military to defend us from possible attack and to protect "American interests" worldwide. Embedded in this rationale is the notion that men will protect women and children. Women who oppose the U.S. military argue that rather than offering protection, it is a constant source of danger, especially to women and children and to the physical environment. U.S. military operations also limit the sovereignty and self-determination of countries that host U.S. bases. This chapter focuses on women's opposition to U.S. militarism and presents examples from the United States, western Europe, East Asia, and the Pacific.

The United States: Living in the Belly of the Beast

Contemporary U.S. women's opposition to militarism has roots in Quakerism and the nineteenth-century suffrage and temperance movements. For example, Julia Ward Howe, remembered as the author of the Civil War song "The Battle Hymn of the Republic," became involved in the suffrage movement as a way of organizing women for peace. In 1873, she initiated Mothers' Day for Peace on 2 June, a day to honor mothers, who, she felt, best understood the suffering caused by war. Women's Peace Festivals were organized in several cities, mainly in the Northeast and Midwest, featuring women speakers who opposed war and military training in schools.[2] During the 1890s, many women's organizations had peace committees. In 1914, the Women's Peace Party was formed under the leadership of Carrie Chapman Catt and Jane Addams.[3] In 1915, despite difficulties of wartime travel, more than one thousand women from twelve countries participated in the Congress of Women in the Hague, the Netherlands, to "cut across national enmities" and to call for an end to the war.[4] The congress sent delegations to meet with fourteen heads of state and attempted to influence press and public opinion. A second congress at the end of the war established an ongoing international organization: the Women's International League for Peace and Freedom (WILPF).[5]

In the 1950s and 1960s, more U.S. women than men opposed the Korean and Vietnam Wars. In 1961, Women Strike for Peace (WSP) was founded in response to atomic bomb tests.[6] The WSP had a younger membership than the WILPF, though it also comprised mainly white, middle-class women. They picketed the White House, organized demonstrations, presented educational programs, and held a one-day women's "strike" on 1 November 1961, around the slogan: "End the Arms Race Not the Human Race." In 1963, the WSP was among those responsible for the passage of the Atmospheric Test Ban Treaty prohibiting aboveground nuclear tests. The WSP called attention to "the fact that after each aboveground nuclear explosion, the level of radiation in milk rose dramatically."[7] Members were encouraged to have their children's lost baby teeth tested for strontium 90, a radioactive isotope found in nuclear fallout and deposited in bones and teeth in place of calcium. They boycotted dairies as dangerous to their children's health, and sent the baby teeth with the lab reports to their senators.

The near-meltdown of the nuclear power plant at Three Mile Island in 1980 was the impetus for a new group, the Women's Pentagon Action (WPA). Thousands of women surrounded the Pentagon in November 1980 and 1981, their Unity Statement an instant feminist antimilitarist "classic."[8] Like the WILPF and the WSP, the WPA included pacifists, Quakers, and socialists, but unlike these groups, there was significant participation of radical feminists and lesbian feminists. They protested the enormous U.S. military budget and the ecological destruction caused by military operations. They challenged the widespread culture of violence manifested in war toys, films, and video games; the connection between violence and sexuality in pornography, rape, battering, and incest; and the connections between militarism and racism. The demonstrations were organized in four stages: mourning, rage, empowerment, and defiance, culminating in the arrest of many who chose to blockade the doors of the Pentagon.[9]

By the 1980s, the WILPF, WSP, WPA, Another Mother for Peace (started in the late 1960s by women in the Hollywood film industry), and Women's Action for Nuclear Disarmament (founded by Australian pediatrician Dr. Helen Caldicott in 1981) were all active in opposing the nuclear arms race through demonstrations, educational campaigns, lobbying, and direct action. The women's peace camp outside U.S.A.F. base at Greenham Common (England), started in 1981, inspired dozens of other peace camps outside military bases and weapons production plants in western Europe, North America, and Australia.[10] These protests were imaginative, colorful, and assertive and had powerful artistic and emotional elements. They were usually organized in a decentralized way, with an emphasis on each woman's personal responsibility. They combined a deep concern for a life-sustaining future with political confrontation; they were oppositional and celebratory at the same time. At the Seneca Women's Encampment for Peace and Justice near Romulus, New York, thousands of women gathered in the spring and summer of 1983 to oppose the shipment of nuclear cruise missiles from the Seneca Army Depot to U.S.A.F. base at Greenham Common.[11] Women also set up peace camps outside the Savannah River nuclear power plant (Georgia), Boeing (Puget Sound, Wash.), and Sperry-Univac (Minneapolis/St. Paul), protesting weapons production at the very gates of the bases and plants where weapons components were produced and stored.[12]

These organizations brought together women of all ages and varied backgrounds, though they were largely white and middle class. Many saw their opposition to war in moral terms—war was simply wrong—or in terms of their responsibility to protect and nurture their children. Although this approach can sentimentalize motherhood, it is powerful because women, as mothers, are expected to support, not oppose, the government. In seeking to protect their children and the children of "enemy" mothers, women are conforming to conventional female roles. Yet they expose fundamental contradictions: that the state, through militarism, does not let them get on with their job of mothering.[13] Others oppose militarism as intrinsically sexist and racist. Militaries depend on people's ability to see reality in oppositional categories: us and them, friends and enemies, kill or be killed.[14] They are organized on rigidly hierarchical lines, demanding unquestioning obedience to superiors. Although the U.S. military uses women's labor in many ways, as shown in this anthology, it does so on its own terms. Sexual harassment of U.S. women military personnel by their buddies and superiors, and high rates of domestic violence in U.S. military families are not coincidences, on this view. Cynthia Enloe's concept of "militarized masculinity" is relevant here.[15] This notion of manhood involves an individualistic heroism of physical strength, emotional detachment, the capacity for violence and killing, and an appearance of invulnerability. Young boys are socialized to this kind of manliness from early childhood. In basic military training, new recruits are punished for any failure or weakness in order to push them beyond the limits of their strength and stamina and to train them to follow orders without question. A key aspect of this process is the way recruits are insulted and reviled by drill sergeants as "women" and "queers" as part of the military promise "to make a man" of them; that is, to make them not-women.[16] Women peace activists make the connection between violence against women and the international violence of war. Another argument concerns the waste involved in war—the waste of lives, as well as of public resources required to maintain the military.

Women of color who oppose U.S. militarism use similar arguments. They also draw on critiques of racism at home and imperialism abroad, and have linked antimilitarist concerns with civil rights activism and anticolonial struggles for self-determination in Africa, the Caribbean, and Central America. The work of African American women writers, organizers, and public figures such as Angela Davis, Coretta Scott King, June Jordan, Sonia Sanchez, and Alice Walker is pertinent here. Native American women link their opposition to U.S. militarism with their history of oppression and near-genocide in this country, the long list of treaties with Indian nations that the U.S. government has broken, and the contamination of native lands as part of the process of weapons production. For example, toxic fallout from nuclear testing on Western Shoshone land in Nevada, which the Western Shoshone people have never ceded to the U.S. government.[17] Barbara Omolade notes the contradictions of militarism for people of color in the United States, many of whom support the military—even if reluctantly—because it provides one of the few avenues for education, a secure income, benefits, social mobility, and the opportunity to get away from crisis-torn inner cities.[18] She comments that people of color in the U.S. military fight for a country where they are oppressed; the people they fight against and are trained to kill are often other people of color; and combatants of color are more likely to be killed compared to their white counterparts, as happened in Vietnam. Although the armed services were officially integrated in 1948, decades before desegregation in southern states, racism is still common. In 1994, a House Armed Services Committee investigation uncovered serious problems with institutionalized racism through-out the armed forces.[19]

Some women of color have been highly critical of white women's perspectives that often did not integrate anti-racist work with opposition to militarism.[20] Huge demonstrations like the peace rally in Central Park (New York City) on 12 June 1982 brought people together across lines of difference. This also happened in local organizations, though for the most part white women's antimilitarist activism was separate from that of women of color. An exception was the opposition to U.S. intervention in Nicaragua and El Salvador, where more diverse groups of women worked together.[21]

Western Europe: Cutting Down the Fence

In 1979, the North Atlantic Treaty Organization (NATO), an alliance of North American and western European countries dominated by the United States, decided to site a new generation of U.S. nuclear missiles at bases in Belgium, Britain, the Netherlands, Italy, and West Germany. The intention was to bring U.S. nuclear weaponry within range of targets in the Soviet Union by using sites in Europe as forward bases.[22] Widespread European opposition to this policy crystallized in the early 1980s. It was based on fear that these countries would become targets for nuclear attack or retaliation, and anger, further provoked by President Reagan's remark that the United States was planning "to win a limited nuclear war in Europe." In all five countries there were tremendous demonstrations and rallies, in some cases the largest ever held in a particular country. Women were especially active and initiated a new kind of public opposition by maintaining round-the-clock vigils and peace camps outside U.S. bases at Greenham Common (England), Comiso (Sicily), and Soesterberg (the Netherlands). WILPF chapters were active in several countries; Women for Peace groups organized in West Germany and the Netherlands; Women Oppose the Nuclear Threat (WONT) and Babies Against the Bomb formed in Great Britain.[23]

Women literally cut down miles of fence around the U.S. Air Force base at Greenham Common. They kept up a campaign of nonviolent direct action that involved gatherings of as many as forty thousand women on occasion, as well as countless smaller actions where women blocked the roads into the base, went onto the base, and blockaded missile convoys that, after September 1993, regularly left the base on maneuvers. These actions were paralleled by others in many towns and cities throughout the country, some of them coordinated on the same day. Women also lobbied politicians, organized educational campaigns, and argued their case in court. As in the United States, this mainly white women's movement emphasized gender over race and class.

East Asia: Colonial Legacies and Cold War Politics

The U.S. military has operated more than three hundred facilities in the East Asia/Pacific region since the end of World War II. Troops are involved in regular maneuvers and military training that include the firing of live ammunition.[24] These activities often destroy cropland; contaminate land, groundwater, and the ocean; and cause a great deal of noise, disruption, and accidents.

In the Philippines, U.S. intervention dates back to August 1898, when the United States took over the country after defeating Spain in the Spanish-American War. The United States developed some twenty-four military facilities there. Subic Bay Naval Base was the largest U.S. Navy base outside the mainland Clark Air Force Base was also very large and highly significant strategically. In 1992, the Philippines Senate voted against continuing the lease for these bases and they were closed, but not before a new agreement had been put in place: the Acquisition and Cross-Servicing Agreement (ACSA), which gives the U.S. military access to ports, airfields, and military installations in the Philippines for resupply, refueling, and repairs, as well as R and R (rest and recreation; often called I and I, intoxication and intercourse).

U.S. intervention in South Korea dates from World War II. Korea had been colonized by Japan in 1910. With the defeat of Japan at the end of World War II, U.S. troops were stationed in the southern half of the Korean peninsula below the 38th parallel, and Soviet troops in the North. Korea was formally divided into two nations, North and South, separated by the 155–mile-long Demilitarized Zone (DMZ), dividing families whose members ended up on different sides of the new border. The Korean War (1950–1953) started when North Korea attempted to take over the South. Together with South Korean and UN forces, the U.S. reversed this attack. The possibility that it might happen again—which contemporary commentators view as extremely unlikely—has been a cornerstone of U.S. military policy to the present day. Now, more than forty years after the end of the Korean War and more than fifty years since Korean independence, the U.S. military presence is still strong, with at least 35,000 troops and 120 to 180 military facilities in a country one-fourth the size of California. The Cold War lives on in Korea because no peace treaty has been signed between North and South. One million or more troops, heavily armed, face one another across the DMZ, a sealed border with no traffic across it. South Koreans cannot visit the North, and vice versa.[25]

A third example is Okinawa, a small group of islands in southwest Japan, formerly an independent kingdom with its own language and culture but annexed by Japan in 1865. Situated midway between Manila and Tokyo, just off the mainland of Asia, Okinawa is a highly strategic location and was the site of three months' fierce fighting between Japan and the United States at the end of World War II. In 1945, the islands came under direct U.S. occupation, which continued until 1972, a full twenty years later than the rest of Japan. The U.S. military appropriated land and homes for military bases, which, like those in the Philippines, were a staging post for U.S. planes and troops for Korea, Vietnam, and the Persian Gulf. Okinawa is the poorest prefecture in Japan. It has an unemployment rate twice that of the rest of the country, and houses 75 percent of the U.S. military in Japan, although it accounts for only 0.6 percent of the land area. There are forty-two U.S. bases and some 30,000 troops together with 22,500 family members in Okinawa.[26]

Violence against Women

The behavior of U.S. troops toward Asian civilians has been an inflammatory issue in South Korea, the Philippines, and Japan. The National Campaign for Eradication of Crime by U.S. Troops in Korea was founded in 1993, growing out of a coalition including women, students, labor, religious leaders, and human rights activists that formed to protest the brutal rape and murder of a young woman, Yun Kumi, the previous year. The coalition organized public demonstrations and demanded that Ms. Yun's murderer be brought to trial, noting, with heavy irony, the slogan of the Second Army Division based in Korea: To Live by Chance, Love by Choice, Kill by Profession. The campaign cites a South Korean Assembly report that estimated 39,542 crimes committed by U.S. military personnel between 1967 and 1987. These included murders, rapes, sexual abuse, arson, theft, smuggling, fraud, traffic offenses, and the sale of PX merchandise off-base. These crimes have continued, as exemplified by the murder of Yun Kumi, though they are not always reported. The Korea Women's Hot Line, a women's organization active around violence against women, has also recently taken up this issue, as has Korean Church Women United, a Christian organization.

In Okinawa, too, violence against women and girls has generated outrage against U.S. bases by many Okinawans. In September 1995, two U.S. marines and a sailor abducted a twelve-year-old Okinawan girl on her way home from a store. They bundled her into their rental car; taped her mouth, eyes, hands, and feet with duct tape; and took her to a deserted road where they beat and raped her, and left her unconscious. Initially, the news of the rape was reported very briefly in local newspapers. But feminist activists, returning from the NGO Forum of the 4th UN Conference on Women, in Beijing, mounted a campaign to publicize the incident more widely.[27] They formed a new organization, Okinawan Women Act Against Military Violence, which has played a significant role in revitalizing Okinawan opposition to the U.S. military presence. For older people, this rape stirred bitter memories of many rapes and other crimes committed by U.S. military personnel, officially estimated at 4,700 since 1972, 509 being particularly brutal.[28] These figures are a conservative estimate because many crimes are not reported. Also, in official records, rape, robbery, and arson were lumped together in one category. Part of the Okinawan women's organizing involves documenting this crime record as completely as possible.

U.S. military officials and personnel were quick to attribute the Okinawan girl's rape to "a few bad apples." Participants in the thirteen-member Okinawa Women's America Peace Caravan, who came to the United States in February 1996 to call for the removal of U.S. bases from Okinawa, see such sexualized violence as a crime produced by the military system, not just by individuals. They argue that military training is an inherently dehumanizing process that turns "soldiers into war machines who inflict violence on the Okinawan community, only a chain-link fence away."[29] Military training also encourages the construction of an aggressive male sexuality in need of regular release—hence the explicit arrangements for sexual servicing of military personnel. So accepted is this practice that the (then) commander of the U.S. forces in the Pacific, Admiral Richard C. Macke, casually remarked, "I think it [the rape] was absolutely stupid. . . . I've said several times, for the price they paid to rent the car, they could have had a girl."[30]

Amerasian Children

Advocates for women's rights in East Asia also critique militarized prostitution, discussed elsewhere in this anthology, and the situation of Amerasian children, an often-neglected and vulnerable group.

Many bar women and former bar women in Okinawa, South Korea, the Philippines, and Vietnam have mixed-race children fathered by U.S. military personnel. Some of these people are now in their thirties and forties, having been born during the Korean War or Vietnam War. Others are young children, born to women recently involved with U.S. troops. Most of them have been raised in poverty and are further stigmatized by their mothers' occupation and their own mixed-race heritage.[31] Many have not had much schooling as a result of poverty, intimidation, and harassment from their peers, and the prejudice and racism in these countries. Amerasians whose fathers are African American may do well in sports or music and gain some acceptance in these stereotypically "black spheres." Some of the girls become bar women like their mothers. Kim Yeon Ja, who notes that she had more than twenty-five abortions in her twenty-five years as a bar woman in South Korea, was determined not to "bring another life into this world if he/she has life like mine."[32] The Pearl Buck Foundation provides small stipends to help support Amerasian children who are registered with the foundation. There is no support from the various governments involved, including the U.S. government. A relatively small number of such children are adopted by U.S. families, but this is expensive and impossible for children whose births have not been registered, and who are, in effect, stateless. Numbers are difficult to estimate. In the Philippines some fifty thousand Amerasian children have been born since the 1940s.[33] The Olongapo Working Committee on Abandoned and Street Children estimated that the majority of the city's three thousand street children were Amerasians.[34] The Coalition on the Rights and Welfare of Amerasians advocates and demands funds for the education, health care, and other needs of Amerasian children in the Philippines.[35] Du Rae Bang and Sae Woom Tuh, shelters for Korean women who service U.S. military personnel, offer night care and educational programs for Amerasian children.

The Pacific: Nuclear Colonialism

The islands of the Pacific are like stepping-stones for the U.S. military across this vast ocean from Hawai'i, colonized by the United States in 1898, westward to Guam and Belau. According to Walden Bello, the Pacific Command is "an integrated and extremely secretive complex composed of mobile forces and fixed bases, linking Japan, Korea, Micronesia, the Philippines and Australia with the ostensible purpose of confronting the U.S.S.R. and China in the Pacific."[36] Micronesia, which includes the islands of Belau, Kwajalein, Rongelap, and Bikini, was administered by the United States as a United Nations Strategic Trust Territory from 1947 to 1969. In return for permission to use land for military bases, the U.S. government offered military protection, money, infrastructure such as roads and airstrips, and educational opportunities in the United States for young people. Despite this pressure on these poor communities, opposition to U.S. military policy comes from various local organizations, many of which are part of the Nuclear Free and Independent Pacific network. The People's Charter declares the Pacific a nuclear-free zone and affirms a shared commitment to "work to ensure the withdrawal of colonial powers from the Pacific."[37] The Pacific Concerns Resource Center has branches in Honolulu, Vanuatu, Belau, and Aotearoa (the indigenous name for New Zealand). Women are prominent in these organizations, though they may not always have formal leadership positions.[38] Women play a crucial role in organizations such as Iepjeltok (the Club of Bikini Women) and Kl-Talreng (Belau).

Atomic Testing

In the 1950s and early 1960s the United States, as well as Britain and France, undertook a series of atomic tests in the Pacific, which irradiated whole islands and contaminated soil and water for generations to come. Subsequent to U.S. tests on Bikini, many Micronesian women have given birth to children with severe illnesses or disabilities caused by radiation, including some "jelly fish babies" without skeletons who live only a few hours. Pacific-island women and men have contracted several kinds of cancer as a result of their exposure to high levels of radioactive fallout.[39] People have had to leave their ancestral lands that had been contaminated by radiation. Given the long-lasting effects of atomic material in the food chain and people's reproductive systems, these disabilities and illnesses are likely to persist for many generations. In 1969, some years after the Partial Test Ban Treaty (1963), which prohibited atomic tests in the atmosphere, the United States ended its trusteeship of Micronesia. Then U.S. Secretary of State Henry Kissinger was openly dismissive of the indigenous people in his comment "[T]here's only 90,000 people out there, who gives a damn?"[40] Film footage of the U.S. tests included in newsreels for U.S. audiences had described the islanders as happy savages.[41] Many Pacific islanders view these atomic—and later, nuclear—tests, which France continued until 1996, as imperialist and racist. The United States government has been very slow to acknowledge its responsibilities to the Micronesian people, despite their protests, lobbying, and lawsuits.[42]

Base Negotiations

In 1979, the people of Belau wrote the world's first "nuclear-free" constitution; it bans the storage, transportation, and testing of nuclear weapons in the islands and its territorial waters. This was quickly challenged by the U.S. government, which wanted permanent land rights in the islands in exchange for money for development and education. In the short term, the U.S. military wanted to develop a port and an airfield in Belau, and has pressured the Belauan government to hold numerous referenda, seeking the 75 percent vote needed to override the constitution.

Women active in Kl-Talreng (meaning "unity of heart and mind" in the Belauan language) organized to protect the constitution.

> We don't want militarism in Belau because we experienced one of the bloodiest battles of the Second World War. We don't want the protection of the military. We want to be protected from them. . . . We have noticed during the last forty years with the United States that their customs are very different. Our tradition is cooperation, while the US custom is very individual and they are ruining our lifestyle. Above all they do not care about keeping the land and the ocean unpolluted. If there were two Belaus we could give one away, but there's only one and we have to be careful with it.[43]

Much opposition to U.S. militarism in Asia and the Pacific stems from the desire for sovereignty and self-determination. The presence of U.S. bases, troops, and regular war games are a daily reminder of U.S. domination and of the acceptance of this by host governments. In Okinawa and South Korea, U.S. troops live in spacious, fenced-off enclaves—some with golf courses and swimming pools—in marked contrast to local people, whose close-packed homes are crowded aside. Under Status of Forces Agreements in Okinawa and South Korea, U.S. military personnel who commit crimes against local people are not usually turned over to the local police, and often are not punished for what they do. Typically, U.S. military personnel know very little about the countries they are posted to—their customs, history, language, and culture. They speak English, pay their way with dollars, buy U.S. goods, smoke U.S. cigarettes, eat U.S. food, and watch U.S. TV programs via satellite.

As well as condemning U.S. military personnel who commit acts of violence against local women, women's opposition to the U.S. military in, for example, the Philippines, Okinawa, and Belau has also turned on arguments for self-determination and local control of land and resources in the interests of local people. Women from the Pacific urged European peace activists to think about European campaigns against U.S. bases in terms of political independence from NATO. In Belau and other Pacific islands, opposition to U.S. militarism is also framed in terms of indigenous views that hold sacred the land and ocean. This deep respect for the natural world is in sharp contrast to the severe environmental contamination caused by military operations.

Women's Peace Activism as Reactive and Proactive

Much, but not all, women's peace activism is reactive. Clearly, if the military did not exist or were not doing what it is doing, women could be doing other things too. Peace activists are not integral to the functioning of the military in the way that enlisted women or military wives are. But because they choose to challenge military activities and policies, their lives and daily routines are also profoundly shaped by the military, which ties up their resources—skills, talents, time, and energy—as it does those of women directly involved as "insiders." Organizing sustained opposition to the military is time-consuming. Also one must be able to drop other commitments in order to react in a timely manner. Like other activists, women peace activists may risk losing sight of wider questions, such as possible alternatives to militarism, as they scramble to keep up with the day-to-day activities involved in being military "watchdogs," keeping the fliers, newsletters, and press releases coming. They are also faced with the challenge of balancing home life, family responsibilities, paid work, or education, especially if they are to sustain their organizing work over the years.

The many fences and "KEEP OUT" signs at military bases are both literal and symbolic barriers to knowing what goes on inside. Peace activists draw attention to military activities—which, typically, receive little critical media coverage—and, thus, expose them to public awareness and scrutiny. In South Korea, for example, activists have protested the murders of Korean women by U.S. military personnel with powerful public rallies displaying photos of the dead women. Women who blockaded the gates of the base at Greenham Common, and those who encircled the Pentagon, chanting and drumming in mourning and rage, also created space for public debate and opposition. These actions are reactive, but at the same time they create new opportunities for public awareness and resistance.

What kind of opposition is thought possible in a given context depends on women's reading of their political circumstances. In the Philippines and Okinawa, opposition to the U.S. military presence has been much more vocal than in South Korea, where political discourse is still dominated by Cold War attitudes. Anti–United States remarks and activism are seen as unpatriotic and procommunist, a serious charge in South Korea, where many social activists have served jail sentences for opposing authoritarian governments, even though many

Koreans are committed to reunification of North and South. Currently, South Korean activists are pushing for revisions of the Status of Forces Act so that U.S. military personnel who commit crimes against Koreans will be punished. They recognize that this is a relatively modest goal, constrained by political realities.

At a personal level, antimilitarist activism can be rewarding and empowering. It provides a vehicle for women's feelings, convictions, and integrity. They learn a great deal about military policy and strategy, the public officials and agencies responsible for them, and the alignments of politicians, labor unions, and religious or environmental organizations. They learn how the media work and develop skills in organizing and public speaking. Their analysis and understanding of what is going on locally often expands to become national and international in scope.

Opposition to military policy also takes up emotional energy. Learning about how weapons kill and seeing the brinkmanship played by politicians may make antimilitarist activists more afraid and frustrated. Often they are outraged about military operations, which can be a potent "fuel" for continuing work. Many people are numb in the face of military realities. Military personnel are trained to distance themselves emotionally from what they are involved in, under the guise of "just following orders." Women peace activists voice emotional reactions. They are often put down as hysterical females by the authorities, who say they are incapable of grasping the intricacies of military policy or the technicalities of military operations. They are told to rely on male experts and not to meddle in things they do not understand.

Indeed, notions of gender are often used to constrain such women, but in contradictory ways. Greenham women challenged accepted gender boundaries as well as physical boundaries. Critics separated the majority, whom they condescendingly characterized as nice housewives, from a few "agitators," said to be communist sympathizers who had managed to dupe the housewives. The mainstream press emphasized the harsh conditions of the peace camp, where women lived in all weathers without electricity or proper toilets, and from which they were often evicted by the authorities. The implication was that "real" women would not choose to live like that.[44] Much more space was given to these details rather than explaining why women had, indeed, chosen to live at Greenham. Some feminists criticized Greenham women for being all too womanly, for inadvertently supporting the conventional "gender regime" by reinforcing the man-as-warrior/woman-as-pacifist dichotomy. Others argued that women peace activists support U.S. militarism by "giving it energy" rather than focusing on women-defined alternative institutions. Mixed-gender peace organizations sometimes criticized women's organizing as divisive and argued that the issues are too important to be left to women.

Despite the strengths of women's antimilitary activism, peace women have had limited success in changing military policy. In 1987, Reagan and Gorbachev signed the Intermediate Nuclear Force (INF) Treaty. This provided for the withdrawal of U.S. and Soviet nuclear missiles from western and eastern Europe, in large part because of concerted opposition, especially by women. At the same time similar missiles were deployed on U.S. warships in the Pacific, and later used in the Gulf War. Women's organizations in the Philippines were part of a concerted prodemocracy movement that ousted President Marcos and, subsequently, the U.S. bases. Women's Education, Development, Productivity, and Research Organization (WEDPRO) made proposals for alternative development of the baselands that would benefit local people. But the Philippines government preferred to encourage foreign investment in hotels, casinos, duty-free shops, and factories with the draw of cheap labor, leaving local people with, at best, minimum-wage jobs, many of them temporary. WEDPRO and other feminist groups have been unsuccessful so far, in getting either the Philippine or U.S. governments to take responsibility for former bar women left without work, or Amerasian children abandoned by their American fathers.

U.S. residents and citizens are in a stronger position than activists from other countries to speak out on these issues, as allies, in this country. We can vote, lobby, engage in direct action, and undertake educational and media campaigns in an attempt to influence policy decisions. Women peace activists in the United States have a responsibility to work in solidarity with their counterparts in other countries. This includes support for projects that aim to enhance the dignity, voice, and agency of women and children affected by the U.S. military presence; making information on associated issues much more widely known in the United States; revitalizing feminist antimilitarist discourse and activism in this country; and linking the effects of U.S. military policy, especially on women and children, at home and abroad. This last point is most important in reframing discussion of security. The government argues that ordinary citizens are not competent to judge foreign policy issues and does not allow dissemination of detailed information about them on the argument that this would hurt "national security." Women should treat foreign policy matters as our business and make links between domestic and foreign policy so that we can trace the various ways women and children are harmed by U.S. military policies and operations, whether in this country or abroad. The ballistic defense system ("Star Wars") program, for example, costs an estimated $91 billion, that could pay for early education for 740,000 children under Head Start for twenty-six years.[45] Currently, 150,000 children with disabilities are having their Supplemental Security Income (SSI) cut to save $800 million, or one-third the cost of building and maintaining one B-2 bomber. Twenty-one such planes have been built at a cost of $45 billion; nine more are planned for a further $27 billion.[46]

Peace activists spend much of their time saying *no*, emphasizing what they are against. But such women are also saying *yes* to the life-affirming values they believe in. The process of demilitarization has economic, political, and technical aspects. It involves a redefinition of manliness and the reconstruction of gender relations. And it requires nonviolent ways of resolving conflict at personal and global levels. Many activists work at practical projects that embody some small piece of this larger vision. Examples include conflict resolution in schools; work as healers, on rape crisis lines or in shelters for victims of domestic violence; establishing community gardens and kitchens; or working with Amerasian chil-

dren. Alternative economic projects to support bar women include sewing projects in Olongapo (Philippines), and a bakery and herb-growing project in Korea.
Such projects may be temporary, small scale, or fragile, but through them women
peace activists are engaged in direct and indirect opposition to the military.
Alternatives may not be something new but a reclaiming of traditional ways of
doing things, for example, teaching indigenous culture and language in Belau,
Okinawa, or Hawai'i, and practicing traditional ceremonies.

Redefining Security

Current notions of security usually involve strength and force. As a society, we
build walls, gates, and fences; lock people up, keeping them in or out; carry
mace, buy guns, and stockpile weapons. These are all ways of separating people
and maintaining hierarchies of haves and have-nots. Women who oppose U.S.
militarism have a very different notion of security based on the following prin-
ciples:

1. The assumption of connectiveness and interdependence among peoples.
   This implies the eradication of gross inequalities between rich and poor
   countries and between rich and poor people within countries.
2. A civilian economy that provides for everyone's needs, and a radical shift
   in public-spending priorities.
3. The central importance of genuinely democratic processes and institutions,
   with local control of resources and appropriate education.
4. Cultures that are generative rather than materialistic, with the definition
   of wealth broadened to include all the ways people are enriched.
5. A recognition that we are nurtured and sustained by the earth's wealth
   and need to live in sustainable ways.
6. Respect for differences based on gender, race, and culture, not demoniza-
   tion of "others" and the creation of enemies.
7. The belief that the world's resources should be devoted to people's basic
   needs.
8. A redefinition of manliness, power, and adventure, all currently tied up
   with violence. Rather, men's sense of well-being, pride, belonging, competence, and security should come from institutions and activities that are
   life-enhancing.
9. A radical change in the current gendered division of labor so that men
   become more involved in the bodily and emotional processes of life.
10. A commitment to solving disputes between individuals and communities
    without recourse to violence.

Women who oppose militarism offer cogent critiques. As the examples in this
chapter suggest, this requires a multilayered theoretical analysis integrating issues of gender, race, class, nation, and the global economy. We must continue to

imagine the possibility of true security based on justice and sustainability, and urge others to join with us to make such visions a reality.[47]

NOTES

1. War Resisters League, *Where Your Income Tax Money Really Goes: The United States Federal Budget for Fiscal Year 1998* (New York: War Resisters League, 1997), 1. Available from 339 Lafayette St., New York, NY 10003.

2. Harriet Hyman Alonso, *Peace as a Women's Issue: A History of the U.S. Movement for World Peace and Women's Rights* (Syracuse: Syracuse University Press, 1993).

3. See Sybil Oldfield, "Jane Addams: The Chance the World Missed," in *Women in World Politics: An Introduction*, ed. Francine D'Amico and Peter Beckman (Westport, Conn.: Bergin and Garvey, 1995), 155–68.

4. Roberta Spivek, "The Hague Congress," *Peace and Freedom* 45 (1985).

5. See Carrie A. Foster, *The Women and the Warriors: The U.S. Section of the Women's International League for Peace and Freedom, 1915–1946* (Syracuse: Syracuse University Press, 1995); Catherine Foster, *Women for All Seasons: The Story of W.I.L.P.F.* (Athens: University of Georgia Press, 1989).

6. See Amy Swerdlow, *Women Strike for Peace: Traditional Motherhood and Radical Politics in the 1960s* (Chicago: University of Chicago Press, 1993).

7. Alonso, *Peace as a Women's Issue*, 207.

8. See Leonie Caldecott and Stephanie Leland, ed., *Reclaim the Earth* (London: Women's Press, 1983), 14–19; Lynn Jones, eds., *Keeping the Peace* (London: Women's Press, 1983), 43–44.

9. See Ynestra King, "All is Connectedness," in Jones, *Keeping the Peace*, 40–46.

10. Alice Cook and Gwyn Kirk, *Greenham Women Everywhere* (Boston: South End Press, 1983); Barbara Harford and Sarah Hopkins, *Women at the Wire* (London: Women's Press, 1984); Sasha Roseneil, *Disarming Patriarchy: Feminism and Political Action at Greenham* (Buckingham, England: Open University Press, 1995); Ann Snitow, "Holding the Line at Greenham," *Mother Jones*, March-April 1985, 30–34, 39–44, 46–47.

11. See the following essay.

12. See Participants of the Puget Sound Women's Peace Camp, *We Are Ordinary Women: A Chronicle of the Puget Sound Women's Peace Camp* (Seattle: Seal Press, 1985).

13. Sara Ruddick, *Maternal Thinking: Toward a Politics of Peace* (Boston: Beacon Press, 1989).

14. See Val Plumwood, *Feminism and the Mastery of Nature* (London and New York: Routledge, 1993), ch. 2; Betty A. Reardon, *Sexism and the War System* (New York: Teachers College Press, 1985).

15. See Cynthia Enloe, *Bananas, Beaches, and Bases: Making Feminist Sense of International Politics* (Berkeley: University of California Press, 1990); Enloe, *The Morning After: Sexual Politics at the End of the Cold War* (Berkeley: University of California Press, 1993).

16. See Richard Cleaver and Patricia Myers, eds., *A Certain Terror: Heterosexism, Militarism, Violence, and Change* (Chicago: Great Lakes Region, American Friends Service Committee, 1993); Cynthia Enloe, *Does Khaki Become You? The Militarization of Women's Lives* (Boston: South End Press, 1983); Helen Michalowski, "The Army Will Make a 'Man' out

of You," in *Reweaving the Web of Life: Feminism and Nonviolence*, ed. Pam MacAllister (Philadelphia: New Society, 1982), 326–35.

17. See Winona LaDuke, "A Society Based on Conquest Cannot Be Sustained," in *Toxic Struggles: The Theory and Practice of Environmental Justice*, ed. Richard Hofrichter (Philadelphia and Gabriola Island: New Society, 1993), 98–106; "The Mortality of Wealth: Native America and the Frontier Mentality," *Radical America*, 1993, 69–79; Paul Rodarte, "Military Maneuvers over Native Lands," *Nuclear Times*, winter 1990–1991, 34–38.

18. Barbara Omolade, "We Speak for the Planet," in *Rocking the Ship of State: Toward a Feminist Peace Politics*, ed. Adrienne Harris and Ynestra King (Boulder: Westview Press, 1989), 171–89.

19. Cited by Citizen Soldier, Nazis, Skinheads, Klansmen (New York: Citizen Solider, 1996), 1. Available from 175 Fifth Ave., #2135, New York, NY 10010.

20. See Valerie Amos and Pratisha Parmer, "Challenging Imperial Feminism," *Feminist Review* 17 (1984): 3–19; Wilmette Brown, *Black Women and the Peace Movement* (London: International Women's Day Convention, 1983); Barbara Smith, " 'Fractious, Kicking, Messy, Free': Feminist Writers Confront the Nuclear Abyss," *New England Review/Breadloaf Quarterly*, summer 1983, 581–92.

21. Examples include MADRE, Somos Hermanas, and Women against Imperialism.

22. See Duncan Campbell, *War Plan UK: The Truth about Civil Defence in Britain* (London: Burnett Books, 1982); Diana Johnstone, *The Politics of Euromissiles: Europe's Role in America's World* (London: Verso, 1984); Michael Randle, *People Power: The Building of a New European Home* (Stroud, England: Hawthorne Press, 1991).

23. See Jones, *Keeping the Peace*.

24. See John Miller, *Bases and Battleships* (Foreign Bases Project, P.O. Box 150753, Brooklyn, NY 11215); Joseph Gerson and Bruce Birchard, eds., *The Sun Never Sets: Confronting the Global Network of U.S. Foreign Military Bases* (Boston: South End Press, 1990).

25. See Ahn Ilsoon, Ahn Hae Roung, Cham-Sarang Shim Teo, Du Rae Bang, Korea Church Women United, National Campaign for Eradication of Crime by U.S. Troops in Korea, eds., *Great Army, Great Father: Militarized Prostitution in South Korea; Life in G.I. Town* (Seoul, 1995); Bruce Cumings, "Silent but Deadly: Sexual Subordination in the U.S.-Korean Relationship," in *Let the Good Times Roll: The Sale of Women's Sexual Labor around U.S. Military Bases in the Philippines, Okinawa and the Southern Part of Korea*, ed. Saundra Sturdevant and Brenda Stoltzfus (New York: New Press, 1992); Daniel B. Schirmer, "North Korea: The Pentagon and Issues of War and Peace in the Asia-Pacific Region," *Monthly Review*, July/August 1994, 66–76.

26. Joseph Gerson, "Japan: Keystone of the Pacific," in Gerson and Birchard, The Sun Never Sets,; Military Base Affairs Office and Public Relations Division, *A Message from Okinawa on Military Bases, Peace, and Culture* (Okinawa: Okinawan Prefectural Government, n.d.).

27. Margo Okazawa-Rey and Gwyn Kirk, "Military Security: Confronting the Oxymoron," *Crossroads* 60 (April/May 1996): 4–7.

28. Okinawa Women Act Against Military Violence, internal research document.

29. Okinawa Women Act Against Military Violence, *Okinawan Women's American Peace Caravan* (Naha, Japan: Okinawa Women Act Against Military Violence, 1996), 7.

30. Eric Schmitt, "Admiral's Gaffe Pushes Navy to New Scrutiny of Attitudes," *New York Times*, 19 November 1995, 6Y.

31. Margo Okazawa-Rey, "Amerasian Children of GI Town: A Legacy of U.S. Militarism in South Korea," *Asia Journal of Women's Studies* 3, no. 1 (1997): 71–102.

32. Quoted in Ahn et al., *Great Army, Great Father*, 11.

33. Sheila Coronel and Ninotchka Rosca, "For the Boys: Filipinas Expose Years of Sexual Slavery by the U.S. and Japan," *Ms.*, November/December 1993, 11–15.

34. GABRIELA International Relations Staff, North America, "Women and the U.S. Bases in the Philippines: Generations without Future," *Peace and Freedom*, March/April 1989, 18–21.

35. Lynn Umali, "Left without Alternatives," *Connexions* 44 (1994): 12–14.

36. Walden Bello, "From American Lake to a People's Pacific," in, ed. Sturdevant and Stoltzfus, *Let the Good Times Roll*, 14–21.

37. Nuclear Free Pacific Conference, *The People's Charter for a Nuclear Free Pacific* (Fiji, 1975).

38. See Zohl de Ishtar, *Daughters of the Pacific* (Melbourne: Australia: Spinifex, 1994).

39. Jane Dibblin, *Day of Two Suns: Nuclear Testing and the Pacific Islanders* (New York: New Amsterdam Books, 1989); de Ishtar, *Daughters*.

40. Women Working for a Nuclear-Free and Independent Pacific, *Pacific Women Speak: Why Haven't You Known?* (Oxford: Green Line, 1987), 5.

41. Dennis O'Rourke, dir., *Half Life: A Parable for the Nuclear Age* (1986).

42. Women Working for a Nuclear Free and Independent Pacific, *Nuclear Free and Independent Pacific Bulletin*, no. 20 (1990): 21.

43. Women Working for a Nuclear Free and Independent Pacific, *Nuclear Free and Independent Pacific Bulletin*, no. 6 (1987): 15.

44. See Alison Young, *Femininity in Dissent* (London and New York: Routledge, 1990).

45. Women's International League for Peace and Freedom, *Women's Budget, 1996*.

46. Robert Scheer, "Our Rained-out Bomber," *Nation* 265, no. 8 (September 1997): 6.

47. Also see, for example, Elise Boulding, *Building a Global Civic Culture: Education for an Interdependent World* (Syracuse: Syracuse University Press, 1988); Jeremy Brecher, John Brown Childs, and Jill Cutler, eds., *Global Visions: Beyond the New World Order* (Boston: South End Press, 1993); Annie Cheatham and Mary Clare Powell, *This Way Daybreak Comes: Women's Values and the Future* (Philadelphia: New Society, 1986); Betty A. Reardon, *Women and Peace: Feminist Visions of Global Security* (Albany: State University of New York Press, 1993).

Peace Work
Women Confront the Military

Francine D'Amico

When peace activists confront the military, they force it to justify itself in terms acceptable to ordinary people—people with diverse values and priorities. When *feminist* peace activists challenge the military to justify itself, they reveal its gender camouflage, that is, the established yet sometimes invisible gender politics of the institution. The military attempts to discredit the antimilitarist message of peace activists by playing the gender card, feminizing peace men as unpatriotic wimps and portraying peace women as un-women who transgress appropriate gender boundaries: mothers who neglect their children or lesbians because without men. Especially since the early 1980s, warriors are revered, honored, and fêted, while peace activists are reviled, degraded, and shunned as we attempt to overcome what some call "the Vietnam syndrome."[1] What does it signify that most warriors are *men*—that is, people gendered *masculine* (indeed, quintessentially defined as masculine!)—and that many peace activists are *women*—that is, people gendered *feminine*?[2] The warrior/peace activist gender dichotomy privileges male authority and permits women's deauthorization: "You don't know war—you haven't been there—so you can't make decisions about when war is needed."

In the 1980s, a confrontation between peace women and the military occurred at the Seneca Army Depot in upstate New York. In an old white clapboard farmhouse just outside the tiny village of Romulus, women from around the country and around the globe gathered in the summer of 1983 to "say 'No to war and Yes to life'" by trying to stop the deployment of U.S. intermediate-range missiles to Europe and by creating "an alternative way of living based on women's experiences."[3] The Seneca Army Depot (SEAD) was believed to be the transshipment point for the missiles. The women held educational sessions, marches, and demonstrations to protest the planned deployment, and they occasionally engaged in civil disobedience by entering the base grounds without permission. To protect the base from these dangerous women, Army officials erected observation towers—reminiscent of those in the television sitcom "F Troop"—at intervals around the base perimeter, strung barbed wire along culvert drain openings and atop fencing, and added extra patrols. This did not deter civil disobedience. In the excerpt below, one peace activist from the camp describes a close encounter between demonstrators and townspeople near the base:

I was part of a contingent of 100 NYC women who came to take part in a 15–mile peace walk from Seneca Falls to the Women's Encampment. We were part of the protest against the neighboring Seneca Army Depot, believed to be the major East Coast shipment point for missiles bound for deployment in Europe this fall, specifically the Cruise and Pershing II missiles.

Along the walk many of us handed out flyers, explaining our beliefs and purposes. Most bystanders were minimally polite and often receptive. But near Waterloo, when I asked a woman, "Would you like a leaflet to read?" she screamed at me, "Stick it up your ass!"

We never made it through Waterloo. Two blocks away, the bridge on Route 96 was barricaded by a solid mass of 250 to 300 protesting, shouting people. Many waved American flags, shaking them at us, or carried signs: "Right idea, wrong attitude." "America, love it or leave it." "Our country, right or wrong."

Police struggled to hold back the crowd. As we reached the edge, it was clear we could move no further. Many of us sat down in the road to defuse mounting tensions. Surrounded on three sides by loud and taunting voices, we were soon encircled. Chants of "Go home, Commies," "Go home, Russians," filled the air. Some hurled anti-Semitic and anti-lesbian taunts. A man stuck his face very close to mine and yelled, "You weren't even born in 1945 when I dropped the A-bomb. What do you know about war?" Another man shouted, "Waterloo is the birthplace of Memorial Day, and you have the gall to march through our town?"

A bullhorn announced that we could be arrested for disorderly conduct. Most of the crowd retreated slowly. A sheriff's assistant again warned us that we were risking arrest if we did not move. We told him we wanted to move forward and continue on our peace walk. He threw his hands up in the air and said, "Fine, just get on the sidewalk, just get out of here."

We started to move towards the partially cleared roadway. The crowd, led mostly by angry men, surged toward us again. The police formed a barricade just in time. Some of us sat down and arrests [of the peace marchers] began in this chaos.

The women who refused to move were carried away. A large man, not in uniform, took my arm and said, "Come on, will you get up and walk? I have a bad back." I decided to walk for fear of being hurt. As I was led to the paddy wagon, I told him, "You're arresting the wrong people." Shaking his head resignedly, he answered, "I know, I know."

The peace camp had informed all the proper authorities about our walk well in advance. We had been told that a permit was not required, and that they guaranteed our right to march. It was clear that the police needed to control the situation, and we non-violent women were much easier to arrest than the Waterloo mob. None of us had started on the peace walk intending to commit civil disobedience that day.

We were taken to the Seneca county jail in Waterloo, where 54 of us spent many hours. . . . We all agreed on bail solidarity—to collectively refuse bail—because we felt we had done no wrong and in recognition of the economic injustices of the bail system.

We also collectively decided to refuse to give our names, again to cooperate as little as possible with the system. I became Jane Doe #9.

As it grew dark, we were each issued a green woolen Army blanket. We were fingerprinted, photographed, stripped of all money, jewelry, even my bandanna ("You might want to hang yourself with that"). We were each served orders to appear in court on August 3, and charged with $50 bail. We were also strip-searched, fortunately by a woman who was neither unkind nor hostile toward us. I was led with 15 other women to the third floor of the county jail. . . . [W]e sat on bare Army cots as lawyers came to talk with us. . . .

Upon the discovery that they could not house us all in the county jail, we were driven, at 3 A.M., exhausted and disoriented, to the Interlaken school. Army cots were set up in the school cafeteria, and we finally slept.

Bella Abzug was there to support us. Gov. Cuomo canceled his trip to Maine to remain in New York and monitor the situation.

I remained in the cafeteria-turned-jail-cell until Monday morning, when after much internal dilemma, I chose to post bail for myself. I knew I was breaking the bail solidarity, but women stressed that it was important that each of us do as we needed (I had to get back to my job). . . .

My sister Jane Does appeared in court on August 3. The 43 women still there collectively decided to non-cooperate as thoroughly as possible. The judge wanted to see each woman individually, and so each woman had to be carried and driven separately from the holding area to the court.

By late afternoon, the judge had had enough and "dismissed the charges in the interests of justice." A terrific celebration let loose in the court.

—Laurie Lytel, Ann Arbor, Mich.[4]

Also during the summer of 1983, while the U.S. military was undergoing its largest peacetime expansion in our nation's history, another demonstrator who climbed over the fence at SEAD explained her reasons for participating in civil disobedience actions this way:

I was one of the demonstrators arrested at the Seneca Army Depot yesterday. I have my "Ban and Bar" letter and the threat of a $500 fine and six months in prison if I am caught trespassing again at the Seneca Depot. I have never been arrested before in my life, but having done it once, I know I will do it again.

If breaking the law, breaking it repeatedly, and going to jail is a way of stopping the nuclear arms build-up in this country, then that is what I will do.

When women wanted the vote in this country they had to put their bodies on the line to get it. They were arrested, they went to jail, they came out, they did it again, and finally they won the battle. . . .

Yesterday, on the march to the Depot, when I heard "Go Home" screamed repeatedly at me and my fellow-marchers from people on the sidelines, I felt an overwhelming pity for them. I was home. This was my land, too.

I am not a tool of Moscow. I wouldn't know if I have ever met a Communist. I am not a lesbian or a witch. I am a native-born pacifist and I feel that I have a personal, ultimate responsibility to do what I can to stop this horror. . . .

Many members of my family have been in the military. Some are still in. . . . I do believe that the men who have gone to war in the past are deserving of every respect and consideration.

But we cannot go again.

It is the responsibility of the American people to put an end to war. Americans are the ones with the biggest guns, the mightiest nuclear weapons in the world. Let them stop now and consider how their tax dollar is spent.

If the defense budget of the country were cut in half, we would still be more than adequately defended and there would be money for better schools and hospitals and roads. There would be time. Time for our children to grow and prosper and spread the message of peace and freedom and democracy to the world.

—Norma Lewis Cummins, Cortland, N.Y.[5]

The Seneca Women's Camp for a Future of Peace and Justice closed in 1991, and the Seneca Army Depot base itself is scheduled to close in 1999 as a result of the post–Cold War military drawdown.[6] Some would say the camp failed in the sense that the women did not stop the missile deployment, but others see the camp as a success because of what the women learned about organizing and about themselves and their possibilities for independent action.[7] Ultimately, the missiles were withdrawn from Europe under the terms of the Intermediate Nuclear Force (INF) treaty between the United States and the Soviet Union, and peace activists around the globe—including the women of Seneca and their sisters of Greenham Common—claim some share of responsibility for this policy change.

NOTES

1. Susan Jeffords, *The Remasculinzation of America: Gender in the Vietnam War* (Bloomington: Indiana University Press, 1989).

2. On the warrior/pacifist gender dichotomy, see Jean Bethke Elshtain, *Women and War* (New York: Basic Books, 1987).

3. Rhoda Linton, "Seneca Women's Peace Camp: Shapes of Things to Come," in *Rocking the Ship of State: Toward a Feminist Peace Politics*, ed. Adrienne Harris and Ynestra King (Boulder: Westview Press, 1989) 242.

4. Reprinted with permission from Mima Cataldo, Ruth Putter, Bryna Fireside, and Elaine Lytel, *The Women's Encampment for a Future of Peace and Justice: Images and Writings* (Philadelphia: Temple University Press, 1988), 71–78.

5. Reprinted with permission from Cataldo et al., *The Women's Encampment*, 93.

6. Under federal legislation, the base must close by 1 July 2001, but the base commander, Lt. Col. David C. Olson, and the officials on the Local Redevelopment Authority (LRA) plan on closure in September 1999; this target date is contingent upon mission completion and funding. See Mary LeClair, "Depot Reuse Progresses," *Finger Lakes Times* (Geneva, N.Y.), 10 September 1997, 3.

7. See Linton, "Seneca Women's Peace Camp," 239–61; see also Louise Krasniewicz, *Nuclear Summer: The Clash of Communities at the Seneca Women's Peace Encampment* (Ithaca: Cornell University Press, 1992).

Twelve

A Well-Kept Secret
How Military Spending Costs Women's Jobs

Marion Anderson

Women are some of the chief victims of fifty years of high military spending by the U.S. government. As taxpayers, it costs them money. As workers, it costs them jobs.

How can spending tax money on the military cost women's jobs? Because expenditures involve choices where to spend and where not to spend. The decision, decade after decade, to spend our taxes on warships, planes, tanks, and nuclear weapons are simultaneously decisions not to spend the money on health care, education, the environment, and consumer goods and services. *And these are the areas that employ the vast majority of working women.*

Women are not heavily employed in the industries that produce weapons for the military. They constitute only about 20 percent of the workers in the durable goods industries that produce military materiel like missiles, tanks, and warships. These heavy, metalworking industries are overwhelmingly filled with male employees. The armed forces, too, are heavily male. Just 13 percent of the uniformed armed forces is female. So, when our tax dollars are diverted from civilian goals like education, health care, and the environment, where many women are employed, to expenditures on the military for purchasing weapons and for the armed forces, there is a net loss of jobs for women.

Women have been some of the chief victims of disordered federal priorities. We have had forty-five years of war—hot and cold—where enormous military budgets sustained by the fear of communism took preeminence over all other expenditures in the federal budget. During these years, the institutions that encouraged and fed upon the fear of the Soviet Union grew to have tremendous power within our society. The military-industrial complex included the armed forces, the Central Intelligence Agency, big and small military contractors, the national labs like Sandia and Los Alamos, academics on Pentagon contracts, and members of Congress who received large campaign contributions and lucrative speaking fees from military contractors. The power of this interlocking set of institutions combined with compliant media meant that basic questions about how much is enough, and what makes a nation secure were never asked. These questions are still not being asked now, a decade after the collapse of the Soviet Union.

The constant emphasis on the military preempted the money, brains, and hands of our society. From 1950 through 1980, about one-third of all American scientists and engineers worked for the military. They were far more lavishly funded than their civilian counterparts. While we were pouring billions into the giant maw of the Pentagon, our chief trade competitors, Japan and Germany, were putting their talent and money into developing and producing reasonably priced, high-quality consumer goods, and were shutting us out of industry after industry, costing us millions of high paying manufacturing jobs.

The sustained focus on an enemy also drained our nation of its spiritual resources. If the national emphasis is constantly on fear and hatred, it cannot simultaneously be on life and hope. So, part of the unseen sacrifice of these years has been of the public vision needed both to dream and to work for investments in educating, healing, and building.

The job cost to women of high Pentagon budgets has been going on for a long time. In our 1981 report, *Neither Jobs Nor Security: Women's Unemployment and the Pentagon Budget*, Employment Research Associates considered the number of jobs generated by military expenditures on equipment, supplies, and services, as well as on military personnel, contrasted with the number of jobs that would have been created for women if people had spent their income on normal consumer expenditures and state and local governments. We found that when the military budget was $135 billion, it cost the jobs of 1,270,000 women nationwide. Women had a net loss of jobs in forty-nine of the fifty states; only in Virginia, home of the Pentagon and the CIA, did women have a net job gain.[1]

In 1991, the Employment Research Associates report *Converting the American Economy*[2] showed the economic effects of cutting the military budget $70 billion a year and transferring these funds into needed civilian expenditures on health care, Head Start, education, job training, mass transit, and the environment. The result: more jobs, especially for women. This transfer of funds would have meant more than 460,000 more jobs for women (see table 12.1). Every $1 billion transferred from the Pentagon to these civilian expenditures generates a net gain of about 6,800 women's jobs. We took into consideration all of the jobs lost from cuts in military spending both in industry and in the armed forces. This figure was then contrasted with the more than 1,000,000 new jobs generated by new civilian expenditures. The total was a net job gain of more than over 460,000 new jobs for women.

The vast majority of occupations in which women are heavily engaged also gained jobs (see table 12.2). Now is the time for change. As General Colin Powell said, "I don't see a single nation that I would identify out here now as being a major threat to the United States or to world peace."[3] He added that the United States may be able to reduce its own military strength. "Think hard about it, I'm running out of demons. I'm down to Castro and Kim Il Sung," referring to the aging Communist dictators of Cuba and North Korea.[4]

No one even pretends that we have any formidable enemies left. In fact, the possible adversaries are all poor nations incapable of making the gigantic invest-

TABLE 12.1

Effects on Women's Jobs, by Industry, of Shifting $70 Billion from Military to Civilian Expenditures

	Net Gain Industries		
	Women's jobs lost from military spending cuts	Women's jobs gained from civilian spending increases	Net jobs gained or lost for women
Durable Goods			
Lumber	−780	+2,580	+1,800
Furniture	−1,460	+1,920	+460
Stone, Clay, Glass	−1,060	+2,840	+1,780
Motor Vehicles	−1,240	+1,540	+300
Non-Durable Goods			
Food	−2,150	+3,550	+1,400
Apparel and Textiles	−5,900	+7,780	+1,880
Paper	−1,200	+2,150	+950
Printing	−5,180	+13,100	+7,900
Other Non-Durables	−3,720	+4,210	+490
Construction	−4,500	+28,240	+23,750
Transportation, Utilities, Mining			
Railroads, Trucking, Mining	−4,700	+5,450	+750
Local Transportation	−400	+2,500	+2,100
Communications	−6,300	+7,920	+1,620
Public Utilities	−2,540	+3,810	+1,280
Finance, Insurance, Real Estate			
Banking	−8,360	+11,500	+3,150
Insurance	−8,420	+15,830	+7,400
Credit & Finance	−6,290	+9,720	+3,430
Real Estate	−10,180	+18,960	+8,780
Wholesale & Retail Trade			
Eating & Drinking Places	−25,330	+28,660	+3,330
Rest of Retail	−38,370	+68,340	+29,970
Wholesale	−19,040	+23,060	+4,020
Services			
Hotels	−9,400	+9,760	+360
Personal, Repair, Pvt. Household	−20,300	+30,090	+9,780
Misc. Business Services	−37,680	+44,970	+7,290
Amusement, Recreation, Movies	−4,280	+6,920	+2,640
Misc. Professional	−14,150	+36,350	+22,190
Education—Public & Private	−20,450	+108,030	+87,580
Non-Profit Organizations	−18,150	+186,650	+168,500
Medical	−28,620	+127,500	+99,000
Agriculture, Forestry, Fisheries	−2,000	+5,960	+3,960
Federal Government-Civilian	0	+20,730	+20,730
State & Local Government	0	+130,570	+130,570
	Net Loss Industries		
Durable Goods			
Primary & Fabricated Metals	−7,890	+6,360	−1,530
Non-Electrical Machinery	−5,120	+4,530	−580
Electric & Electronic Equipment	−27,910	+8,440	−19,470
Rest of Transportation Equipment (missiles, aircraft, ships, tanks, etc.)	−20,240	+1,120	−19,120
Instruments	−8,220	+3,850	−4,370
Misc. Manufacturing	−3,600	+1,670	−1,920
Non-Durable Goods			
Chemicals	−4,050	+3,940	−110

TABLE 12.1
Continued

	Net Gain Industries		
	Women's jobs lost from military spending cuts	Women's jobs gained from civilian spending increases	Net jobs gained or lost for women
Federal Government-Military			
Uniformed Military Personnel	−64,800	0	−64,800
Non-Uniformed Military Personnel	−86,200	0	−86,200
Net Jobs Gained		+461,000	

SOURCE: Marion Anderson, Greg Bischak, and Michael Oden, *Converting the American Economy* (East Lansing, Mich.: Employment Research Associates, 1991). Data modified by utilizing U.S. Bureau of Labor statistics data on women's employment in 1995.

TABLE 12.2
Effects on Women's Jobs by Occupation, of Shifting $70 Billion from Military to Civilian Expenditures

	Net Gain Industries		
	Women's jobs lost from military spending cuts	Women's jobs gained from civilian spending increases	Net jobs gained or lost for women
Managers & Management-Related Occupations			
Educational Admin.	−760	+4,610	+3,850
Financial Managers	−3,620	+9,110	+5,500
Public Admin.	0	+620	+620
Other Managers	−30,880	+52,830	+21,950
Accountants, Buyers, other Managers	−26,330	+38,590	+12,260
Engineers and Architects	−2,160	+3,450	+1,290
Computer, Natural, and Social Scientists			
Computer Systems Analysts	−2,250	+3,600	+1,350
Natural and Math Scientists	−2,450	+3,560	+1,110
Social Scientists	−1,110	+2,240	+1,130
Teachers, Lawyers, Social & Religious Workers			
Pre-K, K–6 Teachers	−7,680	+72,130	+64,450
7–12 Teachers	−2,700	+25,090	+22,390
Post-secondary Education Teachers	−1,330	+5,100	+3,770
Other Teachers, Counselors	−6,460	+37,340	+30,880
Librarians	−930	+3,860	+2,930
Lawyers and Judicial Workers	−1,620	+3,780	+2,160
Clergy & Religious Directors	−670	+6,500	+5,830
Social & Recreation Workers	−2,940	+25,860	+22,920
Health Professions			
Physicians and Dentists	−1,430	+3,260	+1,830
Nurses, Dieticians, Therapists	−10,980	+35,480	+24,500
Reporters, Writers & Artists	−5,700	+11,710	+6,010
Technicians			
Health Technicians	−8,970	+28,400	+19,430
Other Technicians	−14,470	+16,750	+2,280
Marketing and Sales			
Real Estate and Securities	−1,730	+3,120	+1,390
Other Marketing & Sales	−56,160	+90,670	+34,500
Secretaries & Administrative Support	−201,850	+308,770	+106,920
Service Occupations			
Cleaning Workers	−19,160	+37,990	+18,830
Food Service Workers	−32,820	+57,690	+24,870

TABLE 12.2
Continued

	Net Gain Industries		
	Women's jobs lost from military spending cuts	Women's jobs gained from civilian spending increases	Net jobs gained or lost for women
Health Service Workers	−10,000	+39,100	+29,100
Protective Service Workers	−2,830	+6,800	+3,970
Personal and Other Services	−13,060	+43,310	+30,250
Agriculture, Forestry, Fisheries	−4,760	+13,220	+8,460
Blue-Collar Supervisory Occupations	−4,100	+5,900	+1,800
Construction Trades	−680	+2,890	+2,210
Mechanics, Installers, Repairers	−2,700	+4,070	+1,370
Food, Textile, Other Precision Production Occupations	−2,970	+4,450	+1,480
Machine Operators	−12,220	+16,580	+4,360
Transportation			
Motor Vehicle Operators	−3,240	+5,970	+2,730
Rail and Other Trans. Workers	−1,320	+2,550	+1,230
Helpers, Laborers and Material Movers	−8,850	+17,130	+8,280
Net Loss Occupations			
Engineers	−1,610	+1,290	−320
Engineering Technicians	−3,280	+2,430	−850
Precision Metal Workers Testers and Graders	−4,190	+2,850	−1,340
Machine Operators, Assemblers			
Machine Operators	−9,570	+5,520	−4,050
Assemblers	−20,530	+13,040	−7,480
Uniformed Military Personnel	−64,800	0	−64,800
Net Jobs Gained		+461,000	

SOURCE: Marion Anderson, Greg Bischak, and Michael Oden, *Converting the American Economy* (East Lansing, Mich.: Employment Research Associates, 1991). Data modified by utilizing U.S. Bureau of Labor statistics data on women's employment in 1995.

ments in research, development, and production needed to counter our enormous arsenal of weapons (see figure 12.1). Our allies are clearly not worried. Japan spends less than 1 percent of its GNP on its military, and Germany's percentage is also low.[5]

So, why are we still spending $250 billion a year, more than $1,000 for every man, woman, and child in the United States on the Pentagon? *This equals $4,000 of taxes every year from the average family of four*. This is one-half of the discretionary budget—the budget upon which Congress acts. When senators and congressmen and women say that there is no money for education, for medical care for poor women and children, or for cleaning up our polluted lakes and streams, the answer is: "Yes there is. Cut the Pentagon's budget and invest in America."

Women are in an ideal position to take leadership on this issue. They have never been as tied to the military-industrial complex as have men. Nor is their psyche as involved with militarism. The work that most women do is in services—health, education, finance, banking, insurance, real estate, retail trade, and

FIGURE 12.1
Military Spending of United States, "Potential Adversaries," and Russia, 1996
(in billions)

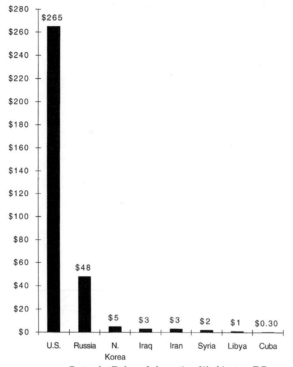

SOURCE: Center for Defense Information, Washington, DC.

state and local government. All of these sectors of the economy will benefit from cutting back military spending and investing in the future.

The Pentagon budget should be cut a minimum of $100 billion a year. About $20 billion could go to reduce the national debt and $80 billion should go for investment in our own and our children's future.

NOTES

1. Marion Anderson, *Neither Jobs nor Security: Women's Unemployment and the Pentagon Budget* (East Lansing, Mich.: Employment Research Associates, 1982).

2. Marion Anderson, Greg Bischak, and Michael Oden, *Converting the American Economy* (East Lansing, Mich.: Employment Research Associates, 1991).

3. General Colin Powell, National Press Club luncheon, 28 September 1993, quoted in Armed Forces Information Service, *Current News Supplement,* 29 September 1993, A7.

4. Ibid.

5. Jim Wolffe, *Defense News,* 8 April 1991, 12.

Conclusion

Francine D'Amico and Laurie Weinstein

The preceding chapters and autobiographical essays illustrate the scope of women's interactions and experiences with the United States military institution. Some women join the armed forces and military nursing services; others remain civilians but work on military installations. Some marry armed forces members; others provide entertainment and sexual services. Some offer moral and material support and advocacy; others challenge the military's legitimacy and criticize its policies. Even women with no apparent connection to the military are affected by its decisions because of the gendered divisions of employment into white-, blue-, and khaki-collar jobs, where men predominate, and pink-collar jobs, where women predominate. Yet despite the many sites women occupy vis-à-vis the institution, the military defines women at its periphery. Even those physically on the *inside*—nurses, servicewomen, and wives of military personnel—are kept outside the gendered space of its core or are made *invisible*, part of the background. The military portrays itself as No-*Woman's*-Land, masking its dependence on *woman*power with *gender camouflage*.

To unravel the military's *gender camouflage*, we must think about why the military seeks to obscure its dependence on *woman*power. Why camouflage women's military participation? What are the *consequences* of portraying women as outside the military or marginal to it rather than allowing them to be visible as contributors, as *insiders*?

A central *political* consequence of women's military exclusion and marginalization has been that arguments that women "don't do" military service and therefore "don't understand" issues relating to the military and national defense have been used to exclude individual women and women's perspectives from decision making, from policy choices, from government itself. The roots of the current structure of political authority lie in this exclusion: to admit women as *insiders* in the military would require a sharing of that authority.

But sharing authority—sharing power—is not willfully undertaken. So, said the military, pressed by the crises of the world wars, let women "in" but only at the margin—as auxiliaries in separate corps with relative rank or as civilians who will work for but not be part of the core institution. And when moving to regularize women's participation during the Cold War crisis that required high peacetime mobilization, keep their numbers small and keep them out of the military's core: combat.

Keeping women's numbers small, keeping them out of combat, and dispersing them to posts throughout the world made women—especially women of color—*conspicuous* in the institution, as Karen Johnson notes in her autobiographical essay. This maximized the military's control of women as a personnel resource and restricted women's ability to organize to challenge discrimination and harassment—and hence the gendered power structure of both the institution and the larger society. As Miriam Ben-Shalom has observed: "I think the idea of women with weapons causes [men] anxiety because it implies that control is no longer theirs—of either women or weapons."[1]

The military uses *gender camouflage* not only to make *women* invisible but also to make *men* invisible, that is, to conceal the ways in which *masculinity* is constructed and that particular *men*—people gendered *masculine*—are privileged by the concept of gender and the construct of gender hierarchy. For example, some critics of women in the military charge that the *gender-norming* of physical standards for today's military personnel is unfair because the requirements for men and women are not the same. But if we see through the military's *gender camouflage*, we recognize how expectations about what it means to be a *man* have shaped the original physical standards: the standards are actually *already* gendered, with men as the norm.[2]

The same is true for other so-called *professional* standards, such as those for officer promotion: officers are assumed to have at-home wives who will voluntarily contribute their time and energy to base programs and activities. If an officer's wife does not do so because she needs to devote more time to her own family, works off-base, or is an officer herself, his chances for promotion suffer. And because women officers confound the traditional gender division and behavioral expectation, their prospects for promotion also suffer, regardless of the contributions their husbands may make to the base community. Similarly, unmarried officers—including those who cannot marry their partners because of the "Don't Ask, Don't Tell" policy and civil prohibitions on same-sex marriage—are hindered in the gendered promotion process.

Of course, while men as a group are privileged by the military's already-gendered standards, individual men are disadvantaged in the institution by race/ethnicity, class/rank, and sexuality. Take, for example, the recent case of Senior Chief Petty Officer Timothy R. McVeigh, a closeted gay serviceman whom the navy attempted to out and to discharge in violation of the "Don't Ask, Don't Tell, Don't Pursue" policy and federal communications privacy law by investigating his personal life and electronic correspondence. Despite his reinstatement, McVeigh has experienced reprisal, including reassignment from his command of a 134–crew member nuclear submarine to a clerk position.[3] More work needs to be done on unraveling the intersecting hierarchies that frame not only military but all social relations.

As the chapters and essays in parts 2 and 3 of this volume clearly show, many women other than those who put on the uniform make significant contributions to the U.S. military or are affected by military policies and practices in a wide variety of ways. Although women's contributions often go unrecognized, they are revealed in the preceding pages as essential to the operation and maintenance of the military institution. For example, before reading Doreen Drewry Lehr's analysis on military wives, we may have thought of military *dependents* as just that: dependent on their spouses and our tax dollars, not contributing to the nation's defense. This view, of course, obscures the countless volunteer hours, fund-raising efforts, and family-support work that military wives do to sustain the members of the armed forces—and hence the institution itself. Now that we *see* military wives differently, now that their military role is no longer *invisible* to us, we can begin to decipher the significance of their *invisibility*.

Keeping military wives *invisible* allows the military institution to benefit from their support work with little compensation—their husbands receive spousal benefits but wives receive no salary—and to control them through peer and command pressure, socialization, and surveillance. Consequently, the military perceives actions that make military wives visible as a threat. Laurie recalls an informal get-together of a group of Navy officers' wives while their husbands were deployed:

> We were sitting in one woman's house on base and chatting when another wife looked me in the eye and said, "My husband doesn't want me to associate with you." Another wife laughed and added, "Laurie's trouble!" Perhaps I was perceived as a threat because I had distributed bumper stickers to other wives which proclaimed, "Question Authority" and "So Many Men, So Few Brains." Or perhaps it was because I unknowingly violated Navy tradition and etiquette on my first "call" to the commanding officer's home in leaving my own business card, which identified me as "Dr. Laurie . . . Ph.D." rather than one that read "Lt. and Mrs. John Doe." I had assumed I was entitled to my identity; I hadn't realized that a new identity had been issued to me: that of "Navy wife."

Men entering military service also go through a transformation of identity; their former identities are shaved and trained away, and their new identities—as soldiers, sailors, marines, and airmen—are created for them. These new identities depend upon a particular vision of *masculinity*. This vision is reinforced by the alternative, feminine-gendered identity of the military wife. So, the military wife is important not only because of the concrete services she provides to her husband and the base community but also because of her role in confirming the gender hierarchy on which the military institution rests. The same is true for other women who provide services to the military but are defined as being at its margin or outside it: If masculine = military, then feminine = not masculine = not military.

Camouflaging wives' contributions to the military limits their ability to organize for change on their own and to secure support for their efforts from civilian organizations. Some have challenged the institution's gendered practices, but the schisms among *military women*—those in uniform and those in military families—and between military women and civilian feminists and peace activists further divide women in these different locations from one another, making solidarity and political action difficult. One way to begin bridging these gaps has been for researchers and women in these different locations to come together to share their work with and learn from one another. This book is part of that bridge-building effort.

Literature on Women and the Military

This volume builds upon a growing body of academic literature on women and the military, a subject neglected by mainstream scholars and obscured by the institution's gender camouflage. Here, we review recent literature on women and the U.S. military and suggest some starting points for further research; full citations for these and other recommended materials appear in the bibliography. A research guide and annotated bibliography compiled by Vicki Friedl and a guide to materials in the National Archives compiled by Charlotte Palmer Seeley, Virginia Purdy, and Robert Gruber provide a more comprehensive list of sources.

Efforts to expose the military's gender camouflage and to correct the official record of women's military contributions have taken many forms. In autobiographies and oral histories, such as Navy Captain Winifred Quick Collins's *More Than a Uniform* and Dorothy Schneider and Carl Schneider's *Sound Off!*, we hear the voices of women who served. In biographies and organizational histories, such as Silvia Sheafer's *Women in America's Wars* and Bettie Morden's volume on the Women's Army Corps (WAC), we hear the stories of individual and collective experiences and trace developments in policies and institutions.[4]

Several monographs and anthologies focus on women *inside* the U. S. military. To hear the voices and stories of more *military nurses*, we recommend the auto/biographical accounts of World War II veterans Juanita Redmond and LaVonne Telshaw Camp, as well as nurse corps histories by Judith Lawrence Bellafaire, Elizabeth Shields, and Sharon Cosner. On nurses who served in Vietnam, see *Nurses in Vietnam*, edited by Dan Freedman and Jacqueline Rhoads; *Women at War*, by Elizabeth Norman; and *A Piece of My Heart*, compiled by Keith Walker. On the experiences of black women as military nurses, see *No Time for Prejudice* by Mabel Keaton Staupers and *The Path We Tread* by Mary Elizabeth Carnegie.

To read more about *servicewomen*, see *Women in the Military: An Unfinished Revolution* by Jeanne M. Holm (USAF, retired), which catalogues women's contributions to, and struggles for acceptance in, the armed forces. An anthology by the same title, *Women in the Military*, edited by Carol Wekesser and Matthew David Polesetsky, examines a wide range of issues on women's military participation. On the experiences of African American women, see *To Serve My Country, To Serve My Race* by Brenda Moore.

Regarding the experiences of women cadets and plebes at U.S. *military academies*, see the autobiographies *Dress Gray* by Donna Peterson and *Inside the Men's House* by Carol Barkalow, and examine Judith Hicks Stiehm's analysis of gender integration at the Air Force Academy at Colorado Springs, *Bring Me Men and*

Women. To read more about *women veterans,* see *Warriors without Weapons* by Donna Dean and *Women Veterans* by June Willenz.

Several recent books are useful for considering the connections between different policies of exclusion and the intersectionality of constructions of gender and sexuality in the military institution. To begin with the voices and stories of real people affected by gay/lesbian exclusion rules, we recommend auto/biographical accounts by Greta Cammermeyer, *Serving in Silence,* and collected voices compiled by Winni Webber in *Lesbians in the Military Speak Out* and by Mary Ann Humphrey in *My Country, My Right to Serve.* Analytic volumes to consult include *Gay Rights, Military Wrongs,* edited by Craig Rimmerman, and *Conduct Unbecoming* by Randy Shilts.

A number of researchers examine the experiences of *military wives.* We recommend for further reading works by Doreen Drewry Lehr, *Madwomen in the Military Attic,* and Joan Biddle, *Do You Speak Military?* The anthology *Wives and Warriors,* edited by Laurie Weinstein and Christie White, provides comparative analysis of the situations of women in uniform and of military wives in the United States and Canada. Another anthology, *Women and the Use of Military Force,* edited by Ruth Howes and Michael Stevenson, examines women's participation in the uniformed military services, the Manhattan Project, national security policy, and the peace movement.

Much has been written about women defense workers and women on the home front in the United States during World War II. To begin, we recommend *Rosie the Riveter Revisited* by Sherna Berger Gluck and *Women at War with America* by D'Ann Campbell. Xiaojian Zhao has compiled a collection of oral histories of Chinese American women defense workers in California, and Gretchen Lemke-Santangelo has examined the home-front experiences of African American women. Other useful resources about women defense workers are *Fleeting Opportunities* by Amy Kesselman, *Gender at Work* by Ruth Milkman, and *American Women and World War II* by Doris Weatherford.

Regarding militarized prostitution, we recommend *Let the Good Times Roll,* in which Saundra Pollock Sturdevant and Brenda Stoltzfus examine the economic and social causes and consequences of prostitution around U.S. military bases in Asia, and *Sex among Allies,* in which Katharine H. S. Moon analyzes the practices, policies, and politics of militarized prostitution in the Republic of Korea.

To read more by and about peace activists, you might begin with *Greenham Women Everywhere,* by Alice Cook and Gwyn Kirk. Other analyses of women's peace work and gender and pacifism include *Peace as a Women's Issue* by Harriet Hyman Alonso and *Rocking the Ship of State,* an anthology edited by Adrienne Harris and Ynestra King.

From Women to Gender

Auto/biographies and oral/organizational histories provide necessary starting points for understanding women's relationships to the military institution. Other feminist researchers move beyond documentation of women's military participation to uncover *gender*, that is, the hierarchical structuring of human relations between people gendered feminine and masculine, whom we call *women* and *men*. To begin, we recommend a new anthology, *The Women and War Reader*, in which editors Lois Ann Lorentzen and Jennifer Turpin have collected reprints and excerpts on gender, war, and peace, by three dozen authors, including Cynthia Enloe, Sara Ruddick, April Carter, and Betty Reardon. We also recommend Cynthia Enloe's full-length work *Does Khaki Become You?*, which examines the militarization of women's lives and the construction of militarized masculinity. This is required reading for anyone interested in understanding the military's gender camouflage. Linda Bird Francke's recent book, *Ground Zero*, and Melissa Herbert's new volume, *Camouflage Isn't Only for Combat*, examine gender politics within the contemporary U.S. military. Francke considers how gender boundaries are (re)drawn to exclude women from the core of the institution over issues such as combat and pregnancy; Herbert analyzes the strategies servicewomen use for coping in a hostile environment and negotiating the contested terrain of sexuality in the armed forces.

A recent anthology, *It's Our Military, Too!*, edited by Judith Hicks Stiehm, explores both the experiences of women in uniform and the significance of gender within the military institution. Jean Zimmerman's *Tailspin* and Jean Ebbert and Marie-Beth Hall's *Crossed Currents* also examine both the lived experiences of military women and the structure of gender in the military institution. Other useful tools for understanding the military's gender camouflage and its consequences are the anthologies *On Peace, War, and Gender*, edited by Anne Hunter; *Women, Militarism, and War*, edited by Jean Bethke Elshtain and Sheila Tobias; and *Women and Men's Wars*, edited by Judith Hicks Stiehm.

Many feminist scholars argue either that apparent wartime disruption in gender roles is only temporary or that war in fact maintains gender boundaries. For example, contributors to *Behind the Lines: Gender and the Two World Wars* analyze the world wars "as events of gender politics" and argue that, although war briefly exposes "the arbitrariness of gender designations," men continue to "dominate the labor market and monopolize political power."[5] They conclude that war is a deeply gendered activity that reinforces society's gender boundaries.

Questions about how and to what extent women's military participation is shaped by and affects gender hierarchy need further exploration. It may be that some women in some locations vis-à-vis the military reinforce gender boundaries; others challenge those boundaries, change our ideas about gender, and thus reshape the institution. For example, we could not have imagined the military addressing issues such as sexual harassment and child care just a few years ago, yet now these subjects are taken seriously in part because women who wear the uniform, along with their male allies and supporters, women who live on and work at military installations, *and* civilian political activists are demanding that they be addressed. Yet questions about gender and the military are not settled, as the recent debate over sex-integrated basic training demonstrates.

Where to Now?

Now that we see—and see through—the military's gender camouflage, what's our next step? This section suggests areas for further research, analysis, and action, including issues that need investigation and possibilities for networking to change policies and practices that make women's military participation seem marginal and invisible.

Our examination of women's roles and locations vis-à-vis the U.S. military is inclusive but not exhaustive. There are many other women connected to the military whose stories need to be heard to get a complete picture of both the military and the gender hierarchy it constructs and maintains. Consider for example, *mothers*: mothers of servicemen and women, of dissenters, of prostitutes, of peace activists. In military histories, mothers are usually visible only in their roles as reproducers of patriots. Gold Star Mothers, women who have had a grown child or children killed in military service, receive a carefully folded flag and honored places on Memorial Day and Veterans Day. Yet in these ceremonies, we see but do not hear them: they are visible but silent. What would they tell us?

And what about *daughters*? How does growing up in the military environment construct gender for young girls? In examining the experiences of children in military families in her book *Military Brats*, Mary Edwards Wertsch found that many women who serve as warriors and nurses or who marry servicemen grew up "inside the fortress" and feel the military, rather than some geographic location, is their home. Other researchers are also exploring this gendered terrain, but more needs to be done.[6]

And what about the many other women whose work links them to the military, such as *diplomats, national security policy makers, espionage agents, scientists,* and *journalists*? How do they fit into the fabric of gender camouflage? If these women operate in "a man's world" where gender boundaries define their presence as inappropriate, how does that affect their range of choice, opportunities, and overall effectiveness? How do those boundaries in turn shape U.S. military policies and foreign relations? For example, consider the experience of *Washington Post* correspondent Molly Moore, who covered the Gulf War. Moore accompanied male marines across the border into Kuwait, but female members of the unit were not permitted to cross the gender line into "combat": did Moore's role as witness challenge or reinforce gender divisions?[7]

Women in these locations are often considered in isolation from one another and from the larger picture of how gender is constructed in a society. If gender is examined, it is often "gender-only" analysis. Future research needs to look for the connections among these women's roles/locations and the military's gender camouflage and to complicate these analyses by addressing the intersecting hierarchies of race/ethnicity and sexuality. Researchers also need to examine the masculine side of gender camouflage more carefully, to reveal both the hegemonic masculinity envisioned by the institution and to make visible the soldiers, sailors, airmen, fathers, brothers, and military and policy leaders who are disadvantaged by intersecting hierarchies of race/ethnicity and sexuality. Looking past the military's gender camouflage, we can see men both inside and outside the institution who unite with women in challenging gender hierarchy.

As we find more women in more locations vis-à-vis the military, we make it possible not only to see the institution's gender camouflage but to envision a military in which gender is "done" differently. What would an *un-gendered* or gender-neutral military look like, and how do we get there? That is, what kind of concrete actions could bring about the kind of changes in policy and practice that would make military *woman*power visible and open gender boundaries and gender hierarchy to renegotiation?

To begin to un-gender the military, we have to recognize that we must also examine and undo other social hierarchies that intertwine with, support, and maintain the current gender divisions. That is, we must simultaneously work to *e-race* the military's racial/ethnic hierarchy and to dismantle hierarchy based in sexuality. The interconnectedness of these hierarchies requires further analysis and manifests itself in a number of ways.

Take, for example, sexual harassment. As Georgia Clark Sadler noted in chapter 2, the DOD's 1995 survey on sexual harassment found that fewer African American women reported harassment than did white women, relative to their presence in the military population. How do we explain this? Either African American women *experienced* less harassment or they were less likely to *report* the harassment they experienced. The first explanation is unlikely because of the way white society portrays black women's sexuality. The second explanation, that African American women were *silenced*, is more likely for several reasons. As Gwendolyn Hall has argued, black women may be denied *credibility* by the military institution because of the intersectionality of race and gender. Thus, black women may not try to report harassment because they think they will not be believed, or they are not believed when they do attempt to report it. If their harassers are also African American, black women may also be silenced by pressure for *race solidarity*, whether internalized or imposed by other African American servicemembers.[8]

Sexuality and the "Don't Ask, Don't Tell" policy of removing openly gay and lesbian people from the services complicates the story of sexual harassment as well. Harassers use the policy as a tool for sexual extortion, threatening to charge a woman with being a lesbian if she refuses sex. So, working to eliminate the "Don't Ask" policy is one step we could take toward reconstructing hierarchies based in not only gender but also race/ethnicity and sexuality in the U.S. military. Other exclusionary policies must also be eliminated, including the remnants of the old combat-exclusion laws, control over which has been ceded by Congress to the individual services.

Simultaneously, "real teeth" must be given to regulations and policies that prohibit and punish sexual harassment and all other forms of discrimination, whether based in gender, race/ethnicity, or sexuality. A first step would be to eliminate adultery as a punishable offense from military regulations; this is a matter between spouses/partners. However, the prohibition on fraternization must be retained and consistently enforced on military personnel (not their civilian spouses/partners) to protect those who are most powerless in the military's class/rank hierarchy.

The newest members of the military need an advocate system, as Aberdeen clearly shows. The solution is not to segregate men and women in basic training but to rethink the basics of the military training format.[9] Perhaps we should integrate basic training facilities with other military installations, such that individuals are trained in the units to which they will eventually be assigned. This might reduce the isolation recruits experience and create greater accountability for instructors within the chain of command. We should also examine the possibility of moving from a garrison-based military installation system to a community-based system, to provide recruits protection from local civilian advocates looking out for their own.[9]

All training and job categories within the military must be gender integrated to remove the appearance of preferences. Because gender-normed physical performance standards continue to create problems for dismantling gender hierarchy, we must work to create gender-neutral standards that consider *both* men's and women's physiological strengths and weaknesses, along with age and other physical attributes, *and* the relevance of such standards to the kinds of jobs/ occupations these personnel perform. Not all servicemembers need to be Rambo to get the job done. We need to make the physical standard one of wellness/ well-being and address health issues such as eating disorders as we would any other condition, rather than requiring women to maintain unrealistic height: weight ratios.

Wives of military personnel clearly need access to confidential civilian support and advocacy networks because they are prevented from seeking help within the institution, where they are ignored, are silenced, or fear jeopardizing a husband's career. We must work to bridge the gap between civilian and military communities so we can communicate with, understand, and help one another. Similarly, women peace activists must seek allies inside the institution because only by pressure from *both* inside and outside can the institution and the system it serves be changed.

We must also extend the support network to women who live in communities around U.S. bases, including sex workers. We can help provide employment options for these women, as well as demand a change in the unwritten U.S. military policy that encourages prostitution through basing agreements with other countries; by prohibiting spouses from accompanying servicemembers to some overseas installations; and by providing medical supplies and services to both servicemembers and sex workers.[10]

How can we start to make these changes? We can begin by contacting the organizations listed in the appendix for more information and to network with others who share our concerns. We can support court challenges currently under way as our knowledge and financial means permit, as in the case of Colonel Margarethe "Greta" Cammermeyer, who was discharged under the gay/lesbian exclusion rule.[11] Finally, we can express our concerns to our congressional representatives and other public officials responsibie for military policy, and we can hold them accountable for making the changes in law and policy that will help dismantle gender, race/ethnicity, and sexuality hierarchies in the United States military.

NOTES

1. E-mail message on MINERVA discussion group on women and the military, posted to H-MINERVA@h-net.msu.edu (6 January 1998).

2. See, for example, Bradley Peniston, "Double Standards? Depends on Whom You Ask," *Navy Times*, 2 February 1998, 1+.

3. "Sailor Fears Reprisals Following Statement" (AP), *Finger Lakes Times* (Geneva, N.Y.), 1 February 1998, 7A; "Judge: Navy Has Gone Too Far" (AP), *Finger Lakes Times* (Geneva, N.Y.), 27 January 1998, 2; "AOL Admits Privacy Error," *Washington Post*, reprinted in *Finger Lakes Times* (Geneva, N.Y.), 22 January 1998, 2.

4. Organizational histories of the WAVES, WAF, Women Marines, and WASP are listed in the bibliography.

5. Margaret Randolph Higonnet, Jane Jenson, Sonya Michel, and Margaret Collins Weitz, eds., *Behind the Lines: Gender and the Two World Wars* (New Haven: Yale University Press, 1987), 6, 3.

6. Gary Bowen and Dennis Orthener, eds., *The Organization Family: Work and Family Linkages in the U.S. Military* (Westport, Conn.: Praeger, 1989).

7. Molly Moore, *A Woman at War: Storming Kuwait with the U.S. Marines* (New York: Scribner's, 1993).

8. See U.S. Department of Defense, *1995 Sexual Harassment Survey*, DMDC 96–014 (Arlington, Va.: Defense Manpower Data Center, December 1996). Lt. Col. Gwendolyn Hall (USAF), associate professor of political science at the U.S. Air Force Academy, presented her analysis of intersectionality at the conference "Military Policy, Military Culture" at the University of Maryland, 4–6 April 1997.

9. On gender integration, see Andrea Stone, "Is Navy Sailing by Others' Integration Woes?" *Navy Times*, 26 January 1998, 2.

10. See Cynthia Enloe, *The Morning After: Sexual Politics at the End of the Cold War* (Berkeley: University of California Press, 1993), 142–60.

11. In *Cammermeyer v Aspin*, U.S. District Court WD C92942Z (1994), gay/lesbian exclusion was ruled unconstitutional; see case materials in Craig A. Rimmerman, ed., *Gay Rights, Military Wrongs: Political Perspectives on gays and Lesbians in the Military*, (New York: Garland, 1996), preface and appendices A, B, xiii–xv, 297–332. This ruling was upheld on appeal on 28 November 1997.

Appendix

Contact information for several support and advocacy groups for, and information sources on, women and the military are listed below.

Linda Grant De Pauw, President
The MINERVA Center
20 Granada Road
Pasadena, MD 21122-2708
410437-5379
MinervaCen@aol.com
http://h-net.msu.edu/~minerva

Joan A. Furey, Director
The Center for Women Veterans
Department of Veterans Affairs
810 Vermont Avenue, NW
Washington, DC 20420
202-273-6193
http://www.va.gov/womenvet/center.htm

Defense Advisory Committee on Women in the Service (DACOWITS)
Office of the Secretary of Defense
4000 Defense Pentagon
Washington, DC 20301-4000
703-697-2122

EXPOSE (Ex-Partners of Servicemembers)
P.O. Box 11191
Alexandria, VA 22312
703-255-2917
703-941-5844

Military Spouse Business and Professional Association
c/o Patti Wells
Army Community Service
201 Custer Road

Fort Meyer, VA 22211-5050
703-696-3047

National Military Family Association (NMFA)
6000 Stevenson Avenue, Suite 304
Alexandria, VA 22304-3526
703-823-6632
families@nmfa.org
http://www.nmfa.org

National Military Family Resource Center
4040 N. Fairfax Drive, Room 421
Arlington, VA 22203

National Women's Law Center
11 Dupont Circle, NW, Suite 800
Washington, DC 20036
202-588-5180

Servicemembers Legal Defense Network (SLDN)
P.O. Box 53013
Washington, DC 20009
202-328-3244
202-328-0063 (F)
sldn@sldn.org
http://www.sldn.org

Survivors Take Action Against Abuse by Military Personnel (STAMP)
Dorothy Mackey, Executive Director
500 Greene Tree Place
Fairborn, OH 45324
937-879-9304
1-888-231-2226 (toll free)

Women Active in our Nation's Defense, their Advocates & Supporters
(WANDAS)
825 Logan Street
Denver, CO 80203
303-860-0905
303-861-2943 (F)

Women Against Military Madness (WAMM)
310 East 38th Street, Suite 225
Minneapolis, MN 55409

612-827-5364
wamm@mtn.org

Women in International Security (WIIS)
CISSM/School of Public Affairs
University of Maryland
College Park, MD 20742-1811
301-405-7582
301-403-8107 (F)
WIIS@puafmail.umd.edu
http://www.puaf.umd.edu/wiss

Women in Military Service for America Memorial Foundation (WIMSA)
5510 Columbia Pike
Arlington, VA 22204
1-800-222-2294
703-533-1155
wimsa@aol.com
http://www.wimsa.org

Women in the Military Information Network (WIMIN)
612 S. Jackson Street
Arlington, VA 22204
703-920-3621
wimin@aol.com

Women Veterans of America
P.O. Box 290283
2056 East 14th Street
Brooklyn, NY 11229
718-375-0565

Women's Action for New Directions (WAND)
691 Massachusetts Avenue
Arlington, MA 021174
617-643-6740
617-643-6469 (F)
wand@world.std.com

Women's Airforce Service Pilots (WASP)
c/o Mary Anna Wyall
P.O. Box 9212
Fort Wayne, IN 46899
219-747-7933

Women's International League for Peace and Freedom (WILPF)
1213 Race Street
Philadelphia, PA 19107
215-563-7110
wilpfnatl@igc.apc.org
http://www.wilpf.org

Women's Research and Education Institute (WREI)
1750 New York Avenue, NW, #350
Washington, DC 20006
202-628-0444
wrei@wrei.org
http://www.wrei.org

Webpages of Interest

Air Force Family Support Centers
http://www.famnet.com

American Red Cross
http://www.redcross.org

American Women in Uniform—Veterans, Too!
http://userpages.aug.com/captbarb

Army Community and Family Support Centers
http://www.armymwr.com

Military Woman Homepage
http://www.militarywoman.org

United Service Organizations (USO)
http://soho.ios.com/~usohq

Select Bibliography

Adams, Judith P. *Peacework: Life Stories of Women Peace Activists*. Old Tappan, N.J.: Twayne, 1990.

Adkins, Yolanda. *Skirt Patrol: Women's Army Corps*. New York: Vantage, 1993.

Alonso, Harriet Hyman. *Peace as a Women's Issue: A History of the U.S. Movement for World Peace and Women's Rights*. Syracuse: Syracuse University Press, 1993.

Alt, Betty Sowers, and Bonnie Domrose Stone. *Campfollowing: A History of the Military Wife*. New York: Praeger, 1991.

Anderson, Marion. *Neither Jobs nor Security: Women's Unemployment and the Pentagon Budget*. East Lansing, Mich.: Employment Research Associates, 1982.

Barkalow, Carol, with Andrea Raab. *In the Men's House: An Inside Account of Life in the Army*. New York: Poseidon Press, 1990.

Bellafaire, Judith Lawrence. *The Women's Army Corps: A Commemoration of World War II Service*. Washington, D.C.: U.S. Army Center of Military History, 1993.

Bellafaire, Judith Lawrence. *The Army Nurse Corps: A Commemoration of World War II Service*. Washington, D.C.: U.S. Army Center of Military History, 1994.

Bérubé, Allan. *Coming Out Under Fire: The History of Gay Men and Women in World War Two*. New York: Free Press, 1990.

Biddle, Joan I. "Do You Speak Military? The Socialization of Army Officers' Wives to Institutional Expectations." Ph.D. diss, Boston University, 1992.

Bigler, Philip. *Hostile Fire: The Life and Death of First Lieutenant Sharon Lane*. Arlington, Va.: Vandamere, 1996.

Bowen, Gary, and Dennis Orthener, eds. *The Organization Family: Work and Family Linkages in the U.S. Military*. Westport, Conn.: Praeger, 1989.

Cammermeyer, Margarethe, with Chris Fisher. *Serving in Silence*. New York: Viking, 1994.

Camp, LaVonne Telshaw. *Lingering Fever: A World War II Nurse's Memoir*. Jefferson, N.C.: McFarland, 1997.

Campbell, D'Ann. *Women at War with America: Private Lives in a Patriotic Era*. Cambridge: Harvard University Press, 1984.

Carnegie, Mary Elizabeth. *The Path We Tread: Blacks in Nursing, 1854–1984*. Philadelphia: Lippincott, 1986.

Cataldo, Mimi, Ruth Putter, Bryna Fireside, and Elaine Lytel. *The Women's Encampment for a Future of Peace and Justice: Images and Writings*. Philadelphia: Temple University Press, 1988.

Collins, Winifred Quick, with Herbert M. Levine. *More Than a Uniform: A Navy Woman in a Navy Man's World*. Denton: University of North Texas Press, 1997.

Cook, Alice, and Gwyn Kirk. *Greenham Women Everywhere: Dreams, Ideas, and Actions from the Women's Peace Movement*. Boston: South End Press, 1983.

Cooke, Miriam, and Angela Woollacott, eds. *Gendering War Talk*. Princeton: Princeton University Press, 1993.

Cornum, Rhonda Scott, with Peter Copeland. *She Went to War: The Rhonda Cornum Story.* Novato, Calif.: Presidio Press, 1992.

Cosner, Sharon. *War Nurses.* New York: Walker, 1988.

Danner, Dorothy S. *What a Way to Spend a War: Navy Nurse POWs in the Philippines.* Annapolis: Naval Institute Press, 1995.

Dean, Donna M./Running Black Wolf. *Warriors without Weapons: The Victimization of Military Women.* Pasadena, Md.: MINERVA Center, 1997.

De Pauw, Linda Grant. *Founding Mothers: Women of America in the Revolutionary Era.* Boston: Houghton Mifflin, 1975.

De Pauw, Linda Grant. *Seafaring Women.* Boston: Houghton Mifflin, 1982.

Dever, John P., and Maria Dever. *Women and the Military: A Hundred Notable Contributors, Historic to Contemporary.* Jefferson, N.C.: McFarland, 1994.

Donahue, M. Patricia. *Nursing, the Finest Art: An Illustrated History*, illus. ed./comp. Patricia A. Russac. St. Louis: C. V. Mosby, 1985.

Dorn, Edwin, ed. *Who Defends America? Race, Sex, and Class in the Armed Forces.* Washington, D.C.: Joint Center for Political Studies, 1989.

Ebbert, Jean, and Marie-Beth Hall. *Crossed Currents: Navy Women from WWI to Tailhook.* 2d rev. ed. Washington, D.C.: Brassey's, 1994.

Elshtain, Jean Bethke. *Women and War.* New York: Basic Books, 1987.

Elshtain, Jean Bethke, and Sheila Tobias, eds. *Women, Militarism, and War.* Savage, Md.: Rowman and Littlefield, 1990.

Enloe, Cynthia. *Bananas, Beaches and Bases: Making Feminist Sense of International Politics.* Berkeley: University of California Press, 1990.

Enloe, Cynthia. *Does Khaki Become You? The Militarization of Women's Lives.* London: HarperCollins, 1988.

Enloe, Cynthia. *The Morning After: Sexual Politics at the End of the Cold War.* Berkeley: University of California Press, 1993.

Feller, Carolyn M., and Constance J. Moore. *Highlights in the History of the Army Nurse Corps.* Washington, D.C.: U.S. Army Center of Military History, 1995.

Forcey, Linda, ed. "Special Issue: Rethinking Women's Peace Studies." *Women's Studies Quarterly* 95, nos. 3/4 (1996).

Foster, Catherine. *Women for All Seasons: The Story of the Women's International League for Peace and Freedom.* Athens: University of Georgia Press, 1989.

Francke, Linda Bird. *Ground Zero: The Gender Wars in the Military.* New York: Simon & Schuster, 1997.

Freedman, Dan, and Jacqueline Rhoads, eds. *Nurses in Vietnam: The Forgotten Veterans.* Austin: Texas Monthly Press, 1987.

Friedl, Vicki L. *Women in the United States Military, 1901–1995: A Research Guide and Annotated Bibliography.* New York: Greenwood Press, 1996.

Gabriel, Richard A., and Karen S. Metz. *A History of Military Medicine.* Westport, Conn.: Greenwood Press, 1992.

Gavin, Lettie. *American Women in World War I: They Also Served.* Niwot: University of Colorado Press, 1997.

Gluck, Sherna Berger. *Rosie the Riveter Revisited: Women, the War, and Social Change.* New York: Meridian, 1987.

Hancock, Joy Bright. *Lady in the Navy: A Personal* Reminiscence. Annapolis: Naval Institute Press, 1972.

Harris, Adrienne, and Ynestra King, eds. *Rocking the Ship of State: Toward a Feminist Peace Politics.* Boulder: Westview Press, 1989.

Herbert, Melissa S. *Camouflage Isn't Only for Combat: Gender, Sexuality and Women in the Military*. New York: New York University Press, 1998.

Hewitt, Linda. *Women Marines in World War I*. Washington, D.C.: History and Museums Division, U.S. Marine Corps Headquarters, 1974.

Higonnet, Margaret Randolph, Jane Jenson, Sonya Michel, and Margaret Collins Weitz, eds. *Behind the Lines: Gender and the Two World Wars*. New Haven: Yale University Press, 1987.

Hodgson, Marion Stegeman. *Winning My Wings: A Woman Airforce Service Pilot in World War II*. Annapolis: Naval Institute Press, 1996.

Holm, Jeanne M., ed. *In Defense of a Nation: Servicewomen in World War II*. Washington, D.C.: Military Women's Press, 1998.

Holm, Jeanne M. *Women in the Military: An Unfinished Revolution*. Rev. ed. Novato, Calif.: Presidio Press, 1992.

Hovis, Bobbi. *Station Hospital Saigon: A Navy Nurse in* Vietnam. Annapolis: Naval Institute Press, 1991.

Howes, Ruth B., and Michael R. Stevenson, eds. *Women and the Use of Military Force*. Boulder: Lynne Rienner, 1993.

Humphrey, Mary Ann. *My Country, My Right to Serve: Experiences of Gay Men and Women in the Military, World War II to the Present*. New York: HarperCollins, 1990.

Hunter, Anne E., ed. *On Peace, War, and Gender: A Challenge to Genetic Explanations*. New York: Feminist Press/CUNY, 1991.

Jeffords, Susan. *The Remasculinization of America: Gender in the Vietnam War*. Bloomington: Indiana University Press, 1989.

Johnson, Jesse J., ed. *Black Women in the Armed Forces, 1942–1974*. Hampton, Va.: Hampton Institute, 1974.

Katzenstein, Mary Fainsod. *Faithful and Fearless: Moving Feminist Protest Inside the Church and Military*. New Jersey: Princeton University Press, 1998.

Keil, Sally Van Wagenen. *Those Wonderful Women in Their Flying Machines: The Unknown Heroines of World War II*. Rev. ed. New York: Four Directions, 1990.

Kesselman, Amy. *Fleeting Opportunities: Women Shipyard Workers in Portland and Vancouver During World War II and Reconversion*. Albany: State University of New York Press, 1990.

Kochendoerfer, Violet A. *One Woman's World War II*. Lexington: University Press of Kentucky, 1994.

Krasniewicz, Louise. *Nuclear Summer: The Clash of Communities at the Seneca Women's Peace Camp*. Ithaca: Cornell University Press, 1992.

Larson, C. Kay. *'Til I Come Marching Home: A Brief History of American Women in World War II*. Pasadena, Md.: MINERVA Center, 1995.

Larson, Rebecca D. *Blue and Gray Roses of Intrigue (Civil War Spies)*. Gettysburg, Pa.: Thomas, 1993.

Larson, Rebecca D. *White Roses: Civil War Nurses*. Gettysburg, Pa.: Thomas, 1996.

Lehr, Doreen Drewry. *Madwomen in the Military Attic: Military Wives*. Forthcoming, 1998.

Lemke-Santangelo, Gretchen. *Abiding Courage: African-American Migrant Women and the East Bay Community*. Chapel Hill: University of North Carolina Press, 1996.

Lorentzen, Lois Ann, and Jennifer Turpin, eds. *The Women and War Reader*. New York: New York University Press, 1998.

Maisels, Amanda, and Patricia M. Gormley. *Women in the Military: Where They Stand*. Washington, D.C.: Women's Research and Education Institute, 1994.

McGlen, Nancy, and Meredith Reid Sarkees. *Women in Foreign Policy: The Insiders.* New York: Routledge, 1993.

Meid, Pat. *Marine Corps Women's Reserve in World War II.* Washington, D.C.: Historical Branch, G-3 Division HQ, 1964/1968.

Merryman, Molly. *Clipped Wings: The Rise and Fall of the Women Airforce Service Pilots (WASPs) of World War II.* New York: New York University Press, 1998.

Milkman, Ruth. *Gender at Work: The Dynamics of Job Segregation by Sex During World War II.* Urbana: University of Illinois Press, 1987.

MINERVA: Quarterly Report on Women and the Military. Pasadena, Md.: MINERVA Center, 1980–.

Moon, Katharine H.S. *Sex Among Allies: Military Prostitution in U.S.-Korean Relations.* New York: Columbia University Press, 1997.

Moore, Brenda L. *To Serve My Country, To Serve My Race: The Story of the Only African American WACs Stationed Overseas during World War II.* New York: New York University Press, 1996.

Morden, Bettie. *The Women's Army Corps: 1945–1978.* Washington, D.C.: U.S. Army Center of Military History, 1990.

Naythons, Matthew. *The Face of Mercy: A Photographic History of Medicine at War.* New York: Random House, 1993.

Noggle, Anne. *For God, Country, and the Thrill of It: Women Airforce Service Pilots in World War II.* College Station: Texas A&M University Press, 1990.

Norman, Elizabeth M. *Women at War: The Story of Fifty Military Nurses Who Served in Vietnam.* Philadelphia: University of Pennsylvania Press, 1990.

Osburn, C. Dixon, and Michelle M. Benecke. *Conduct Unbecoming: The Fourth Annual Report on "Don't Ask, Don't Tell, Don't Pursue," February 26, 1997–February 19, 1998.* Washington, D.C.: Servicemembers Legal Defense Network, 1998.

Pennington, Reina, ed. *Military Women Worldwide: A Biographical Dictionary.* Westport, Conn.: Greenwood Press, 1998.

Pershing, Linda. *The Ribbon around the Pentagon: Peace by Piecemakers.* Knoxville: University of Tennessee Press, 1996.

Peterson, Donna. *Dress Gray: A Woman at West Point.* Austin, Tex.: Eakin, 1990.

Reardon, Betty A. *Sexism and the War System.* Syracuse: Syracuse University Press, 1996.

Redmond, Juanita. *I Served on Bataan.* Philadelphia: Lippincott, 1943.

Reppy, Judith V. and Mary F. Katzenstein. *Beyond Zero Tolerance: Discrimination in Military Culture.* Lanham, Md.: Rowman & Littlefield, 1999.

Rogan, Helen. *Mixed Company: Women in the Modern Army.* New York: Putnam's, 1981.

Sadler, Georgia, and Patricia J. Thomas. "Rock the Cradle, Rock the Boat?" U.S. Naval Institute *Proceedings* April 1995: 51–56.

Salmonsen, Jessica A. *The Encyclopedia of the Amazons: Women Warriors from Antiquity to the Modern Era.* New York: Doubleday, 1992.

Scharr, Adela Riek. *Sisters in the Sky. Vol. 1, The WAFS.* Tucson: Patrice, 1986.

Scharr, Adela Riek. *Sisters in the Sky. Vol. 2, The WASP.* Tucson: Patrice, 1988.

Schneider, Dorothy, and Carl Schneider. *Into the Breach: American Women Overseas in World War I.* New York: Viking, 1991.

Schneider, Dorothy, and Carl Schneider. *Sound Off! American Military Women Speak Out.* Rev. ed. New York: Paragon House, 1992.

Schubery, Frank N., and Theresa L. Kraus, eds. *The Whirlwind War: The United States Army in Operations Desert Shield and Desert Storm.* Washington, D.C.: U.S. Army Center of Military History, 1995.

Seeley, Charlotte Palmer, Virginia C. Purdy, and Robert Gruber, comps. *American Women and the U.S. Armed Forces: A Guide to the Records of Military Agencies in the National Archives Relating to American Women*. Washington, D.C.: National Archives and Records Administration, 1993.

Segal, David R., and Mady Weschler Segal. *Peacekeepers and Their Wives: American Participation in the Multinational Force and Observers*. Westport, Conn.: Greenwood Press, 1993.

Shawver, Lois. *And the Flag Was Still There: Straight People, Gay People, and Sexuality in the Military*. New York: Harrington Park/Haworth, 1994.

Shea, Nancy. *The Army Wife*. New York: Harper and Row, 1966.

Shea, Nancy. *The Air Force Wife*. New York: Harper and Brothers, 1966.

Sheafer, Silvia Anne. *Women in America's Wars*. Springfield, N.J.: Enslow, 1996.

Shields, Elizabeth A., ed. *Highlights in the History of the Army Nurse Corps*. Washington, D.C.: U.S. Army Center of Military History, 1981.

Shilts, Randy. *Conduct Unbecoming: Gays and Lesbians in the U.S. Military, Vietnam to the Persian Gulf*. New York: St. Martin's Press, 1993.

Smith, Winnie. *American Daughter Gone to War: On the Front Lines with an Army Nurse in Vietnam*. New York: Morrow, 1992.

Soderbergh, Peter A. *Women Marines in the Korean War Era*. Westport, Conn.: Praeger, 1994.

Soderbergh, Peter A. *Women Marines: The World War II Era*. Westport, Conn.: Praeger, 1992.

Staupers, Mabel Keaton. *No Time for Prejudice: A Story of the Integration of Negroes in Nursing in the United States*. New York: Macmillan, 1961.

Sterner, Doris M. *In and Out of Harm's Way: A History of the Navy Nurse Corps*. Seattle: Peanut Butter Publishing for the Navy Nurse Corps Association, 1996.

Stiehm, Judith Hicks. *Arms and the Enlisted Woman*. Philadelphia: Temple University Press, 1989.

Stiehm, Judith Hicks. *Bring Me Men and Women: Mandated Change at the U.S. Air Force Academy*. Berkeley: University of California Press, 1981.

Stiehm, Judith Hicks, ed. *It's Our Military, Too! Women and the U.S. Military*. Philadelphia: Temple University Press, 1996.

Stremlow, Mary V. *Coping with Sexism in the Military*. Baltimore: Rosen, 1990.

Stremlow, Mary V. *A History of the Women Marines, 1946–1977*. Washington, D.C.: Government Printing Office, 1986.

Sturdevant, Saundra Pollock, and Brenda Stoltzfus. *Let the Good Times Roll: Prostitution and the U.S. Military in Asia*. New York: New Press, 1992.

Tilley, John A. *A History of Women in the Coast Guard*. Washington, D.C.: U.S. Coast Guard Headquarters, 1996.

Tomblin, Barbara Brooks. *G.I. Nightingales: The Army Nurse Corps in World War II*. Lexington: University of Kentucky Press, 1996.

Treadwell, Mattie E. *The Women's Army Corps*. Washington, D.C.:Office of the Chief of Military History, U.S. Department of the Army, 1954.

Turner Publishing Company Staff and Erika Nau. *Women Marines Association History Book*. Paducah, Ky.: Turner, 1992.

Turner Publishing Company Staff. *Vietnam Women's Memorial*. Paducah, Ky.: Turner, 1996.

Vaught, Wilma. *A Brief History of Women in Combat and War*. SRR 145. Washington, D.C.: Industrial College of the Armed Forces, 1973.

Walker, Keith, comp. *A Piece of My Heart: The Stories of Twenty-Six American Women Who Served in Vietnam*. Novato, Calif.: Presidio Press, 1986.

Weatherford, Doris. *American Women and World War II*. New York: Facts on File, 1990.

Webber, Winni S. *Lesbians in the Military Speak Out*. Northboro, Mass.: Madwoman Press, 1993.

Weinstein, Laurie, and Christie C. White, eds. *Wives and Warriors: Women and the Military in the United States and Canada*. Westport, Conn.: Bergin and Garvey, 1997.

Wekesser, Carol, and Matthew Polesetsky, eds. *Women in the Military*. San Diego: Greenhaven, 1991.

Wertsch, Mary Edwards. *Military Brats: Legacies of Childhood inside the Fortress*. Bayside, N.Y.: Aletheia, 1991.

Whitworth, Shauna. *"The Happy Contagion" Story of the First Military Wives' Club*. Fairfax, Va.: S. Whitworth, 1990.

Willenz, June A. *Women Veterans: America's Forgotten Heroines*. New York: Continuum, 1983.

Williams, Christine L. *Gender Differences at Work: Women and Men in Nontraditional Occupations*. Berkeley: University of California Press, 1989.

Wingo, Josette Dermody. *Mother Was a Gunner's Mate: World War II in the WAVES*. Annapolis: Naval Institute Press, 1994.

Yilianos, Theresa K. *Woman Marine: A Memoir of a Woman Who Joined the U.S. Marine Corps in World War II to Free a Man to Fight*. La Jolla, Calif.: La Jolla Books, 1994.

Zhao, Xiaojian. "Chinese-American Women Defense Workers in World War II." *California History*, summer 1996.

Zimmerman, Jean. *Tailspin: Women at War in the Wake of Tailhook*. New York: Doubleday, 1995.

About the Contributors

Marion Anderson has been the director of Employment Research Associates in Michigan since 1978 and was previously director of the Seminar on Congress and American Foreign Policy in Washington, D.C. She lectures and writes on the economic effects of high levels of military spending.

Judith Lawrence Bellafaire, Ph.D., is curator of the Women in Military Service for America (WIMSA) Memorial Foundation, Inc., in Arlington, Virginia. Dr. Bellafaire has written on women's service in World War II and the Gulf War.

Joan I. Biddle, Ph.D., is a sociologist, a lieutenant colonel in the Army Reserve, and an adjunct faculty member at the U.S. Army Command and General Staff College, Fort Leavenworth, Kansas, and the New School for Social Research in New York. Dr. Biddle researches cyberspace and virtual communities, women, family, and military.

Anne Black (pseudonym) enlisted in the United States Army in 1982, at age seventeen, and became a military photographer. She experienced harassment, found no redress, and left the service. She is now a professional firefighter and a consultant for the National Association of Search and Rescue.

D'Ann Campbell, Ph.D., is Vice President of Academic Affairs at the Sage Colleges. Previously, she was professor of history and Dean of Arts and Sciences at Austin Peahy State University; professor of history and Dean for Women's Affairs at Indiana University; and visiting professor of military history at the U.S. Military Academy, West Point (1989–1991).

Francine D'Amico, Ph.D., writes on race, gender, sexuality, and the U.S. military and is coeditor of two anthologies on gender and international relations. She has taught political science at Ithaca College, Hobart and William Smith Colleges, and Cornell University.

Donna M. Dean, Ph.D., whose Cherokee name is Running Black Wolf, is a trained psychologist and disabled Navy veteran suffering from post-traumatic stress disorder (PTSD) as a result of trauma experienced during her eighteen-year military career. She has written on the prevalence of PTSD among military women.

Joan E. Denman is an independent scholar and an avid researcher on women's experiences in World War II; she is currently compiling a collection of women's oral histories.

Diane M. Disney, Ph.D., is Deputy Assistant Secretary of Defense for Civilian Personnel Policy in the United States Department of Defense in Washington, D.C.

Joan A. Furey is Director of the Center for Women Veterans in the United States Department of Veterans Affairs in Washington, D.C. She served in the U.S. Army Nurse Corps from 1968 to 1970 and has been a nurse, supervisor, and associate chief nurse with the Veterans Administration.

Margaret "Maggie" Gee worked as a welder and then a draftsman in California shipyards during World War II. She later joined the Women's Airforce Service Pilots (WASP). After the war, she became a physicist at Lawrence Livermore National Laboratory.

Leslie Baham Inniss, Ph.D., is assistant professor of sociology at Florida A&M University in Tallahassee. She researches racial and gender discrimination issues and is writing on the long-term effects of being an African American school-desegregation pioneer.

Karen Johnson (USAF, Lt. Col.), retired from the U.S. Air Force Nurse Corps in 1992. During her twenty-year term of service, she completed her M.S. at Yale University. She is currently Vice President for Membership of the National Organization for Women (NOW).

Gwyn Kirk, Ph.D., teaches on women and development at the University of San Francisco. She is a member of the Bay Area Okinawa Peace Network, the East Asia Women's Network against U.S. Militarism, and the Women's International League for Peace and Freedom.

Doreen Drewry Lehr, Ph.D., is a social psychologist and adjunct professor of women's studies at Western Michigan University. She writes and lectures on the military culture of marriage and its psychosocial effects on military wives. Dr. Lehr was an Air Force wife for twenty-three years.

Gale A. Mattox, Ph.D., has been a professor of political science at the U.S. Naval Academy since 1981 and is president of Women in International Security (WIIS), an international, nonpartisan network for women working on foreign and defense issues. She teaches and writes on national security, German, and European issues.

Lynn Meola (pseudonym) is an active-duty Army captain who grew up on military bases all over the world and enlisted in the Army at age seventeen. After her first four years of service, she earned a degree in political science and was commissioned as a second lieutenant.

Katharine H. S. Moon, Ph.D., is assistant professor of political science at Wellesley College. She teaches and researches on international relations and Asian politics. She is currently analyzing how foreign policy elites from different countries and cultures negotiate gender relations in their work.

Lillian A. Pfluke (USA, Major), of Palo Alto, California, graduated with the first class of women from West Point in 1980. A licensed mechanical engineer, she spent fifteen years in the Army before retiring as a major in 1995. She has authored a book on breastfeeding and the active woman.

Helen E. Purkitt, Ph.D., has been a professor of political science at the U.S. Naval Academy since 1979. Her research and teaching interests include political psychology, international relations, and national security issues. Her most recent work is on South Africa and weapons proliferation and the linkages between environmental issues and emerging security threats in Africa.

Connie L. Reeves (USA, Lt. Col.) is a retired Army officer who served as a helicopter pilot, a military intelligence officer, and a foreign area officer. She is completing a Ph.D. in women's military history, writing her autobiography, and researching a biography of Anita Newcomb McGee, founder of the U.S. Army Nurse Corps.

Georgia Clark Sadler (USN, Captain) is president of the Women in the Military Information Network (WIMIN) in Arlington, Virginia, and former director of the Women in the Military Project of the Women's Research and Education Institute (WREI) in Washington, D.C. She served twenty-eight years in the Navy and was the first female faculty member of the U.S. Naval Academy and the first female intelligence briefer to the Chairman of the Joint Chiefs of Staff.

Winni S. Webber (pseudonym) is an active-duty Army medical officer who risked her career to publish a collection of oral histories of lesbians either currently serving in or discharged from the U.S. military.

Laurie Weinstein, Ph.D., is associate professor of anthropology at Western Connecticut State University and codirector of the Women's Studies Program. A former Navy wife, this book is her second anthology on gender and the military. She also researches Native American cultures.

Barbara A. Wilson (USAF, Captain), M.A., M.B.A., served twenty-two years in the Air Force in both enlisted and officer capacity. She was the first enlisted woman to obtain a bachelor's degree by means of "Operation Bootstrap," and the first noncommissioned officer, male or female, to complete Officer Training School and become commissioned.

Judith Youngman, Ph.D., served as a member (1995–1997) and chair (1997) of the Defense Advisory Committee on Women in the Service (DACOWITS). Dr.

Youngman teaches political science at the U.S. Coast Guard Academy, was the first civilian female professor at the U.S. Military Academy, West Point (1978–1981), and researches employment and competitiveness policy and civil-military relations.

Xiaojian Zhao, Ph.D., is assistant professor of Asian American Studies at the University of California at Santa Barbara. She is currently working on a book manuscript on women and the transformation of Chinese American community from 1940–1965.

Index